GUN TALK

GUN TALK

Practical advice about every aspect of the shooting sports from America's greatest gun writers...

edited by Dave Moreton

WINCHESTER PRESS

Copyright © 1973 by Winchester Press

All rights reserved

Library of Congress Catalog Card No. 72-96091
ISBN: 0-87691-105-X

First printing April 1973
Second printing June 1974

Published by Winchester Press
460 Park Avenue, New York 10022

Printed in the United States of America

Contents

Introduction *1*
    Dave Moreton

Hunting from the Saddle *3*
    Col. Charles Askins

What Should a Hunting Shotgun Weigh? *18*
    Pete Barrett

Western Rifles *28*
    Les Bowman

Long-Range Shotgunning: How Long? *43*
    Pete Brown

The Big-Bore Target Rifle—
  King of the Range *53*
    Jim Carmichel

Competitive Shooting *69*
    Col. Jim Crossman

Drilling, Vierling, und Zweiling:
  Reflections on Rifle-Shotguns *84*
    Robert Elman

The Chamberlin Cartridge & Target Co. *105*
    Bob Hinman

Gun Control *117*
    Arnold Jeffcoat

Gun Fit *129*
    Pete Kuhlhoff

Handguns Are for Anything
  and Everything *140*
    Maj. George C. Nonte, Jr.

Some Notes on Big-Game Cartridges *151*
    Jack O'Connor

One Man's African Rifles *165*
    Warren Page

When Your Rifle Goes Sour *177*
    Bob Steindler

Black Powder: Fundamentals for Field Use *190*
    Hal Swiggett

40 Yards Is It *211*
    Ken Warner

Shooting the Old Winchesters and Marlins *226*
    Ken Waters

Introduction

THE WRITERS WHOSE contributions appear on the following pages are a pretty fancy group of gun buffs indeed, for they all manage to earn money at it by writing and editing gun columns and articles for one or more of the top outdoor magazines.

As a group they've had a lot of fun together and developed a lot of respect for each other, for in line of duty their paths tend to cross quite frequently. Such events as the NRA convention and the product introduction "seminars" of the major firearms manufacturers tend to bring them together several times a year, and a lot of marvelous gun talk always ensues.

The present volume owes its inception to just such a conclave, a product seminar several years ago at Winchester's famed Nilo Farm shooting preserve in East Alton, Illinois. A bunch of us were sitting around after dinner, swapping yarns and information with each other, when the thought occurred to me that if you could capture even a small part of the knowledge and experience of the assembled experts within the covers of the same book, it would make quite a treat for the gun enthusiast. (Rarely does the byline of more than one or two appear in the same publication under normal circumstances.)

The idea was batted around a bit, and everyone there agreed to contribute a piece on some specialty or pet subject of his own choice. It took a little while to put it all together, and there was a substitution or two, but now at last the collection of articles is complete. I hope you like it.

Dave Moreton

Hunting from the Saddle

COL. CHARLES ASKINS

Charles Askins has written more than a thousand articles and stories for the gun and shooting magazines over the past three decades, and he has published books on handguns, wing and trap shooting, shotguns, and African hunting. His most recent book is a celebration of the folk and folklore of his native state, Texans, Guns & History. *He is Firearms Editor of* Guns, Shooting Industry, *and* Army Times.

Col. Askins retired from the military in 1963, after more than thirty years' service—first with the U. S. Border Patrol as a Texas National Guardsman, and after the outbreak of World War II as a career army officer. He has hunted on every continent except Australia, and his handgun prowess has earned him more than five hundred medals in state, regional, and national pistol competition. Col. Askins lives in San Antonio.

THE RIDER SAT his horse like a lizard panting in the Mohave sun. He was spread out, loose and unsettled. His shoulders sagged, his back was in bow, his belly, protuberant and flabby, nudged the saddle horn. His feet were shoved deeply into the stirrups, but no weight rested on the oxbows. A big man, grossly overweight, with an upper torso out of proportion to his foreshortened legs, he left the observer with the impression that his balance was as precarious as that of a tightwire walker.

He was sitting a saddle very obviously not meant for him. The tree was too short by inches, and the outfitter had carelessly shortened the stirrups until the rider might just as well have dangled his feet free. His 230 pounds of bone and blubber rested squarely athwart the horse's kidney. After three days of hunting, kidney sores developed and the pony groaned every time the rider shifted position. This was often, for the man in the saddle was galled too. But not over his kidneys.

An outfitter who specialized in quickie elk hunts used to haul his sports out to the end of the road on the Montana side of the state

Typical dude hunters. The last man has no weight in the stirrups; he is spilling over the cantle with all his bulk on the horse's kidneys.

Hunters riding into a camp in the Selway-Bitterroot wilderness area. Many were so sore after the 50-mile trek they had to be put to bed—on their bellies.

boundary and mount them up for a fifty-mile ride into his camp in the Selway-Bitterroot wilderness area. The ride took two days, and at the camp many of the horsemen had to be put to bed on their bellies. The hunt was a seven-day affair, half of which was spent in camp—nursing raw bottoms. The guide-outfitter, a pretty unscrupulous scoundrel, guaranteed the hunt. But when the dude complained he had not shot a bull wapiti—had not in fact even seen one—the entrepreneur would point out that he had spent half his hunt piled up on the bunk.

Les Bowman, one of the saltiest guide-outfitters I have ever known, was a tough one on the hunters. His sports did their elk-deer-sheep questing from the hurricane deck of the equine transport, and Bowman rode along to point out the game and also to shape up the riders. I remember coming to his main lodge late one evening along with several other dudes who had flown into Cody, the distant airport, that day. We traveled to the Bowman diggings in the failing light of the November afternoon.

Next morn, I sallied out to the corral to saddle up, make parley with my assigned guide, and be off to the high sierras. Among the crowd was the very epitome of the Western sportsman. Boots, high-heeled and spurred, by Hyer, hat by Stetson, shirt by Pendleton, pants from Norm Thompson, chaps by Porter, rifle from Champlin, and six-gun by Colt, he toted over his shoulder a pair of handsomely tooled saddlebags. His rifle was encased in a two-hundred-dollar full-length leather case. A scabbard with a cap over it completely enclosed the shooting iron. Rifle and case weighed sixteen pounds.

The saddlebags were the most compelling of the gear. They were stuffed to overflowing. Each bulged until it appeared the retaining straps would burst their lashings. It was obvious our Nimrod was prepared for a long march. Bowman, busy with guides, in catching up horses and tolling them off to his guests, finally looked up.

"What the hell you got in them saddlebags?" he demanded. "You're big, and this pony is going to be loaded just packing you, much less all that extra gear. Dump 'em out and let's see what you can do without," he ordered.

The sport sputtered and protested, but Bowman, tough and unyielding, fixed him with a hard eye. Out came a 20-pound Bolex camera, 3,000 feet of film, a Pentex 35-mm. camera and 12 rolls of film, 100 cartridges, a snakebite kit (the temperature was nudging zero), a three day supply of emergency rations, a first-aid kit, 40 rounds of .357 Magnum handgun fodder, two skinning knives, a whetstone, a rifle-cleaning kit, a set of 10 emergency flares, a pair of binoculars, compass, a pint of brandy, a set of maps, and a copy of the current *Playboy*.

"Leave all that crap right here in the saddle room except the binocs, the compass, a box of rifle ca'tridges and the *Playboy*," old Les ordered. And then, casting a baleful eye over the full-length rifle scabbard, he barked, "Jerk that goodam boot off the end of that scabbard so you can git at that shootin' iron when I tell you to take your bull." It ruined the dude's hunt. He rode for a pair of days, developed a handsomely galled backside, begged a ride with a passing Park Department pickup, and rode to Cody and the airport.

Les Bowman's horses were all big, mountain-bred animals, none under a thousand pounds, but horses ridden every day during the hunting season, sometimes as much as twenty-five miles up and down steep slopes, cannot pack more than 200 pounds. When you consider that the average sport is apt to weigh 175 pounds, the saddle 35 pounds, rifle and scabbard 13 pounds, and such odds and ends as a rain poncho, binoculars, camera, knife and lunch another 8 pounds, it is easy to appreciate why the old outfitter looked over his dudes' gear with a critical eye.

Bowman's sort of outing is no picnic, especially for the horse. So why bother? There are reasons.

Saddle hunting has a lot going for it. The mounted huntsman sweeps broadly through a radius of action two or three times that of the foot slogger. In the high country he expends neither energy nor breath on the shale slopes, and when the shot is offered, he steps down neither shaking from the exertion of the climb nor breathless. He is cool, rested, and ready for the decisive shot.

Critters like elk, deer, antelope, woodland caribou, and bear spook less readily from the sound of the horse's shod feet than from the lesser clangor of the man afoot. The ring of steel shoes in the crumbling granite of the shallow pass is accepted as the passage of other game, and seldom provokes a bolt. The bull wapiti waits to see what comes in view before drifting silently into the blackness of the firs. At times, when compelled by the terrain or wind to ride with the eddying currents, I have overrun game that had surely smelled my sweaty horse. Apparently the equine odor blanketed the human stench so that the wild things did not stampede.

For a long time I had a buckskin in Montana that could smell game. Especially bears. I always concluded that he had been in a bear fracas—probably when a gangling colt—and it had left a permanent impression. Hunting upwind, a habitual practice along the north fork of the Flathead, Cappy would throw his ears forward, snort mightily, and get all humped up like he was going to pitch. On deer or elk he would simply throw his ears forward and stare intently, but bruin brought out all the bronc in him. He would stand quiet while you loaded him with a wapiti or venison saddle, but there wasn't a halter rope stout enough to snub him down while you tied on a bear pelt. Some horses are that way about a mountain lion. I used to run lions in New Mexico with a big black horse called Nigger. When the dogs barked treed you might as well tie Nig and go forward afoot. He wouldn't get within a hundred yards of the cat in the piñon. Mountain lions consider horse colts a rare delicacy, and like Cappy, this horse had probably been jumped when he was running with his mammy.

Pronghorn hunting makes an ideal stalk from sixteen hands up. The antelope see cowboys the year through. A rider can usually injun up on the band to within rifle distance before the leaders grow spooky. It is when the rider pulls to a halt and swings down in full view that they raise those alarm hairs over the rump. The veteran pronghorn gunner knows he must hit the ground shooting. If he is tied up with a pony that stands after he steps down he is in luck. Far too many in my own benighted experience bugger on the report and, reins trailing, strike a high lope for the home corral. Then the hunter's situation is simplified. All he has to do is go over, gut out the buck, and foot slog it back to camp. Incidentally, we always speak about throwing the reins down when we dismount for the quick shot. Actually, it is a lot better to knot the reins over the pony's neck and when you swing off to drop them right there. If he runs out on you, he doesn't put a foot on a rein and bust it.

It looks sort of farmerish to ride a hunting horse with a halter under the bridle, but it never makes you a dime to tie the bronc with the bridle reins. He'll break them just as sure as he gets whiff of a passing bruin. The proper hitch is with a good three-quarter-inch halter shank. By the same token, it is good insurance to always

You need breast straps in the mountains, and sometimes the going is so steep that britching is necessary too.

The oilcloth chaps of the hunter on the left are not heavy or bulky but shed rain and snow. The other hunter wears Ivy League trousers that are too tight in the knee for either riding or walking.

pack a short lariat. Many times you'll drop game where the rope is worth a million to skid the critter out where he can be butchered. Or the rope will take all the work out of swinging the carcass up in a fir to cool and await the coming, next day, of the guide with a pack mule. And if you decide to pack in the meat yourself, walking and leading, the lariat is just the ticket for lashing on the saddle.

It looks pretty far out to wear a pair of chaps when saddle hunting, but if the chase is in heavy timber, and especially growth like the low piñon pine or the mesquite and cactus of the Southwest, the leathern breeches are a real hide-saver. Hunting horses are ridden at a walk ordinarily, but when you have to head a band of elk, catch a bear before he crosses yonder ridge, or ride hell for leather after a pack of kyoodles on a hot lion spoor, you have to put your broomtail into a hard gallop. Times like that the *chaparejos* really pay off. They want to be of heavy skirting leather and "shotgun," that is, without batwings, which simply add weight and contribute nothing. Chaps are a godsend when you are game questing in rain or snow. A good pair will shed water quite as well as the saddle slicker, another piece of essential gear. Saddle makers like Porter's of Tucson and Sam Myres of El Paso make a pair of oilcloth chaps especially for rain, snow, and sleet. These leggings ward off the elements very well but aren't much for barging through heavy brush or cactus at a dead run. Then the heavy cowhide is the real huckleberry.

The best footgear for the saddle huntsman is a pair of riding boots. These should have 15-inch tops to cover the ankle below the chaps bottom. The cowpoke footwear is the most comfortable thing on horseback, and when you step down to lead your horse off the steep slopes, the 2½-inch heels will dig in and keep you from slipping. The boots should be the heavy workaday kind made of bull hide with the flesh side out. With them I like a pair of spurs, which are better than a quirt, for they leave both hands free. There are times when to head a band of game you have got to get full-throttle performance out of your four-legged transport, and there's nothing like a set of *espuelas* for that instant response.

Neither spurs nor chaps are worth a hoot when that moment of truth finally comes and you have to step off and make a stalk to deliver the shot. The chaps are cumbersome and noisy, and so are the spurs. It takes some time to shake out of both pieces of gear, but even though the trophy may decide to take it on the lam, the huntsman will make a lot less noisy stalk if he kicks out of the leather pants and the rib hooks.

More often than not the shot is offered unexpectedly, when you're breaking into a small clearing, edging around a bed in the trail, topping a ridge, or dropping down upon a creek and its ford. The game will be caught, surprised and uncertain, bound to pause for a space of heartbeats to elect a course of action. Then the man in the saddle must do two things, with speed and certainty. He must reach back and with a single one-handed motion sweep the rifle from its sheath and, even as he makes his quick draw, swing groundward. The two actions complement each other; the first accomplished even as the second is well begun. The instant he hits the ground, he is aiming. If the horseback hunter cannot move with all the deft sureness of the old hand, his game will present as a target only the north end going south, a mark recommended by few shooting authorities.

The benighted who has to pull a horse to a full stop, put one hand on the horn and the other on the cantle to let himself down, who has on a pair of Russell's birdshooter boots and hangs one in the far stirrup, who has tied his scabbard on the far side of the pony and has to scramble around the horse's head to extract the shooting iron, or maybe fumble a buckle open and jerk free a leathern cap over the stock, had better give up on saddle hunting and go back to slogging it afoot. His ineptness is bound to cost him some rich opportunities.

This brings us to the best rifle for saddle hunting. This ordnance, let me assure you, is seldom the highly popular bolt gun; of all the firearms, the sorriest for horse carry. The bulky receiver with its protuberant bolt—like a wart on a homely gal's nose—is anything but handy out of the saddle scabbard. The scope atop the obese action aggravates the problem. Quite apart from its cross-sectional dimension, the length of the action tends to produce a shooting iron too long to fit handily aboard the horse. Despite these shortcomings, the bolt gun is exceedingly common among horse hunters. They bear with it, working around its left-handed faults and obvious poor carrying qualities because its other good points are thought sufficiently worthwhile.

A rifle suited to saddle carry should not be more than 42 inches overall and should not tip the scales at over 7 pounds. The scope is a nuisance; a micrometered receiver rear aperture and a gold bead front sight set in a ramp are much better. Such a rifle should be a lever, pump repeater, or autoloader. The Savage Model 99 is near perfect for the saddle; so is the Winchester Model 94 carbine and the recent Model 64 rifle. The Remington Models 742 automatic and 760 pump gun are splendid. So are the new Savage pump repeater, the Model 170, a .30/30, underpowered unfortunately for critters over whitetail, black bear, or pronghorn caliber, but a sparkling good scabbard number for all that.

These rifles are better adapted to the horseman because the receivers are flat and short. There is no bulkiness beneath the leg, no shoulders, angles, or corners about the receiver. Nor yet a knobby bolt handle that refuses to fit in any leather. These rifles slip into a saddle sheath readily and come out quick and easy. They lack weight and thus do not pull the saddle over, unbalancing both the mount and the rider, a common fault of many heavy bolt guns. The rifle, in its scabbard, hangs on one side of the horse, near side or far. If it weighs 9½ pounds, as many do with a big varipower scope and an all-steel mount, together with a sheath made of heavy leather, the total ballast hanging off the pony many times attains 15 pounds. Try hanging 15 pounds off your flank and see how you navigate! The saddle tends to turn in that direction, and unless the girth is kept too tight, the horse is almost sure to get a sore back before the hunt is wound up.

The run-of-the-mill big-game sportsman travels to the headquarters of his guide-outfitter with his battery nestled in a hardshell gun case. This is ideal protection against the depredations of the airlines baggage smashers, but not exactly the kind of a thing to lash on the horse for hunting usage. Up at Frazier's Lake in British Columbia last fall I watched a dude busily lashing the plastic trunk on the far side of his saddle. He was pretty indignant when the outfitter told him it wouldn't do. For all that, the sheath usually proffered by the guide is not much better. Most of them are holdovers from World War II and fit the rifle like the gal said about the Hawaiian mu-mu: "Covers everything and touches nothing." The outfitter, whether he has bought up a lot of old wartime surplus scabbards or has had the local saddle shop whip them up, is intent on getting a sheath that will take any rifle that comes along. As a result, the leather permits the rifle to shift and move every step the horse takes. This is not conducive to either maintaining sights in zero or protecting the finish on wood and metal. Far better to fetch along your own scabbard.

I hunted with a sport who had ordered a custom-sewn scabbard, by Boyd, that covered the rifle from butt to muzzle. You got into it by unzipping the cowhide along its bottom side. While the leather was fairly stiff, it was not strong enough to protect the rifle in air transit. And on horseback the owner had to dismount and jiggle with his zipper to get his shooting iron free. Along with this, the full-length case must have weighed 5 to 6 pounds.

A worthwhile scabbard must be designed and sewn around the individual rifle—with its scope in place. If the hunter has two or three favorite hunting rifles, then he should have that many scabbards. The sheath should be of heaviest skirting leather, the part of the bull that comes out of his back. It runs about ⅜ of an inch in thickness and is as stiff and unyielding as so much sole leather. The gun should be only swallowed up to the pistol grip so that when the gunner reaches for his hardware, he gets it by the small of the stock before he commences to haul it out of the cowhide. Scabbards that engulf a rifle, with only the buttstock free, are slow and awkward. The entire stock should ride outside the mouth of the case with the grip handy to the grasp when the rifle is wanted pronto. This leaves the ocular end of the scope in the open as well, and unless the huntsman uses lens caps of clear plastic, such as Weaver offers, he must either expect his glass to withstand the ravage of the weather or expect to jerk the caps off before he shoots. The Weaver clear plastic can be shot through quite successfully if time is of the essence.

A scabbard, regardless of where it is swung on the *caballo,* collects a lot of trash. Sticks, leaves, dirt, rain, snow, and small rocks work down inside. Sometimes the scabbard will fill with water when the pony stumbles or goes down when fording creeks and rivers. The small end should be open, as in the best sixgun holsters. Then the garbage will work its way on out and not lie in the small end to plug the muzzle of the gun.

The higher the rifle is swung up on the horse, the less he feels the weight, and the smaller the chance of the saddle turning and galling his back from the gun weight. Too, the higher the rifle is carried, the quicker it is to hand when the horseman wants to make

Three bad ways of carrying a rifle. If the sheath is close to vertical, rain and snow will pour into it, and the rider is apt to strike his head on the butt when he bends forward. If it is very low and facing forward, it will interfere when the horse is pulled to the right, it will catch in the brush, and it can be withdrawn only from the ground. And of course a rifle should never be carried riding on its sights.

a rapid shot. You cannot shoot off a horse, even though Matt Dillon often fires between his buckskin's ears and always pinks his man. But while you can't hit from the hurricane deck, that is the place to get a grip on the gun. This hocus-pocus of stepping down and then retrieving the piece is strictly for the birds. Even though the rifle may be swung on the near (left) side, it is still sorry practice. If the game is the breed that scares hell out of the pony, he is apt to stampede when you hit the ground intent on withdrawing the rifle and getting off a hasty opener. He may jerk backward, pulling the reins out of your hand, and take off for camp with the rifle still in its leather. You are then left high and dry. Nope, the only savvy tactic is to reach for that gun before you ever quit the saddle. With it in hand you can then bail out, and when you hit the ground the horse can do whatever he pleases. If he wants to stand hitched, all well and good. Should he snort, throw his tail in the air, and quit the country, you can still shoot your trophy and send the guide to collect the runaway.

Some huntsmen swing the scabbard to the front, the stock of the gun alongside the horse's neck on either the near or far side. The angle of the sheath may be very abrupt, with the stock pointing skyward, or it may be low and parallel to the ground. A lot of dudes have no idea where the best location is and let the outfitter rig the harness for them. He may do a proper hanging job and again may not.

A rifle can be withdrawn from a scabbard hung to the front, but it is a two-handed chore. And slow. When the stock is alongside the pony's head it interferes when the horse is reined around sharply. It hangs in those limbs that work between stock and the animal's neck. And it collects debris continually. If the scabbard is angled abruptly, the stock pointing toward the heavens, rain and snow pour in and the rider, when he bends forward to avoid overhanging limbs, is dangerously apt to crack his skull on the upstanding wood.

The hands-down location for a scabbard is with the gun butt swung to the tail end of the mount—with the muzzle forward. The stock should be considerably higher than the muzzle so that in climbing steep slopes it does not slide out of the leather. The scabbard should be swung high on the far side of the saddle, tucked up under the fender with the rifle action well behind the cantle of the saddle. With the rifle on the right side, all the shooter needs do is to reach back, grasp the gun by the small of the stock, and withdraw it as he dismounts. The right hand has the rifle by the pistol grip and the left is on the horn, a grasp that facilitates a quick dismount.

When the rifle is slung with the stock to the rear, muzzle forward, it not only provides the quickest and handiest position to go into action, but it also permits the rider to move through dense cover without the stock taking a beating from the brush and trees. Less trash is picked up by the open mouth of the leather, and rain and snow don't enter in such quantity. The high position will not turn the saddle and gall the horse's back.

But I meant not just to laugh at the tyros but to convince you that it is all worthwhile.

For stirring a torpid liver, curing constipation, and enlivening the heart muscle, I recommend saddle hunting after a pack of lion dogs. Before hiring on to race lions behind a gaggle of Plott hounds, brush up on those clauses in your accident policy that cover hospitalization for injuries, broken bones, and duration of stay. Also get a briefing on Medicare and Medicaid, for you may need all three.

The handiest carry, shown for both right-hander and left-hander. The rifle may be pulled quickly from the scabbard before the huntsman dismounts.

If you're a bit bored and satiated with the humdrum of everyday existence, try lion running. The old buffalo runners may have had something on lion coursing, but it can't have been much.

In the Sangre de Cristo Mountains of north-central New Mexico, Roy Snyder was the state lion hunter. I threw in with him for a month and we rode after the great cats. We caught more bears than we did puma, but this did not detract from the good clean fun of the chase. Every other day, and sometimes for a brace of days, we would have to loll around camp and let the dogs rest. They tore up the pads of their feet in the shale and flint of the slopes, and a hound—as wise as a mule about taking care of himself—will show little enthusiasm for the spoor when he is footsore.

On those days when men, dogs, and horses were ready, we'd sally forth at dawn. With the pups yoked together, the better to keep them under control, Roy with the lariat doubled to whip back the eager ones, we'd ride to a spring a couple of miles from camp. A lion, like a tiger or the African variety, must drink after he has eaten. Usually we'd cut sign about the watering place and pick up the track of the great cat. Snyder had an old dog, Mose, whom he would signal forward. Ordinarily the lion hunter will not trust his dog to search out the sign and line out on it, for it may be too old. But Roy had lots of confidence in Mose, and if the old boy let out a succession of low, eager cries, we knew it was a hot scent.

The others waited the signal with all the pent-up eagerness of a bunch of young bulls about to be turned into the heifer pasture. Waved forward, away they would tear, every manjack making sweet music to the houndman's ear. And then the race was on!

For hell-and-leather riding nothing can quite touch a lion chase. Cowboys in the mesquite and thorn country of southwest Texas have a hell of a time of it, but the lion hunter in the mountains of typical lion cover is in a class by himself. The dogs have to be kept in earshot. If you lose the sound, then the pack trees the lion, and if you are not hot behind, the feline jumps out and runs again. And again. And will in all likelihood get away.

You gallop, and you'd better have chaps, a leather coat, heavy leather gloves, and a good hat to ward off limbs, trees, downed timber, and rock outcropings. Your St. Christopher medal may also be of some help, especially for your immortal soul. In the Sangre de Cristo where Roy Snyder and I courted the wily game, there were high mesas and abrupt canyons. You would lope across a mountain meadow as sweet as anything you'd ever want to do and then bang; into the piñons and out onto the edge of the canyon. There was no time to pick a spot for a gentle descent. You had to kick your pony off into the little Grand Canyon hoping he'd land at the bottom right side up. Sometimes he did and sometimes he did not, and if you were lucky you gathered yourself up and caught onto the reins and loaded aboard and galloped on. Across the floor of the valley the hounds would be seemingly climbing straight upward. There was nothing for it but to ride over, going all out, and put your winded horse to the climb out of the great wash.

If you were in luck and the sign was fresh, you might hear the pack bark treed within a mile. Sometimes the spoor would last for seven miles, and every foot of it through the worst terrain the cat could find. When you rode up to the trophy, bayed in a low piñon, he'd see you galloping forward and fall out of the tree, boxing a dog or two out of his path, and take off for another thrill-choked mile. At the end of the month I had ripped up a goose-down jacket, had a great unhealed cut down my spine from a low hanging snag, had lost a rifle complete with case, had crippled two horses, one of them fatally, and not a muscle in my body but ached from falls and bumps. For genuine horsehunting thrills, I'll give lion-chasing the nod anytime.

What Should a Hunting Shotgun Weigh?

PETER BARRETT

Peter Barrett has been Outdoor Editor of True *since 1947, and he has also been on the staffs of* Sports Illustrated *and* Outdoor Life. *Hundreds of his articles have appeared in everything from* Reader's Digest *to* Collier's, *from* McCall's *to* This Week. *One reason is that Barrett usually has a lot to write about: he has been on twelve African safaris, and several of his prime trophies are listed in* Ward's Records of Big Game. *He is an honorary member of the East African Professional Hunters Association. Barrett has edited two anthologies on going after the big ones:* Great True Hunts *and* A Treasury of African Hunting. *He lives in Rowayton, Connecticut.*

YOU ARE GOING to buy a shotgun, and the clerk lays a shiny new one on the counter. You pick up the gun, shoulder it, swing at an imaginary bird, and then — regardless of the type and weight — you think: I could knock 'em with this.

Perhaps you could. The hunter who is a fair wingshot can hit some birds with *any* gun, assuming it fits reasonably well and is suitably choked. But getting back to that new gun on the counter, you might hit better if it were lighter. Or heavier. Weight is a more important factor in a shotgun than you might think.

I had to find this out the hard way, blundering about, often not even understanding what I was doing right and wrong. As an example, several years ago I bought a 12-gauge pump with trap stock and 30-inch barrel with full choke. The gun weighed 8 pounds and, like any factory trap gun, fitted me to perfection. I intended to shoot trap with it, as well as high-passing ducks and Canada geese.

The gun arrived a few days before I went west for Idaho bird hunting, and I took it with me untried on the chance there might be ducks. But it was too early in the fall for ducks, and, stubbornly

Shooting grouse in Scotland, with very fast-flying birds, requires a light, fast-handling gun.

wanting to try my new pump on birds, I carried it that first morning, hunting along a creek with Ted Trueblood for mountain quail. Presently he and his pointer got about 50 yards ahead of me on the opposite side of the canyon and into a big covey of quail.

Three came down the canyon bottom below me, nicely spaced, out in the open and about 35 yards away. I took them with three shots. After the retrieves I walked up the canyon and put up two singles, both longish shots above the sagebrush, and I got them also. Never before had I gone five straight on mountain quail. (And never have I repeated, I might add.) Five was the limit then and Trueblood was soon finished.

Had I lucked upon an ideal upland gun? Wait.

Later I found myself on steep, rocky ground beneath a cliff in higher country. Chukars barely waited to be pointed before they were away, curving and hugging the terrain, sometimes zooming up the cliff face. Guns boomed and birds fell . . . but not to me. As we worked along below this huge outcrop, singles got up obligingly close so that there was no panic to hurry the shots.

I could understand missing a bird at 20 yards, for full choke delivers a slim pattern spread at this distance. But I'd also miss the same bird again at 30 to 35 yards, and there was never time for a third shot. By the end of the afternoon I'd scratched down only two chukars, both runners collected by Trueblood's pointer.

"You're having what I call a mysterious slump," my friend

remarked as we drove out of the high country. "I get one sometimes, though usually late in the season."

But "slump" wasn't the right explanation; using a pet 6¾-pound upland gun for the rest of the trip, I had no more problems. What had undone me was that 8-pound gun — too much shotgun weight. Before I explain why this gun worked well in the morning and poorly in the afternoon, let's consider a couple more shooting situations involving a heavy shotgun.

Two years later I had gone to Argentina with Jim Rikhoff for ducks and geese, taking my Winchester 101 trap gun, which has 28-inch barrels bored modified and full and weighs 8¼ pounds. The wildfowling over, we found ourselves with a final morning to kill. We turned to the wind-swept pampas with its shin-deep grass and a partridge-like bird called tinamou.

The only gun available was my heavy 101 and Magnum 4 shells, so we shot miss and out. Walking the vast table-flat fields, we'd jump birds about 25 yards away that flew dazzlingly with the wind, a foot or so above the grass and clover. They were in plain sight, of course, and by the time the gun was swung and the trigger pulled, the shots averaged 35 yards. To my surprise, we knocked them exceptionally well and there it was again: a heavy gun seemingly implacable on upland birds.

I should have known that the tinamou and the mountain quail before them were special situations, but I didn't stop to analyze.

And so when I got invited to shoot driven grouse in Scotland, the *first* gun I picked — remembering the tinamou — was the Winchester 101. The second gun for the pair I'd need (one for incomers, the other for going-away birds) was selected mostly with an eye to tradition. This was a 12-gauge side-by-side Jeffery I'd bought for a song in England during World War II. Bored cylinder and full, and with the same barrel length of 28 inches as the 101, the Jeffery weighed 6¼ pounds.

A trapshooting friend brought a pair of 7¾-pound doubles, his pet trap guns. We joined six other shooters, spaced about 40 yards apart and forming a line just below the crest of a hill. We stood in "butts," chest-deep pits dug in the heather, and after several grouse had hurtled past like cannonballs, I for one had a new understanding of the need for a light gun on close, fast birds.

Mostly the grouse appeared suddenly about 40 yards out, flying toward us at top speed a yard above the heather, though sometimes they were 20 feet high and occasionally 20 to 40 yards up. There would be crossing shots when birds flew parallel to the butts. In short, we were tested by every wingshooting problem except flushing birds.

"When I had to throw my gun up and really swing, it felt like the barrels were full of concrete," my trapshooting friend remarked. He was further handicapped by full choke in both barrels.

I had similar feelings about my 8¼-pound Model 101. It was nearly hopeless on all but high incomers, and not much good on going-away birds till they were well out. In contrast, the 6¼-pound Jeffery, a full two pounds lighter, was a fairy wand just right for the job.

At this point you may well wonder: Is there a "just right" weight for a game gun? When is a heavy gun a good choice? And what about the trend to lightweight models? Can a gun be *too* light?

Let's consider the heavier guns first. Trap and skeet guns commonly weigh about 7¾ pounds and this weight accomplishes two important things — it helps lessen the recoil effect, and it helps the shooter follow through on each swing. In fact, once such a gun is in motion, continuation of the swing is practically built in.

Then why isn't a heavy gun good for general upland shooting? The answer lies in the *way* trap and skeet are shot. You mount the gun carefully. You know what kind of a shot you'll have. And you know when the bird will appear. In trap and skeet, all you need do is move the gun in the right direction and maintain swing as you shoot.

When I saw those mountain quail barreling down the canyon below me and out in the open, I had time aplenty to mount the gun and get a good swing going smoothly. Also, the birds were 35 yards out, just right for full choke. And when I put up the singles, they gave me time to get on them because they were continuously in the clear. Rikhoff and I had a similar situation with the tinamou.

But it's a different ball game when the birds are unexpected and fast-flying besides. Or when they jump close and you must get on them right now or they'll disappear (me and the chukars).

The problem with a heavy gun on game is in *the entire cycle:* picking up or raising the gun, mounting it and swinging.

Just suppose the rules of trapshooting were changed and you had to pick your gun up off the ground *after* yelling "Pull!" Suddenly your 7¾-pounder would be full of concrete. A gun weighing half a pound less would be faster and one three-quarters of a pound less would give you a noticeable advantage.

It follows that a heavy gun is most useful on birds that permit a leisurely shot, game that you can see *coming, going,* or *passing in the open.*

Nothing is absolute in shooting, however, and one man's idea of "heavy" may well be another's notion of "normal." I think particularly of Ted Trueblood, with whom I've often hunted birds in the West for over twenty years. For the last dozen years he hunted with a 12-gauge pump with a 28-inch modified barrel and weighing 7 pounds 10 ounces.

As I like to take pictures of my friends shooting, I have observed him closely taking ducks and pheasants, huns, sage hens, three kinds of quail, and chukars. I have seen him in bad trouble among close-rising, fast valley quail and, watching through the viewfinder, would think: Isn't he ever going to shoot? In my view he was fighting to get a long, heavy gun into fast action. I must admit, however, that most of the time he shot well.

Last year he bought a 12-gauge side-by-side with 26-inch barrels weighing 7⅛ pounds. It was also much shorter on the sighting plane by about half a foot — four inches less because a double lacks the long receiver of a pump or automatic, and two inches less because he chose shorter barrels. Short barrel length contributes to fast gun handling.

After using the double on valley quail and chukars, he wrote:

> I have been amazed how much difference half a pound makes. My shooting with the new gun has not been great, but better than before I got it. I killed 10 valley quail with 19 shots. Don't have a tally on chukars but did kill some I know I would not have with the pump. Example: One flushed at about 20 yards and flew left toward a big rock. I swung fast and shot just before it disappeared. I felt sure I hadn't caught up with it and started around the mountain. Tuck ran behind the rock and brought the bird to me.
>
> The double is several yards faster than the pump. I'd say I get on a bird at least five yards sooner.

I have also been amazed at how much difference half a pound

Leo Martin, head of the gun department at Abercrombie & Fitch, uses Barrett's fishing scale to weigh a Winchester 101.

can make — even a quarter of a pound, in fact. For about fifteen years I used a 6¾-pound over-under with 26-inch barrels bored improved and modified. I do a lot of grouse and woodcock shooting in the East without a dog, so that a flushing bird usually takes me by surprise. I have to get into action quickly while the bird is still in sight, usually in heavy cover.

A few years ago I was in a gun store and was captivated by a handsome over-under with 28-inch barrels, two triggers (which I like) and weighing 7 pounds 1 ounce. I decided to make a grouse gun of it and opened the lower barrel to cylinder and the upper to improved-modified. Yet despite the advantage of cylinder for the first shot, I often seemed just a bit too slow.

The last time I used this gun for grouse I put up a bird in a small, thick cover at about 15 yards and missed. I circled and presently jumped the grouse again at good range. Missed. At this I circled once more, to where the shooting had begun, and so help me, this obliging grouse got up one more time. Only now it fell. gun against a tree and started to light my pipe, when suddenly
 I walked over to the bird, which lay still on its back. I set my

the grouse rolled over, took a couple of steps, and zoomed away as I grabbed frantically for the gun.

On more open shooting — ducks and pheasants, for example — this gun is fine, and I have come to think of it as my "middleweight." But the difference of only five ounces between it and my regular grouse gun got me to thinking seriously about the importance of gun weight, and being of an acquisitive nature where shotguns are concerned, I decided to get a gun a bit lighter than my pet 6¾-pounder.

Taking an accurate fishing scale, I went to a big store and began weighing guns. For contrast, I selected guns that weighed 7¾ pounds, 7 pounds, and another that was an even 6½. Then I picked them up alternately and swung them. The lightest gun was noticeably livelier and quicker and I bought it, even though it was only a quarter of a pound lighter than my old favorite.

Incidentally, if you are interested in saving ounces, try weighing several guns of a preferred model if they're available. Highly figured wood is heavier than plain wood, and there may be a difference of four or more ounces between identical guns because of the wood. European walnut averages 20 to 25 percent lighter than American walnut. And don't overlook mahogany, which Remington uses in its lightest pumps and autos.

It might seem that going down only four ounces on a gun reflects timidity, and at the time it did. However, there was an underlying reason, something the famous Ray P. Holland told me years ago. We spent a fall hunting grouse and woodcock together, and one night I was at his house admiring his three British Woodward over-unders, two 12-gauges and a pretty little 20.

I picked up the 20-gauge, swung it a couple of times, and remarked that it handled wonderfully fast.

"Too fast," Ray said. "Whenever I use it, I throw the gun away."

This is an old expression for wild swinging or overreacting with a light gun. Holland's remark made a deep impression on me, particularly since he favored the heavier of his two 12-gauges and shot exceptionally well with it. He was opposed to weighing guns for some reason, and I believe they never were laid on a scale till last winter, when I called his son Dan and asked about them.

Presently he wrote me, "That big Woodward weighs 7 pounds 15 ounces. No wonder Dad 'threw away' the 20; it weighs almost exactly two pounds less: 5 pounds 15½ ounces."

Barrett's lightest gun, 5½-pound Model ASEL Beretta, is good for fast, close work in woods and uplands. A baby scale is accurate enough for gun weighing.

Ray Holland's preference for a grouse gun weighing practically 8 pounds probably reflects a lifelong use of 12-gauges on the heavy side. And though his use of this Woodward ruins my theory that a gun for fast handling in heavy cover should be light, I must point out that he had damned good dogs and at least had some warning when a bird might flush.

After I'd used the 6½-pound double for a couple of seasons with good results, I got to wondering what would happen if I tried an even lighter gun. Would I throw it away? Would I perhaps shoot *better?* With more than a little trepidation, I took my fishing scale to a store and came away with a 5½-pound 20-gauge over-under with 26-inch barrels and fairly open boring.

From the start I was pleasantly surprised. That little gun was so light I could carry it easily in one hand with the muzzle raised while I fought thick brush with the other. The gun seemed to fly to my shoulder at the thunder of a grouse and I was faster getting on the target. And would that little gun swing!

If I was throwing the gun away, at least I was doing it in the right direction, for I killed three grouse I only *hoped* I'd hit and looked for mostly out of respect for the bird. I had the best grouse and woodcock season ever.

You can carry a lightweight shotgun one-handed without strain, leaving a hand free for fighting brush.

Three classes of gun weights. At the top, 5½-pound Beretta and 6-pound Remington Model 870, both 20-gauge. In the middle, 6½-pound Winchester Model 21 20-gauge and 7-pound-1-ounce Beretta SO4 12-gauge. At the bottom, 8-pound Remington Model 870 12-gauge and 8¼-pound Winchester Model 101 12-gauge.

Later I tried the gun on bobwhite quail and again it did well. Then I took it to a preserve and at last found its flaw: the gun was excellent for getting on a pheasant fast but just about hopeless when I had to take a long crossing shot. Perhaps now I was indeed throwing the gun away, for I could not sustain a smooth swing well enough.

If I had to settle on one gun weight for everything, my ideal would be $6\frac{1}{2}$ pounds, but since I don't have to settle, I vary my hunting between guns of $5\frac{1}{2}$, $6\frac{1}{2}$ and about $7\frac{1}{2}$ pounds. And believe me, each pound you add or subtract makes a considerable difference.

Regardless of what gun weight is "just right" for you, there will come a time when a hunting situation is just plain dismaying. My favorite occurred some years ago when I'd gone to an island on the Snake River in Idaho with Ted Trueblood in his canoe. A ground fog about a yard deep overlay the river, and as the canoe grated gently on the shore, the fog hid us from Canada geese that we suddenly heard nearby.

"They've got to be on the sandbar forty yards down the shore," Ted said quietly. "Let's separate and come on them in ten minutes." He checked his watch and disappeared. I took to the weeds above the bank and eased toward the goose sounds.

At the agreed time we stepped out and there they were, only 25 yards away. A breeze had cleared off the fog, and I'll never forget the spectacle of dozens of the big birds thrashing away.

Confidently I swung on the head of a goose, shot, and then picked another carefully. Trueblood also shot twice. I walked toward him numbly, for neither of us had touched a feather.

There wasn't much to say, but Ted put it into words presently. He looked at the guns with which we'd done so well the day before and said, "Somehow it was us."

Western Rifles

LES BOWMAN

One side of Les Bowman comes across in Col. Askins' piece earlier in this collection—Bowman the hardbitten big-game outfitter. Most hunting enthusiasists also know him from his by-line in several publications: Guns, The Handloader, The Rifle, Gunsport, *and even Australia's* Sporting Shooter. *But for more than thirty years, Bowman's main activity was with aircraft. He was one of the pioneers of the air age, both as a flyer and racer and as an engineer. He and his wife, Martie, were both barnstormers, and their daughter soloed at the age of twelve, maintaining the family tradition.*

Bowman left the aircraft industry in 1951 to concentrate full-time on his business of outfitting and on writing, and since then he has become well known to the gun fraternity. However, he was reared with a gun in his hand, and he brings to his readers a lifetime's experience as a hunter as well as an engineer's interest in precision and a natural talent for explaining the finer points of hunting and hunting equipment.

TO AVERAGE HUNTERS, particularly those not familiar with the physical aspects of our Western hunting country, the term "Western rifle" means just one rifle of the type, caliber and weight suitable for all Western hunting. They would not use this rifle for deer hunting in the heavily wooded areas of the East, where most shots are made at fairly close range and in brushy or timbered country.

This is certainly a misconception and a large one. No one rifle of any caliber, type, or weight can be classed as a perfect "Western hunting rifle." The variety of game animals, ranging in size from moose to antelope, and hunting areas that take in the open plains and the high mountain country, make the use of several different rifles practically a necessity.

With the large assortment of rifles and calibers available to today's hunter, it is easy to select one that will be adequate for a particular kind of hunting area and the type of game in it. From the large number of rifles I have, I could select five of different types and calibers that would be adequate for any kind of hunting in the West, from the far Arctic to Central America. However, I am happy to be able to have more than just five to choose from, because quite often a choice from just these would be a compromise instead of the best gun for a certain kind of game and hunting terrain.

Because every outdoorsman does, or should, own a .22 rimfire rifle for target practice, plinking, vermin, and small varmint shooting as well as for the small game such as squirrels and rabbits, this caliber will not be on the following list of rifles for Western hunting:

1. Pure varmint rifles, short-, medium- and long-range types.
2. Large predator rifles that can also be used for varmints.
3. Combination varmint, predator, and light-game rifles.
4. Rifles for medium-size game animals, up to and including elk.
5. Rifles for the more dangerous game animals of Alaska and Canada. These include the brown and polar bear as well as the big grizzlies.

The rifle should be right for the job it has to do, although it may differ considerably in barrel length, weight, type of action, etc.

Power and velocity classifications are rather standardized for each general group, but within that grouping calibers and cartridges of many different sizes and styles can be used. This is particularly true in the fourth group, where a series of cartridges and calibers such as the .270 Winchester, the .280 Remington, the .284 Winchester, the .308 Winchester and the .30/06 will accomplish the same purpose. Selection of any of these is controlled by personal opinion and preference, just as the choice of any of the many variations in rifle types and styles.

The Varmint Rifle

The group of pure varmint rifles and calibers is a long one, because of many different factors: variations in the locality and areas, which governs the distance most shooting will be done at; the size and habits of the varmint being hunted; and last, but certainly not the least, the personal preference of the shooter.

Varmints of the West include prairie dogs, rockchucks, badgers, ground squirrels, and birds, such as the crow and some types of hawks. The smaller predators like the wildcat, the bobcat, and coyote would also be included in this varmint rifle class.

There are other predators found in certain coastal and inland areas of Alaska and Canada, two being what I consider our largest predators: the big Barren Land wolf and the seal. Wolves can weigh well over 150 pounds and seals run to 250 pounds, so the minimum rifle used for these larger predators should be of a caliber and power overlapping those used for game in the deer or antelope class.

The pure varmint rifles really start with the .22 Winchester Magnum and the rather new Remington 5-mm. Magnum. These are both rimfires, but have nearly twice the power and velocity of the standard .22 rimfire, Long Rifle cartridge. Both are excellent for shooting the smaller varmints in the prairie dog and ground squirrel class, at distances out to 150 yards. They are too light for such varmints as rockchucks, marmots, or the Eastern woodchuck, at distances of more than 100 to 125 yards. For a sure kill you should make head shots at these ranges. Both cartridges are made for different types and makes of rifles. These two Magnums are very accurate.

These cartridges (50 to a box, at a moderate price) are perfect for the shooter who does not handload and wants to keep both rifle and ammunition cost low. Both these cartridges develop quite high pressures and require stronger and better designed rifles to handle them than the standard .22 rimfire does.

For years, the .22 Hornet centerfire was the best of the pure varmint rifles. Using the 45- or 46-grain bullet, at a velocity of about 2,700 f.p.s., in later years it was bettered a little by the .218 Bee, at nearly 2,900 f.p.s. The .22 HiPower and the .220 Swift were real high-speed varmint rifles during the years of the Hornet popularity, with the .220 Swift doing 4,140 f.p.s.

The advent of the .222 Remington and a series of cases with the same head dimensions, giving a 50-grain bullet a velocity of 3,200 f.p.s. to 3,300 f.p.s., yet retaining good case and barrel life, while elevating the positive kill range to 225 or 250 yards, certainly helped the popularity of varmint shooting. Of the ten most popular cartridges in overall sales in this country, the .222 Remington is the only centerfire cartridge to be included.

During the past few years, the standardization of the wildcat .22-250 to factory ammunition status, and the addition of the .225 Winchester and the .224 Weatherby Magnum, have established a group of pure varmint, high-velocity cartridges that attain 3,550 to 3,800 f.p.s. They all shoot the .224 bullet, mostly in the popular weight range of 50 to 55 grains.

Any of these mentioned are good for most varmints, of various sizes, out to 400 yards. They are all powerful enough for good kills on coyote-size predators but are definitely too light for the big wolves. Seal must be killed instantly when hit or they will sink and be lost, and I know several commercial seal hunters who use the .224 calibers for their work, depending entirely on the accuracy of their rifles and making head shots only. My choice for such use would be one of the larger .243 (6-mm.) sizes.

When we select the .243 Winchester, the 6-mm. Remington or the .240 Weatherby, we are out of the class of pure varmint calibers and enter the light-game caliber category. All of these, using the specially constructed varmint-weight bullets of 60- to 80-grain weights, are excellent long-range varmint loads. With 100-grain bullets they are adequate for open-range shooting of deer and antelope.

In my opinion, the new .25/06 Remington is the very top of the line of the true varmint rifles. The 6-mm.'s will kill varmints out to well over 400-yard ranges and the .25/06 may increase this distance another 50 yards or so. Actually, the range of any of these calibers is mostly limited by the shooter's ability, and the quality of his rifle and sighting equipment. Also, as winds can be a problem in open-range country, a shooter should select a bullet that carries some weight.

The Plains Rifle for Light Game

The light-game rifle class, for such animals as deer and antelope, starts with the various .243's (6-mm.'s). One of these rifles, shooting the 100-grain bullet, is an excellent combination for antelope out to the 350-yard range. During my years of guiding hunters for this type of game, I have seen more good one-shot kills made with rifles of .243 or similar caliber than I have when the shooter was using a true big-game rifle in the Magnum class. A principal reason for this, I believe, is the lack of severe recoil, permitting a shooter to make better shot placement.

Many other rifles or calibers are very good for this size game, and some of them are adequate for all big game up to elk-size animals. Now that the .25/06 and ammunition for it is factory produced, it is growing rapidly in popularity. My favorite antelope-deer-weight bullet for this rifle, during the twenty-five years or so that I used it as a wildcat, was 100 grain. Remington is now one of the factories that has structured this weight for game and added it to their line of products. It should perform excellently.

Until both Remington and Winchester brought out a well-structured 120-grain bullet for the .25/06, I had always considered the caliber very marginal for elk-size game, although I have seen many of this size killed with it. Now, the new 120-grain loads, both the Remington and the Winchester, perform very closely to the 130-grain .270 loadings that have always done so well. *Do not* use the 87-grain varmint load or any similar varmint load in the .25/06 for any type of game. It is strictly for varmint or predator use.

Two old favorites of mine for deer and antelope hunting and also for varmints, using the proper bullets, were the .250/3000 and the .257 Roberts. Chamberings on both of these were discontinued by the major gun factories, quite some time ago, but ammunition is still being made. Now Savage has resurrected the .250/3000.

My criterion for minimum remaining energy at point of impact, for deer and antelope, has been 1,000 foot pounds or close to it. The .25/06, with its 120-grain bullet, has just about that at 500 yards, but the .257 Roberts, with the factory-loaded 117-grain bullet, has just under 1,000 f.p.e. at 200 yards, and the 100-grain bullet just a bit over this. The .250 Savage with its 100-grain bullet is now loaded to 1,000 f.p.e. at 200 yards. Keeping this in mind, it is easy to understand that these two calibers cannot be considered as good plains guns, even for deer and antelope.

The various 6.5-caliber rifles are excellent deer-antelope guns. Remington's 6.5 Magnum produces just 1,000 f.p.e. at 400 yards, using 120-grain bullets, and the Winchester .264 Magnum maintains close to elk-killing energy out to 500 yards.

The .270 Winchester, the .280 Remington, the .284 Winchester, and the .308 Winchester are all in a class so close together that a choice of any of them is really just a personal one. All of them are excellent deer or antelope guns to ranges slightly over 400 yards, providing the shooter pays the proper attention to the correct weight and structure of the bullets. All have light recoil and are

The .243 Winchester, a fine varminter, was also adequate for this extra-large antelope. With a 100-grain bullet any of the 243's will do well on light game out to 350 yards.

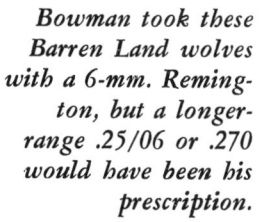

Bowman took these Barren Land wolves with a 6-mm. Remington, but a longer-range .25/06 or .270 would have been his prescription.

pleasant to shoot, and all are on the fringe of true big-game rifles. More North American big game is killed by this group of calibers than all the others put together.

Two more calibers must be included in this list of plains rifles. One is the 7-mm. Mauser. Originally made for extra long bullets for the caliber, the twist was excessively fast. A very limited selection of 7-mm. bullets were available in this country. The 7-mm. never did achieve any great popularity in this country, even with the thousands that were brought in as surplus military weapons. Our arms factories stopped chambering for it, and both major ammunition factories loaded only the 175-grain bullet, which was not at all popular with the sportsmen. This caliber was made up only by the custom gunsmith until Ruger just recently chambered a few of their bolt-action rifles for it.

The 7-mm. Mauser is at a complete disadvantage with bullets of 175 grains, but it is a really good rifle for deer and antelope on open range, with the 130- or 140-grain bullets. It is one of the best for sheep and goat or caribou when 130- to 140-grain bullets are used. For the biggest elk, 160 grain is the top weight that should be used. However, the performance of the 7-mm. Mauser is so nearly identical to that of the other four cartridges that there is little use comparing their relative merits.

The second of these two last calibers in the plains group is the reliable old .30/06, really in a class by itself. It can duplicate most anything they can do ballistically as a plains rifle and goes a step further. It probably is the only standard-case rifle cartridge that can properly be used for game of big bear and moose size, with the proper bullets for each job. For larger-size game, it handles heavy bullets, in weights from 190 to 220 grains, extremely well.

In fact, "if I was charged by a grizzly" (and I have been), I would rather have a .30/06, loaded properly, in my hands than any of the other calibers in this class. As a dyed-in-the-wool .270 fan, I expect I'll get some static from this statement, but the .30/06 is really one of the uncommon ones.

Mountain Rifles

In most of the Western big-game states, where there is little or no need for a large caliber as protection from dangerous game, the type of rifle that I've designated as a plains gun is also quite adequate for all kinds of mountain game, including the southern moose that are a bit smaller than Canadian and Alaskan moose. The four rifles I have grouped together under the plains rifle heading, plus the 7-mm. Mauser and most certainly the .30/06, are sufficient for any type of big game in these areas, including grizzlys. I believe Montana is now the only state that allows a hunter to kill a grizzly without a special permit. A very few special permits are issued by a drawing in Wyoming each year.

During my big-game outfitting years in Wyoming, I guided around sixty or more hunters that were lucky enough to take a grizzly trophy home. All of these, with the exception of a half dozen or so, were killed with calibers no more powerful than the .30/06. The grizzlys I have personally killed were all taken with the .270, the .280, and the .30/06.

For Wyoming moose, I found that any of the general big-game rifles were quite adequate, when used with the right kind of bullets. Bullet placement and bullet structure are far more important than caliber size on these animals.

I rather think that our Western elk is the most popular of our big-game animals. These animals average from 450 to around 800

Prince Abdorezza Pahlavi of Iran and his record elk, taken with his favorite mountain rifle: a Biesen-stocked Model 70 Winchester in 7-mm. Mauser caliber with 140-grain bullets.

pounds, live weight, and I have seen a few that weighed 1,000 pounds. These ones are the real big bulls and usually carry a rack to go with their size. Any animal this big presents a good-sized target. For lung shots there is an area 15 to 17 inches in diameter, and actually, a lung shot is the easiest to make, spoils less meat, and is quite lethal, if the shooter uses modern high-power rifles and well-structured expanding bullets. Unless a shooter is directly behind the animal, a lung shot can be made from any angle, and from directly in front it's a cinch. A direct front shot can blow up the heart and if a bit high will get the spine. Incidentally, if you do find your game with his rear end facing you, unless it's a bear, pass it up. Those rear shots and the so-called raking shots are for the "teller of tall tales." On the bear, since a hunter doesn't usually want the meat, a rear shot will often break the animal down and then a finishing shot does it. Some guides want their hunter to use a shoulder shot, especially on the big ones, for the same reason. If they are close up a shoulder shot is fine.

Ralph Young, Mr. Bear of southeast Alaska, likes his hunters to place their first shot in the lung area and then a shoulder shot if it's necessary.

Shoulder shots on elk with any rifle smaller than the .338 or at least the .300 Winchester with heavy bullets may mean a lost animal, and even with these calibers I have seen bullets fail to go all the way through and break both shoulders. It's surprising how far and fast an elk can go on three legs.

After twenty years or so of big-game outfitting in America's top elk country and witnessing the death of a great many of these magnificent animals, I consider a lung shot to be the surest of killing shots. Neck shot on elk are very uncertain, with any size caliber. There is a very narrow margin for bullet placement in a neck that varies in depth from 9 or 10 to maybe 18 inches. Broadside, the spine is maybe a 4-inch strip, more or less horizontal, and bullet placement for a killing shot is very uncertain in an area this small. If the spine is hit, death is immediate, but an elk with a bad neck wound can travel for miles before he dies.

Bighorn sheep and goats are both game animals for the mountain rifles. Bighorns weigh up to 300 pounds, but are quite easy to kill if hit properly. Although about the same weight as bighorns, goats are harder to kill for some reason. Perhaps sheep, like their domestic cousins, just die easier. Goats are another matter and are as hard to put down for keeps as a prairie dog. Contrary to many stories about them, as a rule bighorn sheep and goats are not killed at terrifically long ranges. My hunters killed quite a number of bighorn sheep during those outfitting days, and very few of them killed at distances of over 200 yards. The average kill was probably less than this, with many under 100 yards. It was almost always possible to make a stalk to within these ranges. Goat kills are made at about the same distances. However, there is always the exception and a hunter does have to make a long shot or he will lose a trophy. By long I mean 300 to 400 yards.

For sheep or goats, any of the plains rifles from the .25/06 on up are excellent choices. My particular favorite is a fast-handling, short-barreled (22-inch) .270 Winchester, rebuilt and restocked for me by Al Biesen of Spokane. The 6.5-calibers are excellent rifles for this kind of game. Also the various 7's, from the standard 7-mm. Mauser on up the scale.

I have read the assertion by some hunter-writers that it takes a rifle of Magnum power to kill a caribou. Well, I guess I just never met any of those tough-to-kill caribou, as my experience on over thirty caribou kills proved them to be about the easiest of all the larger antlered deer to kill. Any good mule deer rifle is adequate for caribou, if the shooter stays within the proper killing range.

Any statement on what kind of rifle it takes to kill a black bear is going to elicit arguments, one way or another. I was brought up in black bear country, at a time when they were extremely plentiful. In fact, they were considered varmints. There was no season and no limits on killing them. My only *high*-powered rifle was a Model 94 .25/35 Winchester. My ammunition was 117-grain factory issue. Money to buy this was scarce, and I had to make every shot count, so I was very sure that each shot was made within the proper killing distance of my rifle. Very seldom did I have to make a second shot.

During the years since then I have killed or seen killed a great many black bear. Our hunters in Wyoming, not really a heavily populated bear state, averaged about twenty a year. Many of these were killed with rifles as small in caliber as the .243 Winchester, using 100-grain bullets. I never saw a bear shot and lost when the hunter was using such a rifle. My personal selection of a black bear rifle starts with a .25 rifle, using not less than the 117-grain bullet. The 7-mm. Mauser, .270 Winchester, the .280 Remington, .284 Winchester, and the .308 Winchester, and certainly the .30/06 are all good black bear rifles, if well-structured bullets are used.

However, black bear are stubborn and tough. I once watched two hunters, both of them trying to get in a first killing shot at a small (250 pounds) bear, shoot and hit him seven times. They were using .06's and good bullets. That little bear ran over a mile before going down. Not one of those shots was properly placed. If they had been shooting Magnums the results would have been the same. These hunters would probably insist that it "takes a lot of killing to down a bear." And I'm just as sure that all it takes is a rifle-and-bullet combination that will penetrate, without premature expansion, the accumulated dust and dirt, thick fur and tough hide of the animal, provided the bullet is placed properly.

Now we come to the list of the high-powered Magnum rifles

Bowman and hunter with a big Wyoming grizzly. Any of the mountain rifles will do the job, with heavy well-structured bullets.

for our mountain rifle class. I do not include the 6.5 Remington Magnum or the .224 and .240 Weatherby Magnums in this list, as they really are not in the true Magnum category, ballistically.

I own and quite often use a number of belted Magnum rifles, in calibers from the .264 Winchester to the 7-mm. Magnums of both Remington and Weatherby, the .300 Winchester and the .300 Weatherby Magnums. My gun rack also houses the .338 Winchester, the .308 Norma Magnum, the .375 H&H, and the .350 Remington Magnum.

The .264 Winchester Magnum is one of the finest long-range deer or antelope rifles made, if a shooter wants that much power and range. It is in the same class with all the 7-mm. Magnums for mountain game. Any of the .300 Magnums are excellent long-range mountain rifles *if* the shooter can handle them well and without flinching. When these Magnums fail, it's the shooter's fault, not the gun's or ammunition's.

Many hunters feel that a Magnum in the .338 Winchester class, or at any rate a Magnum of some kind, is necessary for elk-size game. The fact is that they are more powerful than necessary and have too much recoil for the average hunter. Too many hunters think the bigger the caliber and greater the bullet weight, the easier it will be to get their game. They depend on this rather than proper bullet placement.

Although these larger Magnum rifles kill game very fast and very dead if they are handled accurately, the average hunter just badly wounds and loses more game using one than if he shot a rifle with less recoil, one that he can handle accurately.

In hunting areas where excessively long shots will be the rule and not the exception, a Magnum is quite definitely the best choice. In this kind of hunting country the shooter must be able to handle his rifle very accurately, and if he reacts to recoil it's just not his type hunting.

I kept a two-year record on some seventy-five hunters we had come to Wyoming for big game, mostly elk. The guides all made records of how many shots were fired, at what distances they were made, and all distances at which game was killed. The average distance of the elk kills was a bit under 185 yards. The average of what we called long shots was a little over 225 yards. Only 5 to 7 percent of all kills were over 300 yards. The hunters using the Magnum rifles had more misses and lost game than the hunters using the standard rifles.

For several years I have made a yearly survey of the leading calibers in ammunition sales in this country. Last year was the first time a Magnum rifle made the first ten. This is the 7-mm. Remington Magnum. The .30 caliber (.308 and .30/06) are two of the leaders.

The sales manager of one of the large companies I surveyed added in his answer: "It is interesting to note that J. Q. Shooter isn't too terribly impressed with the views of some of the scribes who think you need nothing less than a .338 Magnum for big game."

The .338 Winchester Magnum is a most excellent rifle for the kind of game it was designed for. It's one reason Winchester named it the "Alaskan," a name that should readily indicate its proper use. Calibers such as the .358 Norma Magnum, the .375 H & H, and others are in the same class.

Mountain Rifles for Mixed Game

Some hunting writers are quite definite about the merits of using a rifle of caliber size and power necessary for any size game in an area, even if that type game is not being hunted. This is especially true if the game is considered "dangerous." Excluding Alaska and its coastal brown bear, dangerous (meaning grizzly) game is nearly nonexistent throughout the Western states but rather plentiful in certain areas of the western and northwestern Canadian provinces and Inland Alaska.

The standard calibers I have listed as "mountain rifles" are all adequate for mountain grizzly, with special emphasis on bullet structure. I bring up this point of bullet structure as it relates to different types of game quite frequently because it is important and is the reason for the immense popularity of the standard calibers I call mountain rifles. The great variety of bullet weights and structure for these calibers makes them useful for most anything from varmints to deer, antelope, or elk. And the .30/06, with its heavier bullets, can even handle the big brown bear and polar bear. The .338 Winchester and other relatively large calibers do not have this large selection of bullet weights and structure. The large ammunition companies and most independent bullet companies produce specially structured bullets for the Magnum rifles.

Western Rifles

Sad to say, many sales people in the shops that deal in ammunition do not know enough about the types of proper ammunition for various calibers. The .30 caliber class is probably the one that is most confusing, and due to the growing popularity of the high-velocity .300 Magnums, it will pay a buyer to be sure of making the right selection as to weights and structure.

For the Western hunter who feels he needs more power and a longer-range rifle for mixed game of any size in the West, there are several choices in belted Magnums in 7-mm. and .30 caliber available. The 7-mm. Magnums, with their rather low recoil, are

Bowman's big bison—2,765 pounds—was taken with a .350 Remington Magnum.

excellent rifles and can be used with bullet weights of 175 grains, well structured for the largest game. They are pointed or Spitzer type for extreme distances.

I believe the various .300 Magnums are definitely the most popular of the Magnum calibers for all types of our Western big game.

Alaskan Rifles

As our hunter progresses through the antelope, deer, and elk hunting, he begins to think of the northern sheep, caribou, and grizzly, all of which can be easily hunted with rifles already listed. However, he will also want to try for the big brown bear of Alaska's coastal areas and perhaps a polar bear.

When Winchester brought out their fine .338 caliber, they gave it a most suitable name, the "Alaskan." It is an excellent choice for hunting the big brown bear and the very large moose they have in Alaska's hunting areas. The only other rifles in this class, the .358 Norma and the .375 H & H, exceed the .338 a bit in power but not in distance.

In general, Western big-game rifles, in all the categories, are bolt-action. A few shooters prefer the lever-action. This action, in such calibers as the .284 Winchester, really utilizes a rotary bolt. There is a scattering of semi-automatics, in appropriate calibers, and some pump-actions, such as the Remington 742.

These rifles are invariably equipped for scope installation. A few rifles have open sights only, and a big percentage have no open sights at all.

The selection of a scope and power is a matter of personal preference. Today's variable power scopes are so rugged and reliable that their popularity is rapidly increasing.

Most Western or mountain rifles have standardized in weight at about eight to nine pounds. Barrel lengths are usually 24 inches, plus an inch or two for some rifles. The stocks on the factory-produced rifles have been so much improved during many years of trial-and-error designs that now the general shape, grip, etc. pretty well fit the majority of shooters as well as a custom-made one would.

The only change in stock fit that now ever seems to be necessary is the minor one of length, and this can be remedied very easily at a minimum cost by any local gunsmith.

Long-Range Shotgunning: How Long?

PETE BROWN

> Pete Brown's first childhood memories are of stalking tumbleweeds with "a Magnum popgun" on the windy South Dakota plains. At eight, armed with a .22 single-shot Hamilton, he declared war on the local prairie dogs and jack rabbits, and by the time he was twelve, he was bagging prairie chicken with his father's 12-gauge double and pursuing turkeys and coyotes with a .38/40 Winchester Model 92.
>
> While studying engineering and ballistics at the U. S. Naval Academy and the University of Illinois, he took up target shooting, and he continued competition after graduation in time off from his job with Western Cartridge Co. During both World War II and the Korean War, Brown held a commission in the Naval Bureau of Ordnance, first as a technical adviser on small-arms and aircraft ammunition and later as assistant to the head of the Ammunition Planning Division. While in the service he began his career as a gun writer with Sports Afield, and he is now Arms Editor there. Brown has written two books, Guns and Hunting *and* Rimfire Rifleman.

RECENTLY I'VE TAKEN what I consider some of the best patterning and game bird data and pulled it all together graphically for a new look-see. If the deductions arrived at by those who have done considerable research are true, then the long-range performance of the shotgun is not as good as some of us think. Not even with the recent great improvements: plastic shot shell tubes, folded crimps, gas-tight wads, protective sleeves for the shot, and better informed shooters. The available data, unfortunately, tends to prove my latest evaluation.

Now I'm thinking in terms of patterns capable of producing a clean kill 95 percent of the time. For example, the maximum sure-kill range of the average 10-gauge Magnum shotgun firing a 2-ounce load is about 51 yards when using No. 2 shot on geese.

The maximum sure-kill mallard range of the 2-ounce load of No. 4 shot comes out to a mere 48 yards. The farther you shoot beyond these ranges, the greater the gamble — even with the bird within the 30-inch pattern circle. However, the superb shot, who can whap the bird with the inner 15-inch circle of pattern, will increase his effective range by as much as 5 yards.

I'll bet most gunners have been led to believe that such a tremendous load will give clean kills at 60, perhaps 70, yards. One reason so many people think this is because part of the time one or two shot pellets happen to hit the right spot and they do drag a duck or goose down out of the stratosphere. Often people overestimate their shells' capabilities simply because they greatly overestimate the range.

Long-range duck and goose shooting is customarily what we call "pass shooting," birds flying to or from feeding areas, or trading back and forth between birds rafting on separate bodies of water. Over the years, the birds have been passing higher and higher as hunters increase and their shells get better. Man has taught waterfowl caution. Now when they fly above land they are inclined to avoid passing over clumps of trees or other cover that might conceal a hunter. If they must fly over trees, they will generally fly that much higher; if they are flying at 50 yards above the ground, they will lift to 50 yards above the treetops. A hunter may actually handicap himself by locating his pass blind in a clump of trees or in a hedgerow.

Otherwise, the peculiar ways of our ducks and geese have changed little during the past centuries. Oh, they will be more cautious when approaching a feeding spot. They have been fooled by sets of decoys many times, and they generally peruse them carefully before deciding on their authenticity.

The puddler ducks are the shallow-water feeders. These include the mallard, black duck, and pintail. They are the slower species and are inclined to be the highest fliers. They approach the feeding area, which may include a set of decoys and the hunter's blind, from on high, then circle and meticulously look things over from a safe elevation. Satisfied, they will ease down and then drop in among the decoys like helicopters. They feed in shallow water and stuff themselves with wild rice and smartweed.

The divers take in the canvasbacks and redheads. They belong to the jet set in the duck family. They fly fast and dive deep to feed on aquatic vegetation such as wild celery The divers are prone to fly lower than the shallow-water ducks. In the style of antelope among land animals, they depend to a large extent on speed for safety. A canvasback may sweep in as low as 40 yards or less, but at a speed of 70 miles or more per hour. He can't possibly slow up enough to flutter down like a puddle duck. He must land like a jet and he needs room. That is why a decoy set for the diver ducks must have a lot of open space in the center. Otherwise these ducks, designed for speed and fast landings, will, in all probability, overshoot the decoys.

Duck characteristics affect long-range shooting. Therefore, a good pass shooter must be able to identify ducks in flight. This helps him judge height, speed, and lead. Divers are inclined to put on a burst of speed when alarmed. That's when they accelerate to better than 70 miles an hour. The puddlers, on the other hand, usually flare upward and tower when alarmed or even suspicious.

Pass shooters are aware that it is the divers that do most of the trading back and forth between different bodies of water. Over large stretches of water, such as wide rivers and lakes, there will generally be a great variety of ducks as well as geese. It is here in particular that the gunner can improve his chances by knowing the various species, their behavior and flying patterns in the area. Before locating his blind, he will be smart to observe flights for a few days if possible. Unless hard pressed, the birds will keep to the same routes.

Whatever the gun, it should have a full-choke barrel, because shots will be mostly at ranges of 40 yards or more. A double makes a fine pass-shooting gun because the shooter can then be prepared for the high-flying puddle ducks or geese and the fast divers that come whizzing over at lower elevations. The double with one barrel full choke and the other improved modified or modified is right— provided the gun has double triggers or a selective single trigger.

Pass shooting is the most difficult to master. The shooter must learn to judge range and speed, and it isn't easy. The distinctness of the duck's markings varies in different light. The direction of approach is a factor in what you see in markings and size. A duck flying in the wide-open sky appears smaller than it does at the same range when framed by trees. Ducks flying near or below the skyline appear smaller. Judging range is a tough problem.

If you can pick your days for pass shooting, take note of the wind. On a windy day the birds will be flying lower than they normally fly during calm conditions.

Judging speed of flight? No one can estimate the speed of a duck within 5 miles per hour! Of course not, but being familiar with the flight characteristics of the various species will help, and the way you lead the duck can make up for considerable error in estimating speeds.

No one can tell you just how much to lead. This depends on personal experience. There are many factors involved—individual reaction time, lock time, etc., which enter into how your personal built-in computer serves you.

I believe in swinging with the speed of the duck, then pulling out in front for lead. Swing past and follow through. Don't stop your gun. Keep swinging for a little, even after you have fired. In this way you tend to swing faster on the faster birds and thereby take a greater lead.

How far will your gun make kills with 95 percent certainty, assuming you put the pattern where the bird is? We may think in terms of sure-kill range but, actually, the term is used loosely. The 95-percent kill figure is used by Oberfell and Thompson in their book *The Mysteries of Shotgun Patterns*. This recognizes the fact that we are dealing with a scattergun.

From calculations based on the results of exhaustive studies of pattern performance and careful analysis of bird kills, I have plotted some graphs to show the maximum 95-percent kill range. I have made use of pattern data found in the *Winchester-Western Ammunition Handbook* and pattern as well as game-kill studies in the Oberfell and Thompson book.

In plotting pellet count versus range, I based everything on a 72 percent pattern in a 30-inch circle at 40 yards. We know that some gun and load combinations will do better and some worse, but I took 72 percent for an average figure. But what is the pattern percentage of such a gun at 50 or 60 yards? To obtain these figures for my plot, I made use of Tables II and III on page 28 of the *Winchester-Western Ammunition Handbook*. These tables provide information regarding the percentages of 40-yard patterns in a 30-inch circle at other ranges. These percentages vary with different sizes of shot as well as range.

For remaining energy of individual shot pellets at various ranges,

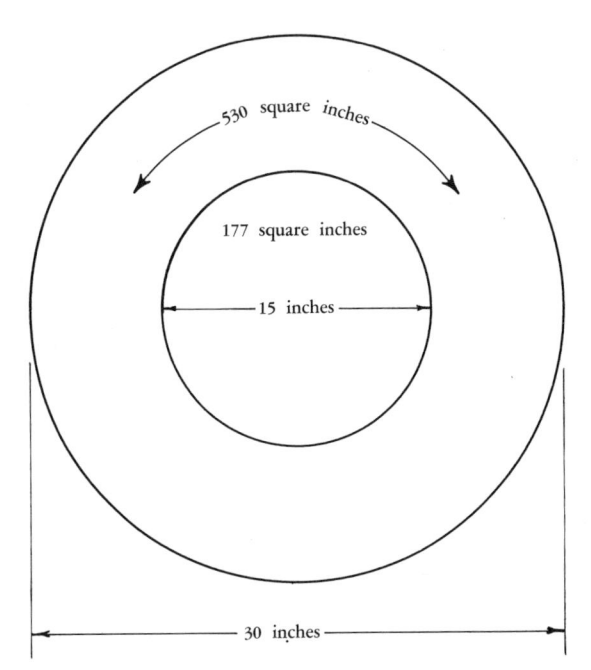

THE WAY THE SHOT SCATTERS. Total 30-inch-circle area is 707 square inches, and the inner 15-inch circle is only 25 percent of this area. However, out of a full choke, the 15-inch circle gets about 38 percent of the shot striking within the larger circle.

I used the remaining energy figures in the table starting on page 33 of the *Handbook*. Oberfell and Thompson developed a formula for arriving at the minimum consistent killing energy for any bird. They found that this energy divided by the "relative target size" was always equal to the constant 11.1. Relative target size was taken to be two-thirds power of the number of pounds corresponding to the weight of the bird. The authors, in Table 34 on page 171 of their book, provide a "Table of Weights and Relative Target Sizes for Water Fowl and Upland Game Birds." The table also gives the trunk area for various game birds.

In order to plot the curve "Minimum pellet count (energy)," I first calculated the minimum energy required to sure-kill the bird in question. I then divided this by the remaining energy of individual pellets at the different ranges. This gave me the number of pellets required to deliver this energy. With this figure I related the area of the bird to the area of the 30-inch circle to determine the number of pellets required in the 30-inch circle to deliver the required energy to the bird.

The plot of "Minimum pellet count (pattern)" is relatively simple. Based on much testing, it has been found that it takes a minimum of four or five pellets of appropriate size to make a sure kill. I have based results on four pellets in past studies. Of course, the plot will be a straight horizontal line. To determine the minimum pellet count in a 30-inch circle in order to put four pellets in the bird, we relate the trunk area of the bird to the area of a 30-inch circle. We thereby arrive at the pellet count in a 30-inch circle required to place four pellets within the trunk area of the bird.

When dealing with long-range shooting, it really makes little difference whether we select four pellets or five pellets as minimum for a sure kill. It seems, from the accompanying graphs, that as we increase range, we run out of energy before we run out of pattern in a full-choke gun. This would not be the case, however, with the more open-choked guns.

Another factor comes into shooting game birds at long range. The pattern gets progressively denser (more pellets per square inch) toward the center of the pattern. This was very effectively shown in a study made by Winchester-Western and reported in the *1963 Sports Afield Gun Annual*. The variation in density is also taken into account in the Oberfell and Thompson book. The change in shot concentration, pattern density, or whatever we might call it can best be expressed by the number of shot per square inch.

Assume, for example, that we shoot a $1\frac{1}{2}$-ounce load of No. 6 shot from a gun giving 72 percent patterns in a 30-inch circle at 40 yards. In the outer ring between the 30-inch circle and the 20-inch circle there will be a shot concentration of about 0.3 shot per square inch. The ring between the 20-inch circle and the 10-inch circle will have about 0.5 shot per square inch and the inner 10-inch circle will have close to 0.7 shot per square inch.

Therefore, the shooter who can center his pattern on the target will be able to make sure kills at longer range. Let's assume that he can always hit the target with the inner 15-inch circle. Chart 2 shows the plot based on a 15-inch pattern. Compare this chart with Chart 1, and you will see why the good shot can make sure kills at about 5 yards longer range than the shooter who is a 30-inch pattern shot.

CHART 1. *No. 4 shot on mallard and teal; 72-percent pattern in 30-inch circle at 40 yards, plotted on basis of pattern in concentric 15-inch circle. Note that the pellet count is low for teal; No. 4 shot is not best for small ducks. Also note that the sure-kill range within 15-inch pattern circle is nearly 55 yards, compared with the 49-yard sure-kill range shown in Chart 2 based on using all of the 30-inch pattern.*

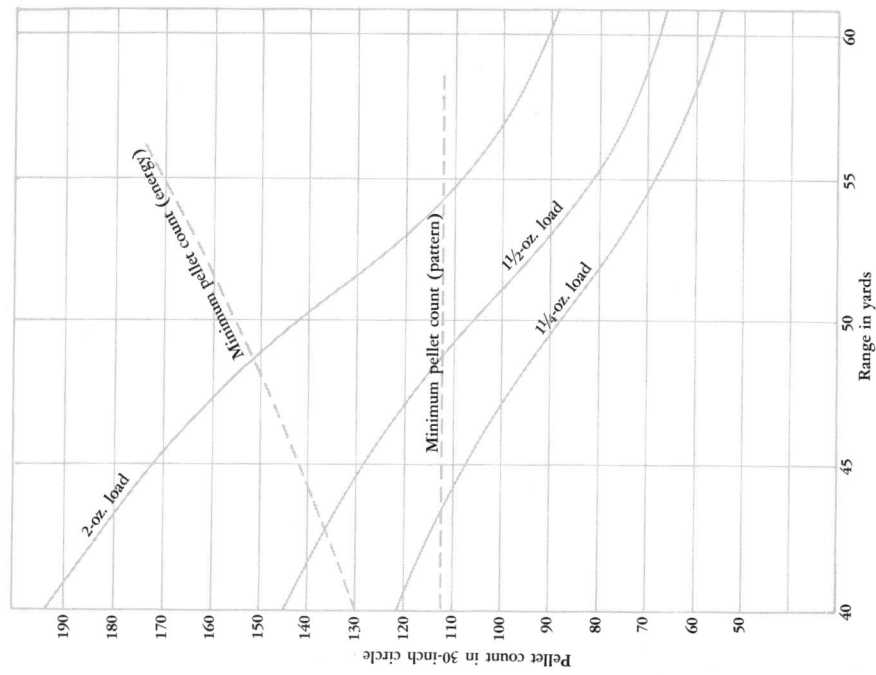

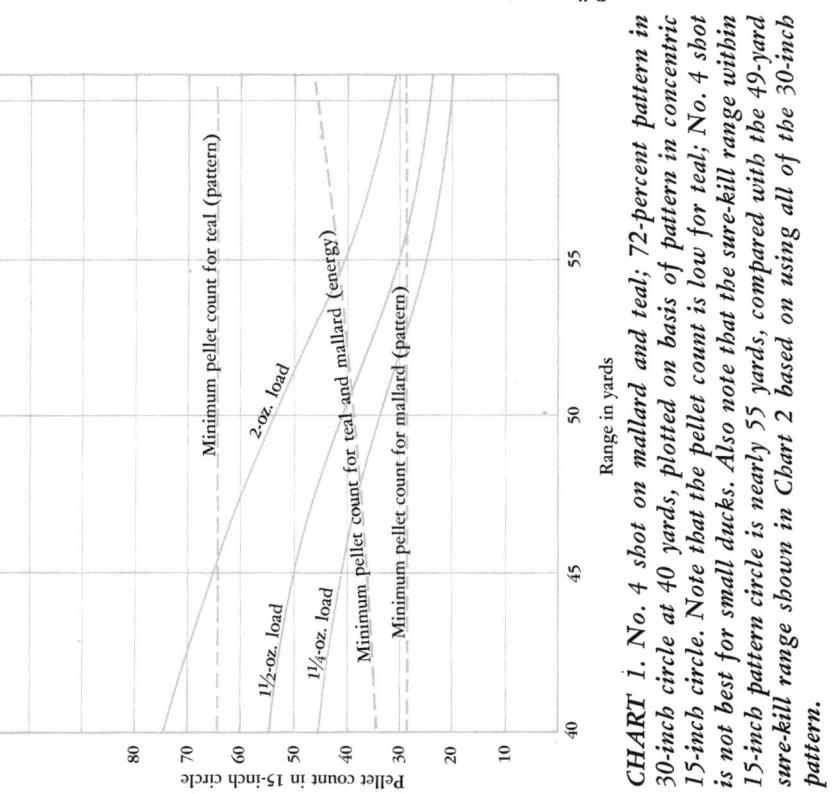

CHART 2. *No. 4 shot on mallard; 72-percent pattern in 30-inch circle at 40 yards.*

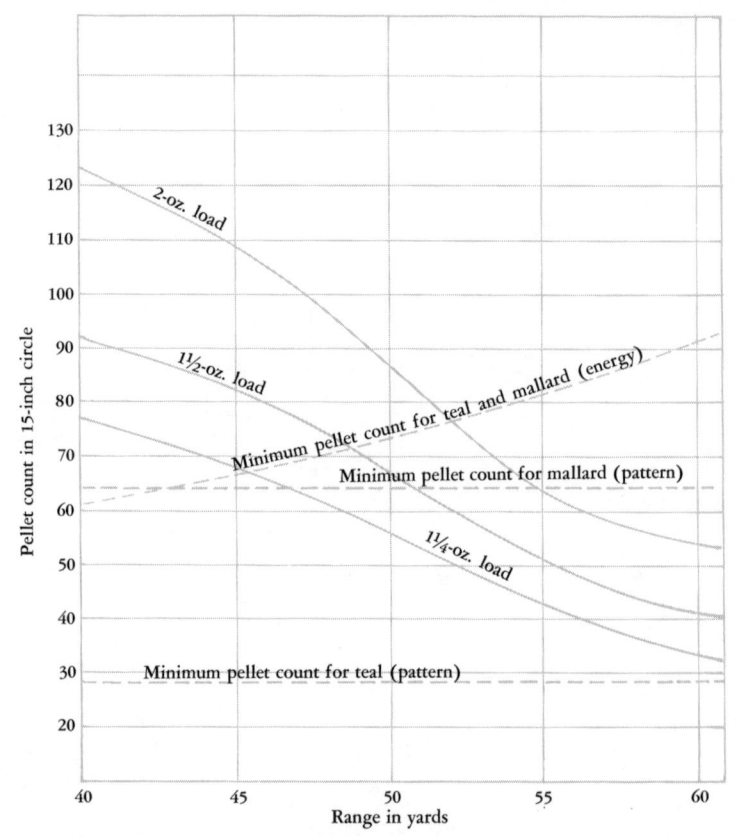

CHART 3. No. 6 shot on mallard and teal; 72-percent pattern in 30-inch circle at 40 yards, plotted on basis of pattern in concentric 15-inch circle. The sure-kill range for teal is 52 yards with 2-oz. load if the shooter can put the inner 15-inch pattern on the bird. Compare with Chart 1 and note that with No. 4 shot the maximum sure-kill range for teal is limited to barely more than 45 yards by minimum pattern requirements.

At this point, someone is sure to invite attention to the fact that there is such a thing as shot-string and that all shot do not arrive at the target at the same time. Then what about passing shots? Sure, this is worth some consideration, but if the shooter is swinging with the bird, the shot column is moving with the target and will get full benefit of all shot with which it is lined up in the shot-string.

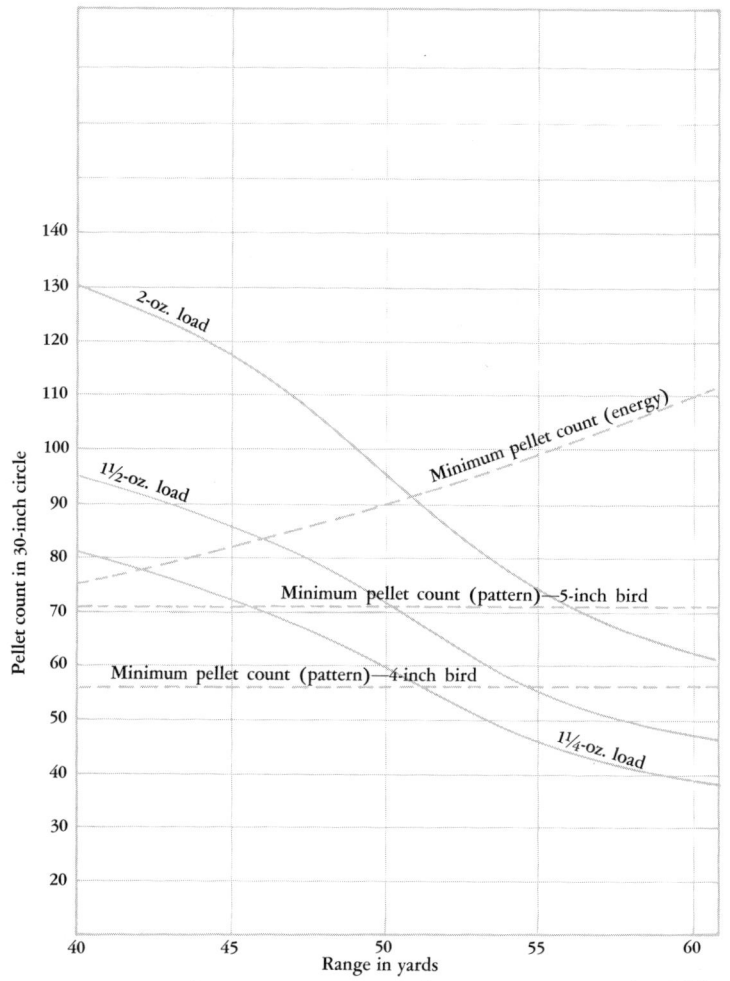

CHART 4. *No. 2 shot on goose; 72-percent pattern in 30-inch circle at 40 yards.*

Chart 1 shows a plot of the calculations for No. 4 shot on a mallard duck. The calculations and resulting plot are based on the required killing energy delivered by pellets penetrating the bird's body. However, a large percentage of birds are bagged because a pellet hit a wing and broke it or a single pellet hit the head. This isn't accounted for in the results picked from the graph.

Here are some of the findings based on my probing of available data:

1. When appropriate sizes of shot are used in a *full-choke gun* for ducks and geese, it is the minimum energy requirement that limits range, rather than the pattern requirement of putting four pellets into the trunk area of the bird. In other words, at long range, it generally takes more than five pellets to make up the combined killing energy requirements.

2. No. 4 or 5 shot is best for mallard-sized ducks at long range, but it is poor for teal-sized ducks. No. 6 shot will produce best long-range shots at teal, particularly when the heavier loads (1½ to 2 ounces of shot) are used. The 1¼-ounce loads are just not in it for long-range teal shooting.

3. If a superb long-range shooter can hit his birds within the 15- or 20-inch concentric pattern circle, he can add about five yards of sure-kill range. Why? Because the shot distribution is denser near the center of the pattern.

4. Chart 2 provides the story for No. 4 shot on mallard-sized ducks. Here are some conclusions based on Charts 3 and 4.

No. 6 Shot—pellet counts based on 72 percent pattern in 30-inch circle at 40 yards:

	Maximum Sure-Kill Range (Yds.)	
	Mallard	*Teal*
2-ounce load	40	48
1½-ounce load	40	40
1¼-ounce load	33	33

No. 2 shot—pellet counts based on 72-percent pattern in 30-inch circle at 40 yards:

	Maximum Sure-Kill Range (Yds.)
	Geese
2-ounce load	51
1½-ounce load	46
1¼-ounce load	42

All of which proves that when Elmer Keith drags his big 10-gauge Magnum way out to the East Coast to shoot passing ducks and geese, he is long on smart.

The Big-Bore Target Rifle—King of the Range

JIM CARMICHEL

Jim Carmichel has been absorbed with guns, hunting, and competitive shooting for thirty of his thirty-six years. Already a skilled gunsmith at an age when most of us have barely graduated from the .22, he earned his way through East Tennessee State University by making stocks for fine rifles and shotguns. His college curriculum was planned to add depth to his knowledge of the mathematics and physics of shooting.

After several years with the Tennessee Game and Fish Commission, Carmichel resigned and moved to Arizona, where he has been active in specialty writing on firearms and shooting. He also serves as Executive Secretary of the National Reloading Manufacturers Association. Carmichel has won many honors in trap, skeet, smallbore rifle, big-bore rifle, and bench-rest shooting, and he is an ardent hunter. Gun and shooting enthusiasts can look forward to seeing his by-line often.

I'VE HEARD IT SAID that the 300-meter free rifle is the queen of rifle competition. If so, there can be no doubt that the big-bore "over the course" gun is the king.

At any rate, no one questions that it calls for the greatest combination of skills of any shooting sport. Not only this, but also a good working knowledge of ballistics and firearms mechanics, plus the poise to withstand the pressures of intense competition. This makes the big-bore rifleman the tall dog among all competition shooters. If you doubt this, just consider the courses of fire the big-bore rifleman encounters in a typical match.

The tournament usually begins with twenty shots standing (offhand) at 200 yards with iron (peep) sights and a twenty-minute time allowance. Some tournaments allow a couple of sighting shots but not usually. Thus, the rifleman must have a thorough under-

Carmichel demonstrates the classic military offhand position with the M1 Garand.

standing of his rifle and know just where and how to set the sights in order to get that first shot on the money.

This is an outdoor event, so if the wind is blowing the rifleman has another factor to consider: How much will the bullet be blown off course? He must estimate this effect and make the necessary changes in his sight-setting. He is not allowed an unlimited number of sighters to "feel out" the wind and make his sight adjustments by trial and error. His first shot is for record, so he has to know his business or flunk out early in the contest.

Not only this, but each individual shot will undergo the critical inspection of at least two other individuals, plus any number of other spectators who may care to look on. As each bullet strikes the target, the man working that target at the butts (two men may even be working each target) lowers the target and marks the location of the hit with a large disc called a "spotter." He also places a scoring disc along the edge of the target to indicate the value of the shot. A scoring disc in the upper-right-hand corner of the target means that the bullet hit dead center for an "X." From there the scoring disc is moved around the edge of the target clockwise to indicate hits of lower value.

In days gone by, shot values were signaled by moving a handheld device. Misses were telegraphed for all to see by waving the infamous "Maggie's drawers"—a red flag. When the current, more complex targets were adopted, the more sophisticated fixed-scoring disc method came into use. Some ranges, however, still keep "Maggie's drawers" handy for shots that happen to go astray.

When the target is raised, the scorekeeper, positioned close by the shooter, notes the position of the scoring disc, records the value on the scorecard, and calls out the value of the shot to the shooter. There is no way to keep a bad shot a secret; it's right there for everyone to see—and hear. Each shot is a complete drama in itself and is played out twenty times over before the shooter can retire from the stage. Under match conditions the performance is exhausting.

The next event calls for twenty more shots at 200 yards, this time from the relatively steady sitting position. (The shooter can shoot from the kneeling position if he prefers, but this is virtually unheard of.) Here the big-bore rifleman is required to exhibit a wholly different facet of his skills: the ability to aim and fire with great speed—*ten shots in sixty seconds!*

This divides up into six seconds per shot—perhaps not too difficult. But there's more to it than that . . . . When the sixty-second time period begins, the shooter must be *standing!* So he has to sit down, get into a comfortable position, and mount his rifle before beginning to fire the ten-shot string. Beginning to sound a bit difficult? Wait, there's more . . . . He must also *reload* during the string! This leaves the big-bore shooter scant seconds to aim, fire, work the bolt, and aim again. Yet the proficiency of some riflemen is astounding. It is not unusual for nearly all of the ten-shot string to hit within the two-inch "X" ring. When the score is recorded, the rifleman rises and awaits the command for a second string of ten rounds.

The next event is rapid fire again, this time from the prone position. But to add a little spice, the range has been increased to *300 yards*. The time limit has also been increased to a full seventy seconds, but the big-bore rifleman still has to begin from an upright position, and he must still reload during the string.

Too, the shooter must adjust the sights to compensate for the greater distance. This is where a solid working knowledge of the rifle and amunition becomes indispensable. If the sights are raised

This awkward-looking position allows the shooter to drop quickly into a comfortable cross-legged position for the 200-yard rapid-fire stage. This position calls for 10 shots in 50 seconds with service rifles or 60 seconds with bolt-actions.

too much, the shots will hit high. Not enough and they will fall low. Either way the score suffers. The rifleman is still trying to get his shots in that two-inch circle.

And then of course the added range presents more problems if the wind is blowing. How far will a five-mile-per-hour wind—or a fifteen-mile-per-hour wind—blow a .30 caliber bullet off course at 300 yards? The big-bore rifleman has to know. He also has to be able to estimate the actual velocity of the wind with a pretty fair degree of accuracy. If he misjudges, his score will suffer. But that's all part of the game.

Next the rifleman moves back to the 600-yard line. On occasion this event will be fired at only 500 yards because of the limited space facility of some ranges. Either way the target is the same, a 24-inch black "bull" that includes the 8, 9, 10, and X rings. The X ring measures a scant six inches, or *one minute of angle*. The 10 ring is one foot wide.

During the rapid-fire events the big-bore rifleman has exhibited a certain flair and dexterity in his form. Now he becomes decidedly deliberate and calculating. The event calls for twenty-two shots

The Big-Bore Target Rifle—King of the Range 57

prone, slow fire. The first two shots are sighters. The time limit is twenty-two minutes.

Of course, it takes some extremely close holding to keep all the shots in the one-foot 10 ring, or for that matter even the two-foot "bull," under the best of conditions. When the wind blows the difficulties are compounded manyfold.

Even with the long, streamlined, boat-tailed high ballistic-coefficient match bullets designed for top wind-bucking efficiency, the effect of a breeze, however slight, can be astounding. Thus, the success of the rifleman largely depends on how well he can estimate the strength of the passing wind and translate his estimate into actual bullet displacement. This is learned by experience.

Too, the wind is seldom constant and as likely as not it will completely change directions several times during the event. The rifleman must be alert to even the most subtle changes of conditions, and his sights are constantly being adjusted in order to keep the point of impact in the center of the bull. Twenty-two minutes of such physical and mental exercises frequently leave the rifleman more fatigued than strenuous physical labor.

Some tournament programs will also include a match at *1,000 yards!* Whatever the reasons—the mystique of long range, the

While the target is being scored, Carmichel notes changes in mirage and wind conditions. Good record-keeping is a key factor in building rifle proficiency.

unique long-range rifles themselves, or simply the idea of hitting a target at over a half mile—few riflemen will dispute that the 1,000-yard match is the most fascinating of all. Likewise, the 1,000-yard winner lays claim to more honors than any other rifle event regardless of the type of competition. The famed Wimbledon Match, fired each year during the National Rifle and Pistol Matches, is the most famous of rifle events.

Actually the big three-foot bull with its twenty-inch V or center circle, doesn't seem all that difficult. It's not at all uncommon for several shooters to fire a perfect score of 100 points during the event. The winner, however, is determined by the number of hits in the V ring. Even so, with a good rifle and perfectly calm conditions the V doesn't offer such an exceptional challenge.

It's when the air moves that the fun begins. A breeze so light that it scarcely ripples the surface of a pond or turns a blade of grass can play astonishing tricks with a bullet that has to travel 3,000 feet.

In such cases the rifleman has to call on his total store of experience to get the bullet to the center of the bull. Even then his resources are often exhausted to the point where all he can do is take an educated guess and hope for the best. What, for example, can one do when the wind is actually blowing in two or more different directions at different places along the bullet's route? Consider also that even such variables as temperature and even the intensity and direction of light affect the performances of rifle, ammo, and shooter.

Though the tournament described above is probably the most typical course of fire, the program may vary considerably. Another popular course of fire is the so-called National Match Course for *service* rifles (meaning the M1 Garand or the M14 military rifles). The standard NMC calls for ten shots in each of the standing, rapid-fire sitting, and rapid-fire prone positions, then twenty-two rounds slow fire at 600 yards. Since autoloaders are used here, ten seconds are lopped off the rapid-fire time allotments. This makes it fifty seconds for the setting phase and sixty seconds for the 300-yard prone phase. Rapid fire is right!

Another popular course of fire is the long-range tournament. These usually will call for twenty-two shots each at 600 and 1,000 yards with iron sights then a repeat of the two events giving the shooter the option of iron sights or scopes (any sights). Or perhaps the tournament will be 1,000 yards only.

This shooter is firing at 1000 yards during the 1968 Wimbledon matches at Oak Ridge, Tennessee. The scorekeeper sits to the right and rear.

Of course, any number of combinations of events will make up a tournament. The host club can select any choice of fire they like or feel will interest the most shooters.

Most tournaments also include team matches, usually for two- or four-man teams. These team matches are usually a repeat of the individual matches, with the exception that the firers are coached during shooting by their fellow teammates or a designated team coach. This means that rather than having to do all the wind-doping and figuring out for himself plus aiming and squeezing the trigger, the coach looks after the wind conditions for him and dictates necessary sight corrections.

This allows an additional degree of precision, because the coach is on the lookout for any change in conditions and can order a change of sights or hold right up to the instant of firing. Good coaching is an art unto itself, and there are lots more good shooters than there are good coaches.

The military in particular puts special emphasis on the team matches because it gives one post or base an opportunity to beat another or, in larger competitions, corps against corps, and finally, service branch against service branch. When the Marines, Army, Navy, and Air Force all get together in a big shoot, the competi-

A few of Carmichel's match rifles. At top, a Roy Dunlap .308 match rifle on a Model 70 action. Scope is a 15-power Lyman Super Target Spot. Second down, a .300 Winchester Magnum Custom Bolt on a Model 70 action; this one is used for 1000 yards only. Stock is laminated walnut by Reinhart Fajen, and scope is a 20-power "3200" Redfield. Third down is a Roy Dunlap .30/06 Model 70 "over the course" rifle with Unertl 16-power target scope. The scope is used only for scope-sight events at 1000 yards and occasionally at 600 yards. At bottom is a 7-mm. Remington Magnum 1000-yard bull gun built on a Model 70 action with Fajen laminated-walnut stock. Scope (which is no longer available) is 6-24-power variable by Bausch and Lomb.

tion is intense—to say the least. As one coach quipped, "Winning isn't everything—it's the *only* thing."

The Big-Bore Match Rifle

By and large, rifles used in these courses of fire fall into three principal groups: Service Rifle, NRA Match Rifle, and Any Rifle. Of these the Service Rifle, which includes the M1 Garand (.30/06 caliber) and M14 (.308 caliber), is the most flexible. By this I mean that it is the only type of rifle allowed in many events (such as many National Match courses) and is nearly always allowed to be used, if the shooter wishes, in events for the NRA-type bolt guns or the "Any Rifle" category. Presumably this means that all you need is an M1 or M14 rifle, a truckload of ammo, and you're in the target-shooting business. Actually this is not the whole story. The M1 you toted back in World War II or the Korean days and those used in top-flight competition are as about as much alike as Elizabeth Taylor and Bella Abzug.

The Big-Bore Target Rifle—King of the Range

Service rifles used in competition are usually the National Match Grades, which are specially built and tuned for top accuracy. Needless to say, a National Match Grade Garand is harder to come by and usually more expensive than a standard service grade. Since the M14 rifle is capable of full automatic fire, they cannot be legally owned by individuals. Thus, civilians who use them in competition do so only on a short-term loan basis. Of course this works a considerable hardship on civilians who must compete against military shooters.

Most civilian shooters get by quite well by using Match Grade M1 Garands they have bought from the DCM (Director of Civilian Marksmanship).

The most widely used big-bore target rifle is the so-called NRA Match Rifle. The rules call for metallic (nontelescopic) sights, a trigger pull of three pounds or more (as opposed to the four-and-a-half-pound pull required for the Service Rifle), and chambering for either the standard .30/06 or .308 (7.62-mm.) cartridges.

The most widely used rifle of this type is the Winchester M-70 Target. Also, Remington now offers a repeater version of their 40-X for this type of competition. Too, quite a few "do-it-yourself" products show up on the firing line based on '03 Springfield, 1917 Enfield, and Mauser Actions as well as super accurate custom rifles based on M-70 or 40-X actions. In fact, many beginning shooters use an unaltered 1903 Springfield rifle in these events. As one's skill increases, however, more sophisticated equipment is usually called for.

Quite a few shooters beat the cost rap by building up their own match rifles. A basic Springfield '03 barrel and action, for example, can be fitted with adjustable target sights and a do-it-yourself semifinished stock for a total investment of under $100. Such rifles give completely satisfactory service. In time, however, the really involved competitor eventually invests in a custom rifle with super accurate barrel, adjustable trigger, the best sights, etc. or at least a Match Grade production rifle such as the M-70.

My first big-bore target rifle was an '03 of Rock Island manufacture with type C stock, a Lyman 48 rear sight, and Dayton Traister trigger. How many rounds I fired through that rifle would be hard to even guess at, but I sure had a lot of fun with it for a lot of years. Though it is now retired to the gun cabinet, I could never bring myself to part with it.

Detail of the Lyman Model 48 receiver sight mounted on a Springfield action. This rifle was made by an amateur gunsmith for less than $100, yet it is entirely satisfactory for big-bore competition.

My present "over the course" battery includes a National Match Garand, a M-70 Winchester Target Grade rifle in .30/06 caliber, a custom M-70 .30/06 with Douglas stainless-steel barrel and Roy Dunlap laminiated walnut stock, and a custom M-70 in .308 caliber, also with Dunlap stock and Douglas barrel. I always take two rifles with me so that if anything goes wrong I'll have a spare. Since I'm prepared, nothing ever seems to go wrong. I understand this has something to do with one of the universal laws.

The third type of rifle encountered in typical competiton is the officially designated "Any Rifle" style. This is a rifle of any caliber or weight, any weight trigger pull and stock style. Set triggers, hook buttplates, and palm rests, however, are not allowed. Not that this makes any difference, because for our purposes the "Any Rifle" is fired prone at long range only. More commonly it is referred to as the long-range bull gun or simply as "the Magnum."

These are remarkable arms, awesome to the shooter and non-shooter alike, and among the most specialized members of rifledom.

Since they are fired slow fire only, they are usually strictly single shots, the magazine cuts being omitted in order to leave more strength for both the action and stock. The weight, without sights, usually runs better than twelve pounds, and the caliber is usually one of the big-belted Magnums.

The most popular calibers for the Any Rifle category are the 300 Winchester Magnums, .300 H & H Magnum, 7-mm. Reming-

The Big-Bore Target Rifle—King of the Range

ton Magnum, and the wildcat .30/338 (.338 Winchester Magnum case necked down to .30 caliber.) One occasionally sees a .30/06 or .308 "Any Rifle" and frequently runs across sundry wildcats such as the 6.5 Weatherby Wright (.300 Weatherby necked down to .264 caliber).

These rifles are most always fixed with bases for mounting both iron sights and telescopic scopes for firing the full long-range course.

Though some programs allow the Any Rifle for 600 yards, they are generally regarded as strictly a 1,000-yard piece. This is the reason for the big Magnum chambering. The big cartridges, with their higher velocities, get the bullet over the range faster with less wind deflection. But the big Magnum target rifles present special problems of their own; they're more expensive to shoot, and some shooters simply cannot tolerate the recoil. Too, barrels for these Big Berthas are notoriously short lived. An accuracy life of 1,000 rounds for a .300 Magnum barrel is considered long. The average is closer to 500 rounds or thereabouts. Despite these shortcomings, the big Magnum target rifle is the Grand Duke of rifles. A really good one will put ten shots in ten or twelve inches at 1,000 yards on a calm day. One that won't keep twenty shots in twenty inches is a sure candidate for a new barrel at least, if not an early retirement.

The 1,000-yard "Any Rifles" in my battery include an M-70 Winchester action in a Reinhart Fajen laminated walnut stock with Douglas 28-inch stainless-steel barrel in .300 Winchester Magnum caliber. A second rifle is identical except for a stainless A & M barrel in 7-mm. Remington Magnum. A third rifle is identical except for a 30-inch A & M stainless barrel in a 7-mm. wildcat chambering based on the .280 Remington case. Any of these rifles will easily group inside the 20-inch 1,000-yard V ring. Firing from a bench at 100 yards with target scope, each is capable of five-shot groups that will go as small as a half-inch center to center of the widest shots.

Sights

Many, if not most, big-bore riflemen agree that the weakest link in the accuracy chain of big-bore target rifles is the sighting equipment. Not that both iron and telescopic sights aren't good—in fact, they're superb—but they simply haven't kept pace with developments in barrels, actions, bullets, etc.

The biggest problem with iron sights is that they don't stand up well to the cruel punishment of an often used target rifle and the constant back-and-forth, up-and-down adjustments that go with match shooting. Solving the problem is much more difficult than it might seem.

By its very nature a good iron sight must be a precision instrument, capable of fine, exact adjustment. This means that the mechanism must be pretty delicate. Herein lies the rub: delicate instruments and big-bore rifles don't go well together. I've known of shooters paying well over $100 for a custom-made rear sight. Yet, so far as I know, no one is ever completely happy with his rear sights.

Front sights are another matter entirely. Other than the occasional fellow who fails to keep the screws tight, the available target front sights sit tight and last forever. The variety of sizes, shapes, and colors in apertures seems to keep everybody happy.

Telescopic sights used in long-range events are invariably of the

Two popular types of receiver sights. At left, the Redfield International Match sight; at right, the English-made John Wilks sight, now available to American shooters.

target variety with Redfield, Lyman, and Unertl getting about an equal share of the action. Big-lens scopes such as the 2-inch Unertls offer the better optical performance, but by the same token the big profile offers more "sail" when the wind blows, thus making the rifle difficult to hold steady. Therefore, scopes with a rather slim profile predominate on the firing lines.

Which magnification is best is largely a matter of personal preference. I prefer a 15X for the few occasions I use a scope at 600 yards and 20X for all my 1,000-yard shooting. I've used every power from 10X to 25X, and I can't really say it makes much difference. It's far more important that the scope and crosshairs be perfectly focused and, of course, properly zeroed.

So far as delivering a bullet to the center of the bull, the scope doesn't have a hell of a lot to offer over iron sights. In fact, my season average of a couple years ago was a bit higher with irons than with scope. The main advantage of a scope, as far as I'm concerned, is a matter of convenience. With a scope I simply hold off to allow for changes in the wind. With irons I must make a sight correction in most cases. In some pretty stiff breezes I've allowed as much as fifteen feet of "Kentucky windage" and had the bullet plunk right in the "V" ring. It's a mighty gratifying feeling. The scope also allows the shooter to catch last-instant changes of wind before pulling the trigger.

Wind

Speaking of wind, how does the successful big-bore shooter deal with the variant breezes? Actually, there are a number of ways: watching the range flags, trees, grass, feeling the breeze on his face, and watching the dust fly when a bullet hits behind the pits. Most shooters try a little of everything. But all and all, the most reliable method is watching the mirage or rising heat waves. These squiggly heat waves have an annoying habit of making the target look out of focus, but at the same time their angle tells the rifleman a lot about the wind.

For example, if the lines seem to rise straight up, there is no wind. When they rise at an angle, they not only tell the shooter which way the wind is blowing but also the velocity. At least up to a velocity of about 10 m.p.h.; beyond that the lines are blown horizontal and the shooter must resort to other devices. But by and large the mirage is the shooter's friend, and success depends in large measure on the ability to "read the mirage."

Ammo

As one might imagine, ammo quality plays an important part in winning, especially at long range. For military events and some National Match courses, high-grade match factory (arsenal) ammo may be loaded. The rest of the time it's pretty much a handloading proposition. The selection of match bullets available to handloaders is superb.

Sierra, for example, offers boat-tail .30 caliber bullets in weights of 168, 180, 190 and 200 grains. Also a 168-grain 7-mm. match bullet and a 140-grain 6.5 bullet. Norma offers an excellent 6.5 bullet of 134 grains. Hornady offer outstanding 168- and 190-grain .30 caliber bullets, and Speer Inc. imports and distributes the fabled Lapua line of competition bullets. Also Remington and Winchester offer 180-grain .30 caliber match bullets.

All the shooter has to do is find the make and weight that works best in his rifle and he's all set. The trick is to find a combination of bullet, powder, primer, and case that works well and stay with it. Those who keep experimenting with different loads usually succeed only in getting confused. The cardinal rule is *keep it simple*.

For example, I stay with two basic loads for my .308 match rifle. For 200- and 300-yard events I use a 168-grain bullet over 39 grains of No. 3031 powder. For long range my load is 48 grains of No. 4350 with a 190-grain bullet.

With the .30/06 I stay with the 168-grain bullet and 52 grains of No. 4320 for short range and 54 grains of No. 4350 and the 190-grain bullet for long range.

With the 300 Winchester Magnum my load is 78 grains of H-4831 with the 185-grain bullet, CCI No. 250 primer and Winchester-Western cases.

For the 7-mm. Remington Magnum I stick with 65 grains of H-4831, the 168-grain bullet, CCI No. 250 primer, and Winchester-Western brass.

These are my "standard" loads for competition. By staying with them explicitly I always know exactly how any given rifle will perform and exactly what sight corrections and adjustments to make for different ranges and conditions. Thus, the likelihood of making a mistake under the pressures and pace of actual match conditions is greatly lessened.

The Competitive Shooter as a Hunter

The competitive rifleman should be a highly successful hunter if for no other reason than his greater skill with a rifle. This, of course, doesn't affect his ability to stalk and locate game, but once the quarry is located, the match shooter is a more capable judge of distance, much more able to place the bullet precisely where he wants it, and probably less likely to get a case of the jitters or "buck fever." The pressures of competition teach one how to deal with one's emotions.

But best of all, the big-bore rifleman probably has more fun than the average hunter—assuming that that's possible.

A few years back when I went on a kick of hunting woodchucks with my .30/06 Dunlap "over the course" match rifle, iron sights and all, my companions were constantly annoyed that I was pretty

Carmichel lines up one of his iron-sighted match rifles on a woodchuck. Chuck shooting is very demanding, requiring a thorough knowledge of the rifle's trajectory and an ability to estimate ranges with a high degree of accuracy.

regularly making right-on-the-button hits out to 300 yards and even a bit beyond. Actually, it wasn't all that much more difficult than making a hit with a scope, though I didn't admit it at the time.

Once I had pretty well determined the range, I simply made appropriate sight corrections and I had a "dead on" zero for that range. Too, I was using the "globe" or circular front sight aperture. So all I did was center the chuck in the globe aperture (even though they appeared no larger than specks at the longer ranges), align the sights, and press the trigger.

Also, competitive big-bore riflemen tend to be especially effective on game, especially varmints, because their long training has conditioned them to take all the variables into account and instantly translate that information into whatever action may be necessary. For example, if the distance and conditions tell him to hold over six inches and two feet to the right, he will unhesitatingly do so with full confidence that the bullet will fall on target. The less experienced hunter tends to be less bold and thus more prone to error.

Most important of all, however, the experienced competitor know his limitations and those of his equipment. He is less likely to attempt foolish shots that at best spook game and at worst result in a poorly placed hit.

I don't ever recall hearing an experienced big-bore rifleman brag about a long shot at game. I suppose this is because they knew for a fact that the game *wasn't* all that far away or simply because they realized that it *was* too far to take a shot.

Competitive Shooting

COL. JIM CROSSMAN

"Col. Jim Crossman" is the pen name of Col. Edward B. Crossman, Ordnance Corps, U. S. Army (Ret.). He has been a competitive shooter and competition official for 40 years, at innumerable events at regional, national, and international levels. Both in and out of the service, his life has been almost entirely concerned with guns and related matters, and his expertise is widely recognized—he has acted as consultant to manufacturers, civilian and governmental investigative bodies, insurance companies, and other organizations, and he is an expert witness who has given ballistic testimony in many legal cases.

Crossman retired from the Army in 1964—his last assignment was with the Army Materiel Command, Research and Development, working on all weapons and ammunition except guided missiles. A writer for more than 30 years, he was formerly Firearms Editor of Sports Afield and is now Contributing Editor to Ordnance and Firearms Editor of The Sporting Goods Dealer. He has written articles for many other magazines, including The American Rifleman, Guns, Guns & Ammo, Mechanix Illustrated, and The Gun Digest, and he is the author of the Boy Scout Merit Badge booklet "Rifle and Shotgun Shooting."

YOU SAY YOU'RE NOT interested in competitive shooting? C'mon now, don't kid me. Of course you are. You may not have rosy visions of standing on the winner's platform in a huge stadium while thousands of hero-worshiping eyes watch you crowned Champion of the Universe. But I'll bet that when you and buddy Bill go out to do a little tin-can shooting, you try to hit the can a little more often and a little farther away than Bill. And that's competitive shooting!

There is enough variety in this competitive shooting game so that something should strike your fancy. If you're not the shy and retiring type, and you like a little make-believe, consider the North-South Skirmish. These Civil War buffs form themselves into units and adopt the name, insignia, and uniform of a local Civil War unit. They get together locally fairly often and nationally twice a year to have big shooting matches. They use muzzle-loading percussion guns of the time or modern reproductions. Much of the shooting is at moving targets: balloons, clay birds hung on a panel, flour-filled cups suspended by a string, etc. With targets of this type, everyone can see how a team is getting along, and there is loud rooting by the spectators. Oh yes, all this is in full uniform—and a handsome sight they make!

If you don't like the small guns, you might at least like to get in there with your big gun in the cannon matches. The North-South Skirmish Association has a 250-acre campsite and range near the Virginia town of (appropriately enough) Winchester.

The Skirmish is confined to the eastern part of the country, but you will find much widespread interest in other types of muzzle-loading shooting, smoothbore and rifle, flint and percussion, shoulder arm or handgun. Besides local shoots of various kinds, the muzzle loaders get together for their annual championship at the National Muzzle Loading Rifle Association range near Friendship, Indiana. Wear fringed buckskins, with beaded moccasins, topped by a coonskin cap, and you will be right in style!

Are you a perfectionist? Does everything have to be just right? And do you have the necessary patience to check and recheck every little detail? You might like to have a look at the bench-rest game. In this sport you don't shoot for score, but for the smallest possible group. Shooting is usually at 100 and 200 yards, in five-shot strings. Measurement of groups is done optically, to the nearest one thousandth of an inch. And they need to be measured accurately, as there is usually only a gnat's eyebrow difference in group sizes. Present records for all classes show five-shot groups at 100 yards which measure less than one tenth of an inch from center to center of widest shots!

Various classes of rifles are used, the unrestricted class including almost anything you can carry up to the firing line. Other classes have some restrictions on the gun. Use of a high-power scope sight is universal. Since accuracy is of prime importance, many shooters carefully make their own bullets and are very fussy about the cartridge case, primer, powder, and all the other little details of reloading. The shooter also has to be a good "wind doper," to know how much allowance to make for a breeze. All these activities are coordinated by the National Bench Rest Shooter's Association.

Now wait just a minute—I can see that sly expression in your eyes. You are thinking that with tiny groups like that, after you have put two or three shots on the paper, no one can really tell how many shots you have in there, so why not dump the others off the paper somewhere, so you won't spoil what you have? I regret to say that this probably has happened. But to thwart such larcenous ideas, a moving paper screen behind the target shows every shot you fire— or don't fire. Golly, there's always someone trying to keep you honest!

The smallbore rifle shooter likewise must be something of a perfectionist, but not in the reloading line, as everyone uses factory .22 ammunition. Smallbore shooting comes in several flavors: prone, conventional position, and international.

Prone, or "belly," matches are usually held outdoors at distances of 50 yards, 50 meters, and 100 yards, both with metallic and telescope sights. Smallbore rifles are often sensitive to the type of ammunition, and it may take the shooter some experimenting to find the right combination to produce tiny groups, since the 100-yard ten-ring is only two inches across, and the X ring only one inch. Small groups, combined with the shooter's ability to sight carefully, hold steadily, and squeeze off each shot precisely, go together with ability to "dope" the wind to produce a winner.

During the winter months, when smallbore shooting moves indoors in the cold country, most gallery work is in three or four positions. Standing, kneeling, and prone are the basic positions, with sitting often added as the fourth. Position shooting outdoors is becoming more popular, especially as international events—Olympics, Pan Am Games, World Shooting Championships, etc.—call for three-position shooting.

The high-power rifle shooter is a philosophical soul. He thinks nothing of picking up his rifle, scope, ground pad, and assorted other gear to trudge a half mile to the firing line. And when he is there on the line, he fully expects broiling sun, gale winds, driving rain, and various other vagaries of nature. In between spells of shooting, he plans on keeping score for other shooters, probably followed by a trip to the pits, where he has to mark targets. But he has a great time at it.

High-power shooting varies somewhat with the range capabilities, but usually includes shooting slow fire standing, rapid fire sitting and prone, and slow fire prone. Distances are whatever the club has available, but where there is a choice, they include 200, 300, 600 and 1,000 yards although 1,000-yard ranges are scarce. Basic equipment includes a rifle chambered for the .30/06 or .308 (7.62 mm.) cartridge, a spotting scope, and some ammunition. Hand loading is popular, to keep the cost down and to provide the right load for the range and conditions.

Conventional handgun shooting in this country involves shooting strings of slow fire (one minute per shot), timed fire (20 seconds per five shots) and rapid fire (10 seconds per five shots). Outdoors, the slow-fire stage is shot at 50 yards and the others at 25 yards, using targets with the same sized scoring rings for both distances. Indoors, the same stages are fired, but usually at a single distance, with different sized targets for slow and the combined timed and rapid stages.

Indoor shooting is usually for the .22 handgun only—and in practice this means the .22 autoloader. Outdoor matches usually include events for the .22, the centerfire, and the .45 caliber handgun. Many people shoot the .45 in both the centerfire and .45 matches.

Handgun shooting doesn't require you to grovel in the dirt, as all shooting is done standing. Consequently, you can dress as fancy as you wish or hit the range in your business clothes without feeling too conspicuous. Pistol shooting requires much self control. It's impossible to hold the gun perfectly still, and there's a great tendency to yank the trigger when the bull's-eye comes wandering by the sights. But that yank is likely to put you way out in the scoring rings, or even off the paper. The handgun requires great concentration on a few fundamentals.

If you wear the blue and want to compete against other police officers, the National Rifle Association's police program will interest you. The courses of fire and the conditions are laid down by working police officers to represent practical methods of shooting the handgun in police work.

In the National Police Championships, the revolver is presently the specified handgun. Shooting is within a time limit and includes drawing from the holster and reloading the cylinder at least once. Distances includes 7 and 15 yards standing (usually holding the gun in both hands), as well as longer ranges in the sitting and prone positions and with right hand and left hand from behind a barricade. The National Police Championships have recently been held at the Mississippi Highway Patrol Academy in Jackson, and are limited to active-duty, working police officers. No civilians, reserves, or military are allowed, according to the present rules of the NRA.

The National Rifle Association, in Washington, D.C., is also the guiding light for high-power rifle, smallbore rifle, and handgun shooting. NRA committees establish the rules, which are used countrywide. Since 1903, the National Championships have been usually held at Camp Perry, Ohio, on the fine ranges of the Ohio National Guard.

Skeet is an American sport developed in the '20's as a means of getting field practice during off season. Clay birds are thrown from two traps on fixed flight lines. The shooter moves around the field to various posts, which gives him a variety of birds: going away, coming towards him, and crossing at various angles. Most of the shooting is with the 12-gauge gun, but specified events require the 20-gauge, 28-gauge and .410-gauge guns, with appropriately reduced shot loads. The National Skeet Shooting Association in Dallas heads up this activity and annual championships are held in various parts of the country.

In trapshooting, the birds are all going away from the shooter, varying from a hard-right angle through straightaway to a hard-left angle. An automatic trap changes the angle from shot to shot so the shooter does not know what angle he will get next. In doubles, two birds are thrown simultaneously, but over fixed and known flight paths. A handicap event is usually included in big matches, where the shooter is moved back away from the trap, the distance varying with his past average. The Amateur Trapshooting Association has its headquarters in Vandalia, Ohio, where it also holds its annual championships.

Want to travel and see the world—at no cost? Take up international shooting and get good enough to make a U.S. team. Every four years we send a shooting team to the Olympic Games, last in Munich. Every four years, halfway between the Olympics, a World Shooting Championship is held, the last in Phoenix, the next in Switzerland. One of the in-between years is taken up with the Pan American Games, next scheduled for Chile. World Moving Target Championships are normally scheduled for the off year. So, if you are good enough and shoot the right event, you can get a fine trip overseas almost every year. Of course there is the little matter of a whole bunch of other people who have the same idea and are more interested in going themselves than in having you go, so you may have to work at it!

Teams for the World Championships are selected by the National Rifle Association, which also pays the expenses. Teams for the Olympic and Pan American Games are nominally selected by the U.S. Olympic Committee, but the NRA acts as their agent in this matter. This applies to rifle, pistol, and shotgun shooters.

The NRA has also sent teams overseas, on an irregular schedule, to compete with high-power rifle or smallbore rifle against other English-speaking countries. Here's another chance!

It sometimes seems that everyone is out of step except Willy, Willy in this case being the U.S. Our shooting developed from a different background and from different causes than most European shooting, so we find that the equipment, courses of fire, and techniques are different. We do have some things in common with our English-speaking friends, but even here there are considerable differences. I shot in the Canadian matches for a few years and found it fairly easy to switch over, as did other Americans who came up north. But the International game, as shot in the Olympics, Pan Am Games, and World Championships, is something else.

We have been involved in international for a long time. The Paine brothers won shooting gold medals in the first of the modern Olympics, back in 1896. But it has been difficult to get U.S. shooters to change to the international game, and there has been a constant wail over the years about the difference in courses, techniques, and equipment. Although this area has improved considerably in recent years, some of the best equipment is still foreign.

International shooting includes two high-power rifle events fired in three positions—prone, kneeling, and standing—at 300 meters. All other matches are at shorter range, with the smallbore rifle events at 50 meters, including prone and three positions. For the hunting type, there is the Running Boar match, shot at 50 meters with .22 rimfire rifles. Pistol matches include the precision Slow Fire affair, at 50 meters, and its opposite number, the Rapid Fire, at 25 yards, which requires the shooter to fire five shots in less than four seconds. A Centerfire match, at 25 meters, combines features of slow and rapid fire, while the Standard Pistol match is for .22's at 25 meters and is based on the U.S. National Match Course. The shotgun shooters have a chance for glory in International Skeet and Clay Pigeon, which is somewhat like U.S. trap shooting. For those who don't want to burn powder, there are the air rifle and air pistol matches, which call for equipment and shooting of the highest precision.

Special events are held for the ladies in World Championships. In addition, any woman who shoots well enough can take her place on the U.S. team. Margaret Murdock won gold medals as a member of our Pan Am team. Nuria Ortiz was one of the two skeet shooters on the Mexican Olympic team—and did very well.

Due to problems of time and space, the Olympics do not include all of these international events. In Mexico City, 1968, we shot seven events, but an additional event was included at Munich. International matches are shot in various places throughout the U.S. during the year, with the National Championships and team selection scheduled for Phoenix during late spring or early summer, conducted by the NRA.

If none of these things set you on fire, but you have visions of the big time, a couple of other shooting events might appeal to you: the Biathlon and the Pentathlon. I guess you wouldn't call them shooting events, strictly speaking, but shooting is an important part.

The Biathlon was dreamed up by the folks living in the cold north country. It combines skiing with shooting. The cross-country course is pretty strenuous, especially as you have to carry your rifle with you. But periodically during the course you get a chance to stop and rest—by shooting at a group of targets at various ranges. The whole thing is against time, and if you take too long in the shooting phases, this hurts. But if you don't take time enough to be sure of making hits, they arbitrarily add time for every miss. So it pays to take just the least amount necessary to be sure of all hits. And if you plan on winning this one, you'd better be pretty handy on the skis!

The Modern Pentathlon is a tough one, requiring a great deal of talent and skill. The five events take place on different days and include riding, fencing, swimming, running, and pistol shooting. This takes a mighty good all-around athlete.

Many of the ladies take to the competitive game like ducks to water. Some don't have the time, ability, or competitive drive to make it all the way to the big time, and matches therefore often have special events or special prizes for the ladies. Other gals will give the men a run for their money and no quarter asked.

U.S. International teams generally have no limitations. Way back more than fifty years ago, my mother was the first woman to make a U.S. International Rifle Team. Many have followed in her footsteps since then. The only requirement is that they shoot well enough.

In U.S. rifle and pistol shooting there is no such thing as a professional. Everyone shoots on the same basis. Generally, there is no money up in rifle and pistol matches. At one time, we used to shoot for dough—but not much! At the National Matches, for example, you could enter for money by paying an extra fifty cents. All this money went into the pot, and if there were over 500 entries, the winner got the magnificent sum of $35, with the other prizes scaling down, ending up with a lot of two-buck awards. Money shooting lasted at least until 1946. I was the Statistical Director of the matches that year, and I have vivid memories of worrying about the money prizes. But by 1953 money prizes were out of the program.

The situation is different in the shotgun sports. Money is involved here, and sometimes in generous quantities. It comes in two forms: added money or guaranteed purse, put up by the shoot organizer. Money for this comes from the club treasury, from profit on sale of birds, from advertising, etc. The other source of money is the optional entry by the shooter. The optional money is normally all given back according to an acceptable formula. In a big event, it is easy to get several hundred bucks tied up in entering the optionals.

The scattergun sports have professional shooters, whose mission in life is to sell their company's shooting product and who get paid for shooting. In big shoots, there are separate events for the pros, but if there are not, they can't shoot against the common folks. This is common sense, since the company concerned wouldn't win any popularity contest if its paid shooters were taking prizes away from its own cash-paying customers.

The pro or industry representative classification really goes to the holder of a specific type of job, but only so long as he is in that job. Provision is made to revert to amateur status a few months after he leaves that job. This is quite different from some other amateur rules, where once you lose your virginity it is gone forever!

The Amateur Athletic Union considers anyone who shoots for money a professional and ineligible for all forms of AAU competition. The Olympic Committee takes a very dim view of combining sport with money. The International Shooting Union, the governing body for worldwide shooting, does permit you to win limited amounts of money. If you have any ambitions towards the international shooting game, find out what the latest ground rules are by writing the NRA before you make any mistakes and ruin your career.

At one time the International Olympic Committee passed a ground rule that said that you were ineligible if you had ever competed for money. Later, they modified this to say that if you hadn't been bad for a certain period, you were back in good standing again. It is unfortunate that this problem has come up, particularly in the rifle and pistol events, where there just isn't any real money. And in shooting, every time you pull the trigger in practice or match, it costs you money for ammunition.

It all started on the basis of the winner taking the turkey home. But after a while it developed that a few people were taking all the turkeys, while other good folks, who paid their entry fee time after time, were not even getting a feather. To spread the joy and good tidings among more people, it was decided to reduce the value of the big prize, and to give some of the place winners a little something to take home.

This did help spread the wealth, but once again, after a little while you could pretty well predict most of the hot shots who were going to take the prizes. Eventually it dawned on a lot of shooters that they just didn't have the talent, money, or time to be among the winners. The newcomer, too, found it rather discouraging to see such a big gap between the kind of scores he was shooting and the scores it took to get an award.

So there grew up various methods of handicapping, again to spread the wealth around, but more specifically to give some of the poorer shots a chance at a prize. In US rifle, pistol, and shotgun shooting it is common to handicap by classification. You are put in a class based upon your past record. In skeet, for example, there the six classes in the 12-gauge, with a 97.5 average putting you in

AA, while under 86 percent is worth an E class assignment. In a match, you shoot for the top prizes, according to the schedule. But if you don't make it here, your score is put down with the scores of other people in your class, for awards only within your class. So even if you shot a poor score in comparison with the match winner, you still have a chance at a prize in your class.

The NRA has long used four classes: Master, Expert, Sharpshooter, and Marksman, which sounds simple. But it isn't quite that simple, since there are classifications for different guns and different courses of fire. There are four sets of classifications for the smallbore rifle shooter, plus other breakdowns for high-power rifle, handgun, and shotgun. It soon becomes a real bookkeeper's nightmare.

Generally, when you start a shootin' match in a particular class you shoot through the whole thing in that class. But I still have horrible memories of my job as Statistical Director of the 1946 National Matches. This was the first big match after World War II and many people had been too occupied to shoot for classification. So, according to the ground rules established to cover this problem, I reclassified folks after they had fired three scores—and the reclassification applied to the rest of the events. That was a real mess!

While trapshooting uses the class system for some events, one does not use classes. This is the handicap event, in which shooters are put at various distances from the trap, according to their average. The man with the low average will be standing 18 yards from the trap house, while the hot shot will be way back on the 27-yard peg, with other shooters in between.

In all the class systems, as you begin to shoot better, your scores go up and are periodically reviewed to see if you shouldn't get promoted up to the next class. Such promotion is automatic and is usually accompanied by much weeping and wailing and beating of breasts. Being low man in class B doesn't get you as many awards as being high man in class C! Unfortunately, going down is not so easy. The keepers of the books view with horror the idea of moving a man down in class: It can be done, but it does take a little special effort, as well as some poor shooting.

Development of the class system in shooting inevitably led to the development of the grand old game of "sandbagging." In fact, if you have a little larceny in your heart, you may already have come up with this bright scheme for beating the classes: you only shoot good when the prizes are good and shoot bad the rest of the time! By picking the occasions when you shoot well, you can take home a nice bit of loot. To keep from getting promoted out of your class, it will be necessary for you to throw off and deliberately shoot low scores on many other occasions, so that you can hold your average down.

Although you may think of it as a cunning way of beating the game within the rules, other folks call it cheating. The guys you beat at these big shoots have a way of remembering, and if you come up top man in your class too often, they get mighty suspicious of those low scores you turn in at the palooka shoots. It doesn't take long for the word to get around!

This is not to say that you shouldn't win class prizes as you learn more about the game and get better and better. You probably will start out in a low class and shoot your way out of that to the next one and so on up. Logically, you would be expected to win some prizes along the way. But if you frequently win one of the lower classes with a phenomenal score but don't work your way out of that class, it is time to be suspicious.

Other cute little tricks have been tried from time to time by people not content to fight it out on the basis of shooting skill alone. There are various ways of getting ahead without having talent, and you may run into the man who is trying to win by cunning or subterfuge rather than skill. Eventually he gets found out, and sometimes the rules get changed to keep other people from straying in the same footsteps.

In trapshooting, the object of the oscillating trap was to give you unknown angles. The trap oscillates back and forth, driven by a motor. Since the bird is called for at indeterminate and unspecified times, the trap can be any place, and so you get unknown and variable angles. But the wise ones found out that the trap had a regular period of oscillation. By fixing that period in their minds and watching a couple of birds to see where the trap was and which direction it was going, they were then able to tell pretty closely what the angle would be at any time. By shooting unusually quickly or unusually slowly, they could, within limits, get the bird where they wanted it to be. To break up this little game and spoil their fun, it has recently been decreed that traps used in ATA-registered shooting must be provided with an interrupter of some sort. This irregularly stops the oscillation of the trap for a short time and raises heck with trap-reading.

Back in the pre-World War II days of skeet, you had to hold the gun off your shoulder, so that part of the stock was visible below the right arm. If you wanted to hold your gun high, you beat the object of the rule by raising your right arm high. If in international skeet you see the referee out on the field pawing at the beautiful damsel, you needn't be distressed. He is merely trying to find her hipbone, as the international rules say that the butt of the gun must be held against the shooter's hip when calling for the bird.

I guess we will always have the rule-bender with us. He leans up against the rules as hard as he possibly can, and doesn't even mind breaking them, if no one calls him on it. In the rifle shooter's prone position, for example, the elbows are permitted to be on the ground, but no other part of the arm. But if you take a very low position, with the left hand well out, and if you wear a coat with thick padding on the left sleeve and a big bulky shooting glove, you can practically rest your whole left arm on the ground, especially if you thoughtfully pick out a small depression for your left elbow. And if you pick a rifle stock that is deep from top to bottom at the butt, in your low position you may be able to rest the toe of the stock on the ground.

With these few tips, I'm sure you will be able to come up with other ways to succeed without real talent. But it has been my observation that people who indulge in these cunning little games don't gain anything by it. The other competitors are going to be watching, and if they find someone taking unfair advantage, they will straighten out the situation. I've often thought that if he spent his time in learning how to shoot, the rule-bender would be a world-beater!

There are several variations of these popular shooting sports we've been covering, as well as some less popular endeavors. Somewhere you should find a competitive game that appeals to you. Maybe it is the Mexican Silhouette, popular in the Southwest. Here you shoot at steel plates, cut in the silhouettes of game animals of the region. Various silhouettes are used at different ranges. Object is to knock all of the silhouettes over with fewest shots. You might even like to try live-bird shooting, which is popular in some parts of the country. While you're a little old for it now, on your next trip through this world you might try the BB-gun championships, sponsored by Daisy, with a National Championship run by the Jaycees.

Okay, so you don't have the tiger spirit and don't want to embarrass yourself by shooting in public competition and making a poor showing. Especially when you don't know how good—or poor—you are. There is still an out for you in the competitive game.

Shoot against yourself. Sound silly? It's really not. You can shoot for qualification scores. You don't shoot against anyone else, you merely shoot for score. When you have scores of the necessary value, you send in your results and can get a colorful qualification brassard for your jacket, a lapel pin, and a medal, all testifying to your skill. As you improve, you will shoot better scores and can earn higher qualification badges. Shooting against yourself this way is a pleasant and relatively painless way of getting some competition at your own level and at your own pace. Besides, you begin to get an idea of how good you are.

As did many others, I started out years ago shooting for qualification awards in the Winchester Junior Rifle Corps. This was a fine program, starting with easy scores for the Pro-Marksman medal, but leading up to some mighty tough scores for the top qualification. About 1926, Winchester turned this over to the National Rifle Association, to combine with their somewhat similar programs. Since then it has been greatly enlarged, to cover a big variety of guns, positions, and conditions. It includes rifle, pistol, shotgun, and air gun in many forms, with resultant brassards and medals. This program has issued something like ten million qualification awards! They can be won by anyone, of any age. There's bound to be something here that would interest you. Write the NRA for dope on qualification in the guns of interest to you.

Even if this doesn't appeal to you, you can still shoot against yourself. Keep records of your shooting. Each time you go out try to make a few less mistakes than last time and try to put into practice the things you learned. If you do, you will find that your records will show a gradual improvement and you will have the satisfaction of knowing that you are beating yourself.

The future of competitive shooting looks good. With more people having more leisure time, I would expect shooting to increase. Competitive shooting is essentially a doer's, not a watcher's, game. While some of the shooting sports have a considerable amount of spectator appeal, in this country, at least, they suffer in comparison with football, baseball, and others. In many foreign countries, however, shooting is popular among spectators.

Worldwide, shooting is one of the most popular sports. In the roster of countries that belong to the International Shooting Union or send shooting teams to the Olympic games, our sport is up there among the top two or three.

Shotgun shooting has been growing rapidly in the U.S. The rapid development of handloading keeps the cost down. Handloading is popular among pistol and high-power rifle shooters for reasons of cost, as well as getting the right ammunition for the conditions. Pistol shooting continues to grow, as the range requirements are not too restricting and it is not too demanding physically. Small-bore rifle shooting is big among the younger set, in high school and college, as well as among the old-timers. Again, range requirements are not too restricting. Conventional high-power rifle shooting, fascinating as it is to those of us who grew up in it, is having some problems, mainly because of range space. Thousand-yard ranges are scarce in this country and even many 600-yard ranges have given way to the developer's bulldozer. But there are ranges and there is activity. Many clubs run a good high-power program on a 200-yard range.

The Europeans, with their more crowded areas, have long faced up to this problem. There are only two international courses at 300 meters, with all the other rifle and pistol events at 50 yards or less. The Europeans have built many "safety" ranges to accommodate shooting in their crowded areas. They build ranges in the heart of a developed area, with adequate baffles and backstops to keep all bullets inside the range. We may come to this in order to keep shooting within a reasonable distance of our people. This is not something entirely new, either, as practically all indoor ranges are built to keep bullets inside the range, although they are mostly short distances—usually 50 feet.

Competitive shooting is a fine sport that appeals to a wide variety of people. Men and women, young and old compete shoulder to shoulder. Many with physical handicaps of one sort or another find that shooting is a sport in which they can compete on an even-up basis. On occasion, special positions or special equipment are permitted, so that they can compete without a handicap.

No matter which competitive shooting sport you take up, I'm sure you will find it fascinating and you will meet a lot of fine people. It's a sport that will stay with you as long as you want to shoot!

Organizations Concerned with Competitive Shooting

Amateur Trapshooting Association
P. O. Box 246, Vandalia, Ohio, 45377

National Bench Rest Shooters Association
607 W. Line St., Minerva, Ohio, 44657

National Muzzle Loading Rifle Association
Box 67, Friendship, Indiana, 47021

National Rifle Association
1600 Rhode Island Ave., Washington, D.C., 20036

National Skeet Shooting Association
212 Linwood Bldg., 2608 Inwood Road, Dallas, Texas, 75235

North-South Skirmish Association
P. O. Box 114, McLean, Virginia, 22101

Drilling, Vierling, und Zweiling: Reflections on Rifle-Shotguns

ROBERT ELMAN

Bob Elman is a writer and editor who resides (reluctantly) in New York and escapes as often as possible to Vermont and points west. Formerly editor of The American Sportsman *quarterly and several outdoor magazines, he is now shooting-history consultant and Outdoor Editor for Ridge Press, specializing in hardcover publications. He has hunted in various parts of the United States, Canada, and Europe, and his articles on hunting and on antique and modern guns have appeared in national magazines. His latest books are* The Great Guns *(with arms historian Harold L. Peterson)* The Atlantic Flyway, *and* The Great American Shooting Prints.

IT WASN'T THE SUBDUED silvery glow of the receiver that I first fell in love with, or the deeply engraved scrollwork, or the splendid bluing of the barrels and top lever. I admired those details, just as I admired the richly figured European walnut, hand-checkered with close, Germanic precision on the pistol grip and ample fore-end. But I had expected refinements of that sort on a sporting arm costing over $600. Perhaps what really got to me was the smooth immediacy with which the leaf sight flipped up from the matted top rib when the barrel selector was thumbed to the right. Or perhaps it was the wide black, sleekly beveled trigger guard, carved from the horn of a Cape buffalo.

"A typical German touch," Larry called that, an extra dash of restrained elegance, and not pretentiously nonfunctional, since horn is more comfortable than steel against the fingers when the weather is cold.

The gun under discussion was a Krieghoff *drilling,* a three-barreled piece with a pair of 20-gauge smoothbores, chambered for 3-inch Magnums, set side by side over a 7-mm. Mauser rifle barrel.

It was one of the last guns ever used by Larry Koller, who was among the most perceptive outdoor writers of this country. He had obtained it in 1966 from Europa Arms, an importer in Miami, Florida. He died the following August. By then he had bagged woodcock and ducks with it, and a single shot from the rifle barrel had given him a nice whitetail buck.

He had lent the gun to Bob Zwirz, another outdoor writer and admirer of good drillings, for a couple of hunts in Maine and New Brunswick. Bob and his wife, Glad, took three whitetails and a black bear with it—all one-shot kills with 150-grain Norma factory loads that printed almost dead-on at 100 yards—as well as seven grouse and 41 woodcock they flushed in the Northern woods.

Late the next spring, Larry propped the Krieghoff against the desk in his study and began typing a magazine article about it. He glanced up and, through the window, saw a woodchuck that had been raiding his garden. He picked up the gun and one of his hand-loaded 7-mm. cartridges—42.5 grains of DuPont No. 4064 powder behind a 139-grain Hornady spire-point—and went to the door. He sat down in the doorstep and watched the chuck grazing some 80 or 90 yards away. Then he chambered the round and put a sudden end to the garden raids.

If I'm not quite sure what it was that most appealed to me about that particular drilling, I do know Larry's reasons for so admiring it. First, there was the obvious versatility which, between the onset of one autumn and the end of the next spring, accounted for ducks, woodcock, grouse, deer, bear, and a woodchuck. This was not just a matter of combining smoothbores with a rifle but of combining the right smoothbores with the right rifle. Next, there was the surprisingly light weight (only seven pounds despite the *ménage à trois* of barrels) and perfect balance, right at the rear of the fore-end. And finally, there was the rather Americanized stock design, wonderfully unlike older European rifle-shotguns in that it had a sufficiently high, well-rounded comb and wide enough fore-end.

Why, then, have rifle-shotgun combinations never become really popular in this country? Many American sportsmen seem to consider them awkward curiosities, conversation pieces, but no more practical than the hybridization of elephant and donkey, if I may poach an image from the political preserve.

A couple of reasons have already been hinted at. A 1925 Stoeger's catalog lists Merkel Brothers drillings that weighed as little as Larry's Krieghoff, but combination guns tended to be quite heavy until the twentieth century was well under way, and some of them were ill-balanced. And until much more recently, it was the European fashion to provide such arms with skimpy, uncomfortable stocks.

Then there was a dissatisfaction with chamberings. For the smoothbores, 16-gauge was most popular and was a fine, versatile choice until it was overwhelmed by the Magnumizing of the 20. But the rifle chamber usually took a rimmed case like the 7 x 57R long after Americans had advanced to excellent rimless cartridges. Even those drillings made for the American market suffered from a paucity of caliber selections.

That 1925 Stoeger catalog displayed a revealing array of two-, three- and four-barreled combinations. There was a side-by-side double with a smoothbored left barrel in .410, a rifled right barrel in .22 Long Rifle, and an underlever to break open the action. The receiver was engraved with hunting scenes, and you got all that for $39.50. Combination guns for more serious shooting (and pride

Illustrations from 1925 Stoeger catalog, showing various combinations as well as a double-barreled rifle and three-barreled shotgun. All of these were in Stoeger's line of Merkel imports.

MERKEL BROTHERS THREE-BARRELED GUNS

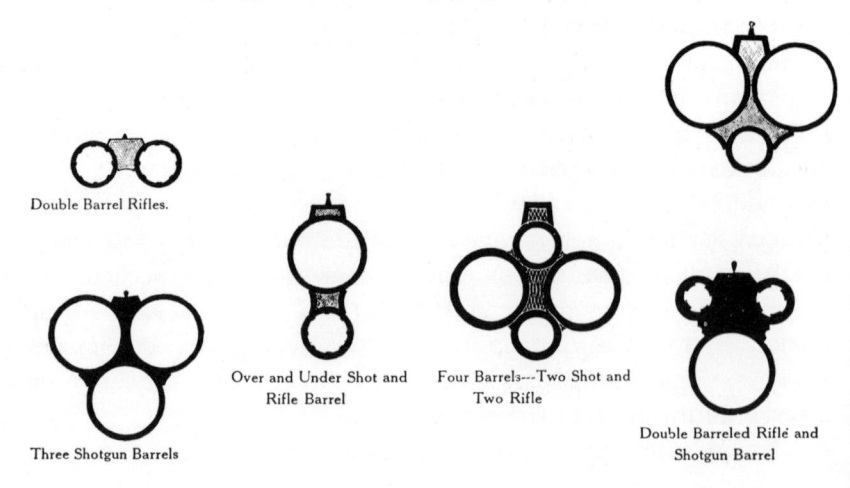

Double Barrel Rifles.

Three Shotgun Barrels

Over and Under Shot and Rifle Barrel

Four Barrels---Two Shot and Two Rifle

Double Barreled Rifle and Shotgun Barrel

Exposed-hammer German drilling from Bob Zwirz collection. Note folding peep sight on tang, plus low notch sight on rib. (Photo by Bob Zwirz)

of ownership) began at $255, climbed a gentle trail of optional features such as peep sights and automatic safeties and ejectors to $375, then leaped from sight with a "Prices on Application" line. There was a choice of 12, 16, or 20 bore for the shotgun barrels — so far, so good. But in all cases the standard rifle chambering was .30/30 or .25/35, with an extra charge for ".30-06 Govt. or Other Rimless cartridges."

There were further drawbacks. A three-barreled combination is even more costly to produce than a good double shotgun. The prices just quoted seem low by today's standards, but they were fairly high for their time. With few exceptions, drillings and *vierlings* — the four-barreled models — have always been expensive. I don't know why no one calls the two-barreled models *zweilings,* and I shall proceed to do so. Zweilings, then, have sometimes appeared in economy models, the most famous being the American-made Savage Model 24, but the European ones have usually been high-priced.

Another objection arose when this nation's hunters became obsessed with repeaters that could keep right on firing to furnish some excitement long after the missed game got bored and went away. (This obsession now shows signs of waning slightly.) Finally, although the rib of a combination gun can be drilled and tapped for scope mounting — and sometimes is — this interferes with wingshooting, and the *raison d'être* for most combination arms is the opportunity to switch instantly from rifle to shotgun or vice versa.

Today's light, well-balanced, properly stocked combination arms, offered in a variety of attractive chamberings, have overcome most of the objections, though vierlings remain awkward and heavy. Drillings are enjoying a mild revival among those who can afford fine guns and appreciate such arms for wingshooting and scopeless timber hunting. Their advantages were nicely summarized by Larry Koller, who wrote that they had never lost their popularity in Europe,

> where hunters have never gone overboard for repeat firepower, and I personally like such guns . . . I've often hunted where it was legal to take both birds and big game on the same day; there have been many times when I could have killed a good whitetail while hunting grouse, or taken birds while out for deer.

L. C. Smith drilling, from Russ Carpenter gun collection. Made in the early 1900's, it has 30-inch Damascus barrels and weighs just over nine pounds. The top barrels are 12-gauge; centered under them is the rifled .44/40 barrel. It has a folding rifle sight on the tang, where the top lever would normally be; the action is released by pushing the front trigger forward. The lever in front of the triggers is the barrel selector. (Photos by Russ Carpenter)

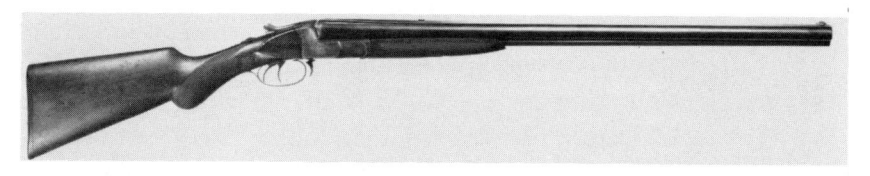

A drilling made by the Three-Barrel Gun Co., from the Smithsonian Institution. The top lever opens the gun, and the lever in front of the trigger guard is the barrel selector. The rear sight is a low notch. (Photo courtesy Smithsonian Institution)

Combination guns have not always gone unappreciated in America. To youngsters like myself, the name L. C. Smith brings only visions of a nice double shotgun, but during the early 1900's the Syracuse, New York, factory also produced a good drilling with 30-inch Damascus barrels and a weight of just over nine pounds. Beneath a pair of 12-gauge smoothbores was a .44/40 rifle barrel. The front sight was a blade low enough to serve as a shotgun bead, and the rear was a combination notch and peep on an elevating ladder that folded down onto the stock. A barrel-selector button, protruding down inside the trigger guard, could be pushed forward for rifle fire, rearward for shotgun use. The gun broke open like a standard double, but since there was a sight on the tang where the top lever would normally be, the release was incorporated into the front trigger. It was pushed forward to open the action.

Somewhere among the Smithsonian Institution's multitudinous possessions is a fairly similar piece made by a firm so specialized as to call itself the Three-Barrel Gun Co. The rear sight on this drilling, however, is a low notch on the rib. There's a conventional top lever and, in front of the trigger guard, a selection lever.

These drillings were pretty heavy for American tastes, and they went out of style by about the time of the First World War. Long before that, however, a different type of combination gun had experienced a small surge of popularity in this country. It was a two-barreled rifle-shotgun, made in the style of the Kentucky rifle. Which brings us to the evolution of the combination gun.

No one knows where or when the first rifle-shotguns were contrived, but in the mid-sixteenth century over/under wheel locks began to appear in Germany. There were double rifles, shotguns, and pistols, with no attempt to wed smooth and rifled bores. Two separate locks were employed, as these were fixed-breech guns. Another century passed and then, with the widespread acceptance of the flintlock, came the *Wender* (the German word for "turner"). Employing pivoting barrels with a single lock, it was a fairly common design throughout Europe by the mid-eighteenth century. There were seven- or eight-barreled guns, too, but the marriage of bore types awaited the advent of lighter, smaller arms, since a shotgun was often swung at moving targets.

Even the early side-by-side fowling pieces were too muzzle-heavy to win great favor until 1787, when the Englishman Henry Nock invented his wonderful new ignition system. His fast-ignition flintlock incorporated a small chamber of powder behind the full charge,

Multi-barreled arms from the Winchester Gun Museum in New Haven, Connecticut. At top, a drilling made in Kentucky (though far removed from the "Kentucky style" of older, Pennsylvania-made zweilings) circa 1865-1875. Center, a vierling made in Pennsylvania, circa 1860. Bottom, a four-barreled rifle made in New York, circa 1850-1860. The vierling weighs over sixteen pounds, though its graceful lines make it look lighter. Its stock and trigger guard show influence of late ("decadent period") Kentucky rifles. (Photo courtesy Winchester Gun Museum)

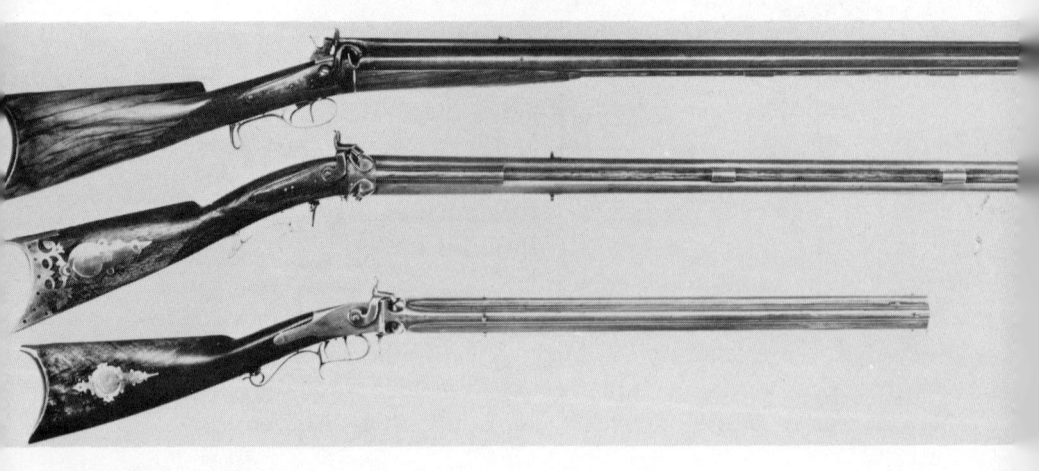

to spurt a flame through the propellant. Ignited in this manner, powder burned so quickly that there was no longer a need for a bore of 40 inches or more.

Barrels became shorter and lighter, and the time had come to mate rifle and shotgun. Traditionally, Germany produces the most and the finest combination arms, and the great German gunsmiths of the early nineteenth century are usually credited with originating these guns. One of the oldest specimens may be a German over/under displayed at the Winchester Museum in New Haven, Connecticut. It was built in the 1780's, originally as a flintlock, though it was converted to the percussion system in about 1825. It has round barrels only 26⅜ inches long and it weighs eleven pounds — less than many guns of its era. This handsome piece employs a 60-caliber rifle barrel over a .62 smoothbore. It has two independent locks, with a trigger on the right to fire the rifle and one on the left to fire the shotgun.

Here was a wonderful innovation for the European sportsman, who never knew whether his next target would be a red stag or a partridge; and what held true for the Continent also applied to England and America.

The Kentucky rifle, which, contrary to the popular nineteenth-century ballads, most often came from Pennsylvania, traced its lineage to the much shorter but very fine German hunting rifle known as the *Jaeger*. Not long after the graceful design of the Kentucky reached its zenith, another German idea — the rotating *Wender* — reached Pennsylvania. During its chief period of manufacture, between 1810 and 1840, it very quickly evolved into a rifle-shotgun. Though a few Kentucky-style side-by-side combination arms have survived, most were over/unders. The barrels pivoted, to fire both loads with the same lock, and the occasional early flintlock examples were soon superseded by percussion mechanisms.

The late Joe Kindig, Jr., probably America's most knowledgeable student of the Kentucky, observed that these combinations were almost invariably made and used in the rugged northwestern mountains of Pennsylvania, where the paltry homesteads had little livestock and farmers hunted for meat, not sport. They carried the relatively heavy combination arms in order to be prepared for any game they encountered, and these American zweilings seldom show the luxurious craftsmanship of the pure Kentucky rifle.

Combination, or Shot and Ball Gun—

W. P. JONES'S THREE-BARRELLED GUN.

Jones Damascus-barreled drilling. Note the flip-up tang sight of early Lyman type, side lever, and separate hammers. In addition to a peep sight, the gun has a series of notch sights on the barrel. This was a lightweight model, "from 7 pounds upward," depending on chamberings.

Still, to some hunters cumbersome weight was a minor consideration. A percussion vierling in the Winchester collection, made in Pennsylvania in about 1860, weighs sixteen pounds six ounces. Its four rotating barrels are positioned so that the shooter always has a smoothbore at the top left and a rifle at the top right for instant choice. Since each of the two hammers engages a sear connected to the single trigger, the choice is simply a matter of which hammer is cocked. The open sights between the barrels are typically low, to permit wingshooting.

Before the century ended, all sorts of barrel juxtapositions had been tried, both here and overseas, and the problem of weight had been partially solved by shortening barrels and trimming stocks and locks. "Exceedingly useful," one writer called drillings such as the W. P. Jones Three-Barrelled Gun, which he described as having

> two barrels side by side as in an ordinary shot gun, but with a rifle barrel on the top taking the place of the usual top rib. This rifle barrel is useful for shooting deer and other small game. The weight of this weapon ranges from 7 lbs. upward, according to the size and power of the cartridges to be used. The firing arrangements are simple and not liable to get out of order.

Drilling, Vierling, und Zweiling: Reflections on Rifle-Shotguns 93

Strong disagreement came from W. W. Greener, that arbiter of English (i.e., definitive) shooting taste. The first edition of his classic work, *The Gun and Its Development,* issued in 1881, lists seven kinds of European big game and nine kinds of game birds in addition to waterfowl. Yet, strangely, he restricts his coverage of combination guns to disapproving observations about side-by-side models much in use in Africa, ignoring both over/unders and the drillings, which were finding wide acceptance. Admitting that the side-by-side combination "is much esteemed by South African sportsmen," he then says,

> The rifle barrel, usually the left, may be rifled on any system. Henry rifling is still most in favour at the Cape . . . the proper proportions . . . being .450 rifle barrel and 16-bore shot barrel, or .500 rifle barrel and 12-bore shot barrel. These arms are only useful in countries where the kind of game that may be met with cannot be determined beforehand, and for emigrants who cannot afford more than one gun . . . The weapon is too heavy as a shot-gun . . . The balance, of course, is bad. As a rifle, the weapon is too light . . .

In a later edition, Greener corrects the oversight regarding drillings. He condescends to print a drawing of the barrel arrangement that was now becoming almost standard, remarking:

> The three-barrelled weapon, usually if not always, consists of a double shotgun, with a small rifle barrel placed between them and below . . . Occasionally similar arms are seen having the rifle barrel on the top. It is difficult to decide which type is the more objectionable. Either arrangement interferes with the breech mechanism, and whether with hammers or hammerless the lock and firing mechanisms are rarely satisfactory . . . The extra barrel quite spoils the arm as a shot gun . . . and as a rifle it is rarely as accurate as a like barrel in a single or double rifle . . . Endeavors to construct them of approximate weight to shot guns have resulted in dangerously light weapons being issued, with disastrous consequences.

(Many years later, after praising his drilling's lightness, safety, and reliability, Larry Koller said of its shooting qualities that he had used it for a fine round of skeet, and that he attributed the 7-mm.'s "excellent accuracy to the stiffening effect of the two shotgun barrels over and around the rifle barrel." *Tempus fugit.*)

Meanwhile, back in London in 1906, Henry Sharp was publishing his third or fourth gun book, a fascinating tome entitled *Modern Sporting Gunnery.* Mr. Sharp, too, omitted mention of any combination except the side-by-side, which he described as most often having a 12- or 16-bore right barrel, and a left barrel chambered for the .450 Westley Richards No. 1 Carbine cartridge (380-grain bullet, sighted to 1,000 yards), the .450 Westley Richards No. 2 Musket cartridge (480-grain bullet, sighted to 1,200 yards) or the .450 Martini (480-grain bullet, sighted to 1,200 or 1,500 yards). These guns were on the order of the well-known Cape rifle made by Jeffery and others, with one smoothbore barrel, one two-groove barrel, and an "Express-type" series of folding-leaf sights in graduated heights for different ranges, plus an adjustable tangent sight forward of the leaves for still greater ranges. Mr. Sharp disagreed with Mr. Greener, declaring that these guns "are extremely useful and effective weapons for mixed shooting and have long been popular in Cape Colony and other parts of South Africa, and they still continue in large use."

America, as usual, absorbed what was wanted of the European trends and went its own way. During the 1850's, for example, Colt's famous revolving shotguns and rifles could be purchased

An illustration from Henry Sharp's Modern Sporting Gunnery *(1906); hammerless Westley Richards double had .450 rifle barrel and 12- or 16-gauge shotgun barrel. Note folding tangent and leaf sights, graduated for rifle shooting at various distances out to 1000, 1200, or sometimes 1500 yards.*

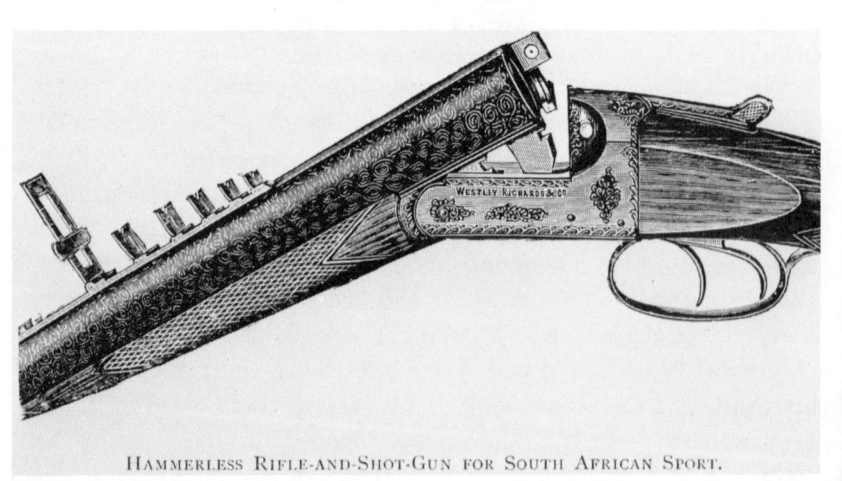

HAMMERLESS RIFLE-AND-SHOT-GUN FOR SOUTH AFRICAN SPORT.

LeMat "grapeshot revolver" carried by Confederate General J. E. B. Stuart and now at the Confederate Museum, Richmond, Virginia. The upper barrel had a .42 rifled bore. The cylinder held nine lead balls plus a heavy scattergun charge for the smoothbore around which the cylinder revolved. The smoothbore was about 18-gauge. The hinged hammer nose could be flipped up or down for barrel choice. Later variations included a sporting carbine with 20½-inch barrel. (Photo courtesy Confederate Museum)

with interchangeable rifle and scattergun barrels and cylinders. In the years since, Colt has been followed by the old Savage take-down version of the Model 99 lever-action rifle, which could be obtained for a while with an interchangeable .410 shotgun barrel; by the Remington Model 219 single-shot rifle, discontinued in 1948 but once available in four rifle calibers and with an interchangeable 12-, 16-, or 20-gauge barrel; and by the Harrington & Richardson Topper Model single-shot, which is still popular and still can be bought with interchangeable rifle and shotgun barrels.

Such arms, obviously, do not permit instant switching, but they represent only one of several approaches. Even handguns have undergone the Great Combination Experiment. The most famous example was the LeMat revolver, patented in 1856 by a French-born physician named Dr. Jean Alexandre Francois LeMat who became a Louisiana colonel, and carried by such distinguished Confederates as Generals P. G. T. Beauregard (coincidentally LeMat's business partner) and J. E. B. Stuart. This revolver utilized a nine-shot

We can recommend our No. 20 and 21 Rifles as superior to any in the market for the money. They are gotten up expressly for our Retail Trade, and we guarantee every one of them to give satisfaction. Every one is tried before we ship it so as to be sure that the sights are properly adjusted.

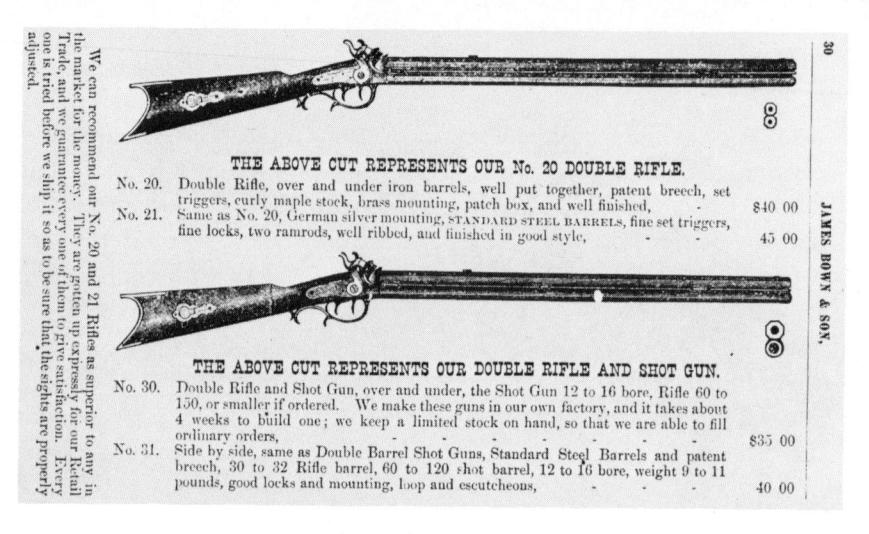

THE ABOVE CUT REPRESENTS OUR No. 20 DOUBLE RIFLE.

No. 20. Double Rifle, over and under iron barrels, well put together, patent breech, set triggers, curly maple stock, brass mounting, patch box, and well finished, - $40 00

No. 21. Same as No. 20, German silver mounting, STANDARD STEEL BARRELS, fine set triggers, fine locks, two ramrods, well ribbed, and finished in good style, - - 45 00

THE ABOVE CUT REPRESENTS OUR DOUBLE RIFLE AND SHOT GUN.

No. 30. Double Rifle and Shot Gun, over and under, the Shot Gun 12 to 16 bore, Rifle 60 to 150, or smaller if ordered. We make these guns in our own factory, and it takes about 4 weeks to build one; we keep a limited stock on hand, so that we are able to fill ordinary orders, - - - - - - - $35 00

No. 31. Side by side, same as Double Barrel Shot Guns, Standard Steel Barrels and patent breech, 30 to 32 Rifle barrel, 60 to 120 shot barrel, 12 to 16 bore, weight 9 to 11 pounds, good locks and mounting, loop and escutcheons, - - 40 00

A page from 1876 catalog of James Bown & Son.

ILLUSTRATED CATALOGUE. 23

AMERICAN BREECH-LOADING GUNS—Continued.

PARKER GUN.

Fine English Twist Barrels, Fine American Stock, no Checking or Engraving. Pistol Grip; No. 10 Gauge $70 00
Ditto, with Straight Grip 65 00
Fine English Twist Barrels, Fine American Stock, no Checking or Engraving. Pistol Grip; No. 12 Gauge 65 00
Ditto, with Straight Grip 60 00
Plain Twist Barrels, no Engraving or Checking. Pistol Grip; No. 10 Gauge 60 00
Ditto, with Straight Grip 55 00
Plain Twist Barrels, no Engraving or Checking. Pistol Grip; No. 12 Gauge 55 00
Ditto, with Straight Grip 50 00

Straight or high ribs put on all grades of Guns when desired. Patent Fore-end lock, where not specified on above list, $5.00 extra. Nos. 8, 16 and 20 Gauge Guns are only made to special order, and can be made to correspond with any of the above grades at an advance of $15.00 for Nos. 16 and 20 gauge above list for 12 gauge, and $35.00 extra for No. 8 gauge above list for No. 10 gauge.

Shelton's Auxiliary Rifle Barrel for Breech-Loading Shot Guns.

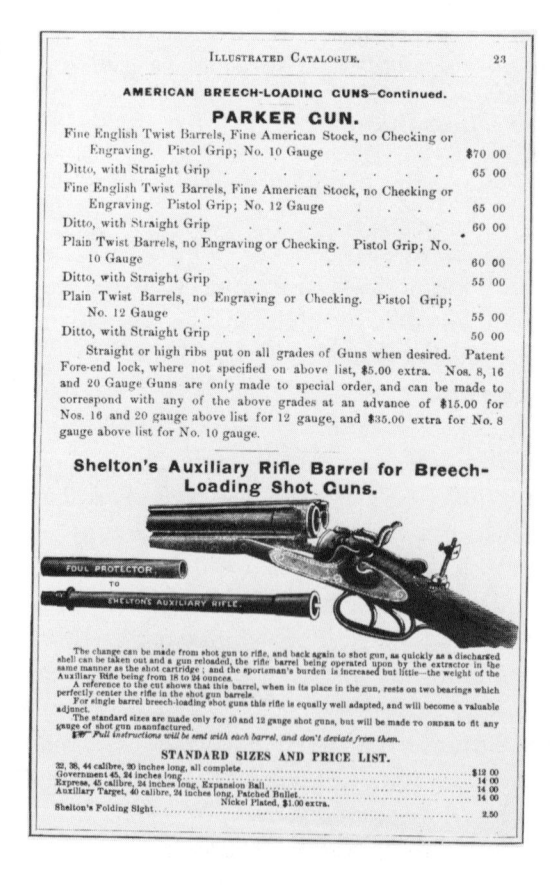

The change can be made from shot gun to rifle, and back again to shot gun, as quickly as a discharged shell can be taken out and a gun reloaded, the rifle barrel being operated upon by the extractor in the same manner as the shot cartridge; and the sportsman's burden is increased but little—the weight of the Auxiliary Rifle being from 18 to 24 ounces.

A reference to the cut shows that this barrel, when in its place in the gun, rests on two bearings which perfectly center the rifle in the shot gun barrels.

For single barrel breech-loading shot guns this rifle is equally well adapted, and will become a valuable adjunct.

The standard sizes are made only for 10 and 12 gauge shot guns, but will be made to ORDER to fit any gauge of shot gun manufactured.

☞ Full instructions will be sent with each barrel, and don't deviate from them.

STANDARD SIZES AND PRICE LIST.

32, 38, 44 calibre, 20 inches long, all complete....................$12 00
Government 45, 24 inches long................................. 14 00
Express, 45 calibre, 24 inches long, Expansion Ball............. 14 00
Auxiliary Target, 40 calibre, 24 inches long, Patched Bullet..... 14 00
    Nickel Plated, $1.00 extra.
Shelton's Folding Sight... 2.50

A page from Homer Fisher's 1880 catalog. When used in a double shotgun, "Shelton's Auxiliary Rifle Barrel" created a temporary rifle-shotgun.

.42-caliber cylinder, aligned to an ordinary, rifled pistol barrel but revolving around a central .63-caliber "grapeshot" barrel. The hammer nose was adjustable to fire ball or shot. Before the maker eventually went out of business, other bore sizes were offered and — what is perhaps not as well-known — so were shoulder-arm versions. They were said to be effective, but failed in competition with all the other post-Civil War innovations.

As late as 1876, the catalog of James Bown & Son of Pittsburgh was offering a percussion zweiling that looked like the overweight progeny of a late Kentucky and a heavy plains rifle, suckled perhaps by an uncultured trade gun. It cost $35 in over/under form, $5 more as a side-by-side. A number of bore sizes were offered.

By then the proliferation of self-contained ammunition began to have an impact. One is familiar with the Four-Tenner bore-reducing insert tubes for break-open shotguns, marketed today by Savage. But what about Homer Fisher's 1880 catalog, offering (at $12 to $14, depending on caliber) "Shelton's Auxiliary Rifle Barrel for Breech-Loading Shot Guns"? Though standard models were made only for 10- or 12-gauge guns, other sizes could be obtained on special order. The device was a short, rifled barrel, inserted into the breech end of a smoothbore in the same manner as a modern bore-reducer. (An even smaller gadget, on the same principle, is manufactured today for .22 plinking with a shotgun.) In a single-barreled gun, it provided reasonably fast interchangeability. In a double, such as the Parker shotgun advertised on the same page of Fisher's catalog, it provided a smoothbore on one side, a temporary rifled barrel on the other.

Not that America had forsaken European tradition (or ingenuity). A 1902 catalog for Sears, Roebuck, which then identified itself as "Cheapest Supply House on Earth," advertised "our $17.10 Belgian combined rifle and shotgun," a side-by-side breechloader with a 12-gauge smoothbore on the right, a .38/55 rifle barrel on the left. Though the rifle barrel was fairly thick-walled, it was slightly out of proportion with its mate. Appearance notwithstanding, the thing weighed a mere 8½ to 8¾ pounds with its 30-inch barrels, and it did offer the versatility of a combination gun. Like most zweilings of its period, it employed a separate trigger and hammer for each barrel, the simplest possible design.

Enter the previously mentioned L. C. Smith drilling, the Three-

Part of a page from the 1902 Sears, Roebuck catalog.

Barrel Gun Co., and plenty of European competition until the outbreak of the First War To End All Wars. Thereafter, for a while, most Americans turned to strictly one-purpose, domestically produced arms or to a few imports that might have fared better if the Great Depression had not descended.

The Germans, as we all know, busied themselves during that period with a lot of unpleasant new ideas and one pleasant one. (A couple of my relatives would argue that the Germans developed *nothing* pleasant during that regrettable era, but they must be pardoned for a certain bias, subsequently nurtured at Anzio and during the Battle of the Bulge.)

The pleasant idea was to continue making fine combination guns, particularly drillings, often departing from traditional designs or with unusual optional features. The firm of Sempert & Krieghoff, for instance, offered double shotgun barrels as an accessory for drillings. (Double rifle barrels were also made separately, though they were not listed in the catalog.) These side-by-side barrels were interchangeable with the triple-barrel units. On the bottom of the doubles, extending downward from the rib, was a short, plugged cylindrical tube to fill the action space normally taken by the rifle barrel. The lumps were attached to this cylinder in order to adapt the unit to the gun's frame. When the piece was assembled, the cylinder was concealed in the fore-end. Farther forward was a short cylindrical block which filled the rifle-barrel channel flush at the front of the fore-end. This converted the drilling into a lighter, faster double for more specialized hunting.

In those days, Krieghoff was located at Suhl, in what is now East Germany. It has since relocated in the Western sector, as have several other makers. But so many drillings were, and are, made in or near Suhl that these arms are sometimes called Suhl guns. At this writing, two- and three-barreled combinations are made by Franconia, Hege, Heym, Krieghoff, and Sauer in West Germany and by Buhag, Fortuna, Hubertus, Merkel, and Simson in East Germany. Ferlach and Sodia are in Austria. The price range varies from moderately expensive to extremely expensive, and the arms are of exceptionally good quality.

Having digressed into the present, I must now return briefly to the twenties and thirties when, as noted, departures from the generally accepted norm were common. In addition to the Krieghoff barrel sets, two Merkel types are worth describing because both were imported to this country.

One was a drilling built on the Anson & Deeley action, with side-by-side rifle barrels above one centered shotgun barrel. The smoothbore was available in 12, 16 or 20 gauge, but since this drilling was produced on special order only, the customer could specify *any* rimmed or rimless chambering he desired for the rifle barrels. Strength was an obvious requisite for such a gun, and the advertisement stipulated a double Greener crossbolt and "extra strong double underbolts." There was a choice of doll's-head or straight extension rib, and a flip-up leaf sight high enough for dead-on shooting at 100 or 150 yards as desired. Features included two safeties, one of which incorporated the barrel selector and flipped up the sight, a horn butt plate, engravings of hunting scenes or English-style scrollwork, and so on. Barrel length was 27 to 28 inches, weight eight to nine pounds, and scoping was common, usually with a German instrument such as the Zeiss or Hensoldt.

The other notable Merkel was a vierling with a .22 barrel on top (and a substantial sighting rib over that), side-by-side shotgun barrels in 12, 16, or 20 bore below the .22, and a .30/30 or .25/35 barrel centered under them as on a standard drilling. The ads stipulated that the chokes were modified and full, and the gun employed the Blitz system, with the locks mounted on the trigger plate, so that the action was positioned farther forward than in the Anson & Deeley system. The simple, reliable Anson & Deeley design is probably the world's most popular for guns that don't utilize sidelocks. (Only a very few of the most costly drillings and zweilings do use sidelocks.) The sun may never set on Anson & Deeley as it has on most of the British Empire, but the Blitz has long been popular in Germany. I suspect that preferences for one or the other have often had more to do with chauvinism than with functioning quality. At any rate, this gun had a Greener-type side safety, a second safety-selector on the neck of the stock for the rifle barrels, an adjustable rear sight, and a barrel length of 28 inches.

The weight was about nine pounds, which seems more suitable for a trap gun or long-range varmint rifle than for a hunting arm whose chief attraction is versatility. This is the inevitable flaw of vierlings, yet they are still made by Buhag, Franconia, and possibly others.

In American manufacture during the thirties, the trend was toward lower costs and fewer rather than more barrels, but two combination guns — both zweilings — did materialize shortly before the Second World War. One was a special edition of the well-known Marlin Model 90 over/under shotgun, employing a two-trigger boxlock action. The top barrel was a 20-gauge smoothbore, the lower one a rifle. Several calibers were offered, of which the .30/30 was probably most popular. The war so disrupted the manufacture of arms for sporting use that the return to peacetime production was tortuous. Among the guns discontinued in the late forties were the Model 90's.

The other zweiling was an inexpensive little Stevens over/under, with a .22 barrel over a .410 smoothbore. Originally, it had two triggers, two side-by-side hammers, and a tenite stock and fore-end, but it was almost immediately improved, with a single, centered hammer, a barrel-selector button on the side of the frame, a wood stock and forearm. In .22 and .410, it was nothing more than a plinking and small-game gun, or a knockabout barn and camp gun. This model was successfully revived after the war. Stevens had long ago been acquired by Savage Arms, and in 1950 the gun's name was changed from the Stevens .22/.410 to the Savage Model 24. In 1960

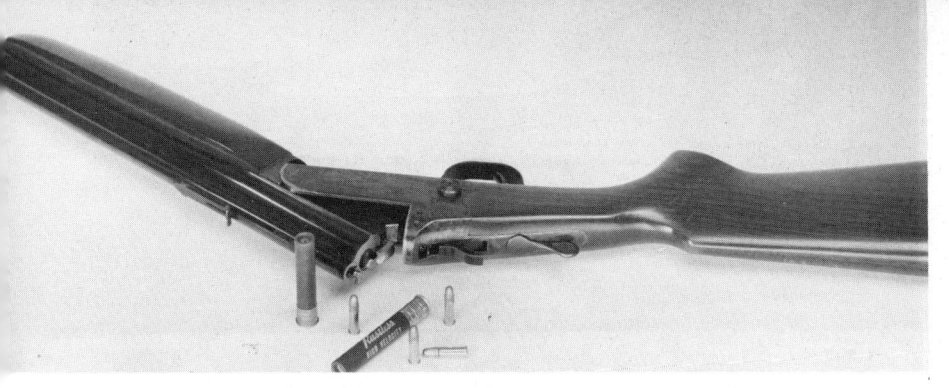

Early Savage Model 24 over/under rifle-shotgun, with the .22 Long Rifle and .410 shells for which it was chambered. In later versions the side selector button was replaced by a hammer-spur selector reminiscent of the old LeMat revolver design.

a version was introduced with a top barrel chambered for the .22 Winchester Magnum Rimfire cartridge. That added moderate-range varmint shooting to its capabilities. Soon afterward, a 20-gauge bottom barrel was offered, further increasing the gun's versatility. Also in the sixties, the barrel selector was moved to the hammer. It's a conveniently positioned, serrated top knob that moves the hammer nose up or down for firing-pin choice. Dr. LeMat would have been pleased to see the concept of his Confederate grapeshot revolver rise again.

There have been other changes. One version has the opening lever on the side rather than on the tang, for easy operation by youngsters with small hands. A more important addition was the 1966 introduction of the Model 24V, which has barrels chambered for the .222 rifle cartridge and the 3-inch Magnum 20-gauge shotshell. The barrels have no full-length joining ribs; instead they're held secure at the front by a barrel band and at the rear by a hefty pin-and-monoblock arrangement. The gun is pleasantly light — just under seven pounds — and accurate enough for 2-inch groups at 100 yards when scoped.

A gun of this sort cannot compare in any way — including versatility — with the costly, beautifully fitted and finished, handsomely engraved foreign combinations. However, with the addition of the centerfire caliber, it is handy not only for small game, chucks, and the like, but for fox or turkey hunting—either of which pursuits may on occasion call for an instant switch of bores. Somewhat similar but more expensive guns have been introduced by Tikka in Finland as well as Hege and Ferlach.

In Savage promotional photograph, hunter aims scoped Model 24V. This modern zweiling has separated .222 (upper) and 20-gauge Magnum barrels.

For a while after the war, it looked as if imports of high-quality combinations might find an eager market in America. Alexander F. Stoeger II, in the 1954 edition of his firm's catalog, proclaimed: "The little Carinthian Mountain village of Ferlach in southern Austria . . . is again buzzing with activity since here . . . are produced the many combination guns otherwise produced almost exclusively in Suhl."

Drilling, Vierling, und Zweiling: Reflections on Rifle-Shotguns 103

But fewer and fewer combinations were listed as the drab sixties progressed, and I notice that the Stoeger *Shooter's Bible* listed none at all in 1970. Yet we proselytizing eccentrics have cause for hope that the barbarians are beginning to see the light of drillings, if not zweilings or vierlings.

The Krieghoff "American" drilling is now imported — in a higher grade than Larry Koller's gun — by Harry Owens of Sunnyvale, California. Alas, the Cape buffalo horn has been replaced by prosaic nylon, but in all other respects this is a very sumptuous piece. The little refinements include cocking indicators, split extractors to lift the brass case higher than the shotshells — one knows the sort of thing. The gun still employs a barrel-selector lever on

German drilling in Bob Zwirz collection has grouse engraved on frame. This is a field-grade drilling; many fancier models feature engraved hunting scenes or elegant English-style scrollwork, as well as beautiful wood with much finer checkering, but less expensive versions were still popular two generations ago.

the tang, which works very nicely. Of course, prices have risen somewhat, to $1,500 to be precise. But this Krieghoff now comes with a .22 WMR insert barrel (shades of Homer Fisher's 1880 catalog!) fitted inside the right shotgun tube, which, like its mate, is 12-gauge. With the insert, the smoothbore, and the rifle proper (7-mm. Magnum or .30/06) a shooter owns three different bores. Four if, having laid out $1,500, he does not balk at another $24 for an extra .22 LR insert barrel.

Then there is Flaig's Lodge in Millvale, Pennsylvania, an importer prepared to order drillings for those of sufficient financial standing, or a $650 Ferlach boxlock two-trigger over/under zweiling —12-, 16-, or 20-gauge, on a rifled foundation of .22 Hornet, .222, .243, .257, 6.5 x 55 mm., .270, 7 x 57 mm., or .30/06.

For only a few more Deutschmarks, Roy Weatherby himself, the esteemed Southgate, California, entrepreneur, will supply you with an exquisite Sauer BBF over/under zweiling or a Sauer 3000-E drilling. Prices for the zweilings begin at $735; the drillings start at $830. The over/under's smoothbore is in the over position and is a full-choke 16-gauge barrel. The drilling has modified and full chokes and is chambered for 12-gauge shells. Both have 25-inch barrels, with the hammer-forged rifle available in .222, .243, .30/30, .30/06, or 7 x 65 R. And both have a front trigger that serves as an adjustable set trigger for the rifle. The engraving (arabesques on the budget-priced versions, hunting scenes on the more elite numbers) is, of course, a many-splendored thing. That also goes for the wood and the checkering and all the other expected refinements.

The stocks are of a modified Monte Carlo persuasion and will satisfy the discriminating American taste in contours (14½ x 1⅝ x 2¾, for the benefit of doubters). The weight of the zweiling is a mere 6 pounds or so, that of the drilling 6½ to 7¼, depending on caliber.

It has occurred to me that I may never tramp the Black Forest in search of black grouse or with the legs of a roe buck daintily crossed upon my chest. But should the opportunity present itself (together with a modest foundation grant), I shall arm myself in style for the occasion. As my grandpa would have said, *"Ach, wie schön, ein drilling!"* Or as Larry Koller put it, in his carefully considered, finely understated manner, "I personally like such guns."

The Chamberlin Cartridge & Target Co.

BOB HINMAN

Bob Hinman has been a keen student and skilled exponent of the shotgun for most of his life, and he has shot skeet and trap or hunted in most of the United States, Canada, and Mexico. He is the man behind Bob Hinman Outfitters of Peoria, Illinois, a successful mail-order house dealing in hunting, fishing, and camping equipment and gear.

Hinman is Shotgun Editor of Shooting Times and is a prolific magazine writer. He has always been interested in gunning history, and over the years he has built up a file on early guns, shells, and related subjects such as game laws and market hunting that may be the most complete in the country. Out of this research came not just the piece below but his book The Golden Age of Shotgunning, *a close study of the period from 1870 to 1900 that saw so many technological and social changes. When he is not being a businessman or an author, Hinman manages to slip away to the bird field or duck blind, or to add to his string of skeet and trap trophies.*

THE EARLY HISTORY of most of the American companies that have been significant factors in the arms and ammunition field has been exhaustively explored. It has been documented, researched, printed, and reprinted to death until the dedicated collector and arms historian can find books and articles recording everything from Oliver Winchester's necktie preferences to the timing of John Browning's daily activities.

Thus I was surprised to learn, when I first attempted to establish who first had manufactured the modern fixed shotshell, that nobody really had the answer. Most experts, when queried, assumed that it was either the old Union Metallic Cartridge Co. or Winchester. But they proved wrong. Further investigation turned up the name of a company that is scarcely mentioned in the shooting literature, and then by name only. This was the Chamberlin Cartridge & Target Co. of Ohio.

I became interested in this obscure company and pursued it further, with considerable help from researcher Dan Wallace. Eventually I discovered that Chamberlin and its affiliate, the Cleveland Target Co., had not only originated the mass-production shotshell, but had also pioneered with several other important innovations that continue in service even today. It is surprising that the firm that invented, improved, and marketed advanced forms of shells, targets, and traps has never received proper recognition in print, and I have waited for a long time to write up this little-known chapter in America's gun history. Here, then, is the story.

For most of the long history of firearms, every shooter has also of necessity been a handloader. Today we are spoiled, though some of us still, for reasons of economy or experimentation, prefer to "roll our own." But prior to the turn of the century, most shotgunners had no choice but to do their own loading. True, there were hardware and sporting goods firms that had a loading service and would whomp up to order whatever load a man desired and could pay for. But even these "manufactured" shells were basically a hand-loaded operation. Mass-production machinery simply didn't exist, and in the opinion of as good an authority as W. W. Greener, it was impossible to build it with the technology and materials available in 1882.

Moreover, most of nineteenth-century America was rural, a country more of villages and towns than of cities, and only those living in metropolitan areas had access to a big sporting goods store. The countryman bought power, shot, and brass or paper hulls from the general store, and loaded his own as best he knew how. The big ammo companies like Winchester, Remington, and U.M.C. sold components only, in the beginning, and it was strictly up to the individual to put together a shootable shotshell.

This was the situation in the fall of 1883 when one Frank Chamberlin of Cleveland, Ohio, invited the president of the Pittsburgh Firearms Co., J. Palmer O'Neil, to go duck hunting with him. Chamberlin furnished the shells, and O'Neil thought they were fine. But he was flabbergasted when Chamberlin told him that he'd cranked them out himself, on a machine of his own invention, at a rate of 400 per hour—adding that three or four

An early advertisement for Chamberlin cartridges.

times that capacity was perfectly feasible. J. Palmer O'Neil was the breed of industrialist for which nineteenth-century America was famous. In his mind he could instantly see what Chamberlin's reloading machine would do—it would give the shooter, at a reasonable price, factory-made, store-bought shells in a handy box, ready to use. He wanted in.

So with O'Neil's money and Chamberlin's invention, the Chamberlin Cartridge & Target Co. came into being. Their first automatic loading machine was built in a Cleveland building and produced from 1,200 to 1,500 shells per hour. Since the 10-gauge was the most popular shell of that day, this was the size of shell first made.

O'Neil and Chamberlin soon found that in order to expand, outside money would be needed, and this they obtained from J. H. Webster, the Cleveland mill owner who employed Chamberlin. Chamberlin's machine was put on exhibition in Cleveland, Pittsburgh, and New York, and apparently aroused some interest for the next year, 1884, found Mr. O'Neil in San Francisco arranging for machines to be installed and operated by the Selby Smelting & Lead Co.

Selby made its own contribution to the operation by inventing a machine that would automatically sort wads, which were not uniform in thickness at that time. This simplified and standardized seating pressures, crimping, and the length of the loaded shell.

In view of the transportation difficulties of the day, it was decided to set up three different manufacturing plants to cover the market for loaded shells: San Francisco to serve the West; Cleveland, the Midwest; and the Atlantic Ammunition Co., Ltd., to supply the East. The last firm, owned by O'Neil, was in the business of loading shells to order prior to the formation of C. C. & T. Co. Atlantic fit nicely into the new company network. In 1887 the Western Arms & Cartridge Co., 108 Madison Street, Chicago, Ill., was licensed to load shells on Chamberlin machines.

At first, Chamberlin shells were sold loaded with either black or wood powder. Prices were $2.50 per hundred black and $3.50 for smokeless, adding 10c per hundred for chilled shot. For three or four years the Chamberlin organization had the factory-loaded shell market to themselves. Then Winchester entered the field in 1887 with their own machines, and soon the large and complex Union Metallic Cartridge Co. was forced to follow suit.

Compared to U.M.C. and Winchester, the Chamberlin company was small and undercapitalized. They felt the competition at once and realized that their position in the market was seriously jeopardized by two such powerful giants. What was even more damaging to the Chamberlin position was their dependency upon competitors for shell casings and wads. Chamberlin did not make hulls or primers, and in spite of prohibitive duties the firm was soon forced to import English hulls and load them to be sold on a break-even basis just to keep in the market.

In 1898 they were offering Leader, Climax, New Club, or Rival casing with nitro card and blackedge wads, 2¾ drams black powder and 1⅛ ounces of shot in 12 gauge for only $1.25 per 100. They also had a brand called Klondikers in the same cases and wads but with 42 to 45 grains of Gold Dust smokeless at $1.60. Their famous Blue Rock shells, called Snuff-'Em-Outs and loaded with duPont, Troisdorf, or Hazard smokeless, were $1.75. Their High Grade brand was any length of Leader case with above powder at $2.00 per 100. Shells were made in 10, 12, 14, 16 and 20 gauge. The High Grade brand was offered in thirteen different loadings and named Woodcock, Snipe, Teal, Mallard, etc., an idea picked up by Remington some years later and used on their own shells to simplify load selection for the hunter. At various times, Chamberlin used almost all American-made powders available.

The Chamberlin Cartridge & Target Co.

The standard over-the-counter box of 25 shotshells we buy today is also, indirectly, another Chamberlin contribution. For when his machine with its capacity of 1,500 loaded rounds per hour revolutionized the industry, it also presented a new problem — that of how the shells should be packed for transportation and sale.

At first Chamberlin reused the boxes in which the empty shells came to the plant for loading. But these boxes, which held 100 empties, proved too fragile to hold the weight of loaded shells. Now with the added weight, it was thought to pack the box in wood. This was both laborious and expensive. And a box of 100 shells was more than the average sportsman cared to purchase at one time.

To solve this problem, O'Neil took a U.M.C. box holding 100 shells and quartered it exactly to hold 25. He then took his model box to Myers, Shinkle & Co., bookbinders of Pittsburgh, and had them cut and glue a two-piece box to hold 25 rounds. They packed the box with 10-gauge shells, alternating the brass and crimped end, and then packed 20 boxes to the wooden case of 500. And thus it is today.

Shotshell loading and packaging innovations were only the beginning of the Chamberlin firm's gifts to the American shotgunner, for in conjunction with its affiliate, the Cleveland Target Co., this

---

Chamberlin cartridges came in boxes of 25, just as cartridges are sold today. The wording on the box suggests that the Atlantic Ammunition Co. loaded for Chamberlin; actually, Chamberlin only licensed Atlantic to use their machines.

20 GAUGE.
BERLIN CARTRIDGES,
Loaded by
atic Ammunition Co.
(LIMITED.)
NEW YORK.

Chamberlin Cartridges

THESE cartridges were loaded on the Chamberlin Patent Automatic Cartridge Loader, which is not an implement, but a machine, so constructed that it performs all the operations of loading shells and does the work with absolute accuracy, giving uniform charges with suitable and unvarying pressure upon the wads. With this machine each wad is put into the shell separately and forced home in an absolutely level position, an advantage that cannot be secured in hand-loaded shells.

innovative firm played a major role in developing the modern form of trapshooting. The Expert trap, still in use today, originated with Chamberlin; also the first automatic trap, the first electric trap release, and the common name for the clay pigeon Blue Rock, which was a Chamberlin trademark.

The connection between Chamberlin and the Cleveland Target Co. is a complicated one. They shared the same stockholders and many of the same officers, and were probably formed at the same time, although the Cleveland firm is not listed in business registers for 1883-84. In practice they seemed to operate interchangeably, even though separate offices were maintained.

Targets and traps were the other major part of Chamberlin's business, and the 1880's was a good time to be in that business. The era of glass-ball shooting was gradually on its way out, because of George Ligowsky's invention of the "clay" pigeon in 1880. Many small companies were producing claybirds in many shapes, but all on a limited-production basis due to poor methods and inadequate molding and baking equipment. There was also a great variety of traps for throwing the new targets, but they, too, were often primitive and unreliable in use. For an innovative firm like Chamberlin, the field was a bonanza, and though Chamberlin gradually ceased to be a factor in the shotshell business after the turn of the century, Chamberlin and Cleveland were to remain important in the trap and target field for many decades after that.

Indeed, the Findlay, Ohio, factory that Chamberlin and Cleveland set up to manufacture Blue Rock targets is still in operation today, turning out a huge volume of claybirds for Remington, who purchased the business in August 1933. The story of the Findlay plant is an interesting one, and I am indebted to a former Chamberlin employee, Don Smith of Findlay, for many of the following details.

Chamberlin's early production of clay targets and traps was concentrated, along with everything else, in their Cleveland plant, but as the Blue Rock gained acceptance, it rapidly became apparent that room for expansion was needed. Accordingly, on June 11, 1889, the Cleveland Target Co. purchased a factory site in Findlay, Ohio, from the Buckeye Land Co. This firm was one of a number of private land syndicates formed to sell land at Findlay, which was experiencing a natural gas boom, and attracting outside industry to the city with almost free gas and land. In addition, Findlay possessed good local clay. To start with, Cleveland planned to use a 40-horsepower steam engine to run their machinery, and to use three or four gas-fired pitch melting kettles as well as a gas-fired clay drying oven. They were to get the gas they needed at $100 per year for a five-year contract.

The money for the Findlay venture was to come from the then president of the Cleveland Target Co., J. H. Webster, also owner of the Variety Iron Mills, at Cleveland. Frank Chamberlin was secretary of this iron mill, and picked his shooting partner, Paul North, to be vice president and general manager of the Cleveland Target Co. Together they chose a mutual friend and fellow shooter, F. C. Damm, as factory superintendent. Damm held a number of patents on targets and traps and had worked closely with Fred Kimble and Charles Stock during the early days of the clay pigeon. Another famous shooter of the day, Al Barton, worked for the firm and is generally credited with being the designer of the Blue Rock target. Probably no other company in the industry at that time had a greater array of talent and inventive genius at its service.

Manufacture of cartridge-loading machinery and most traps was to remain at the Cleveland plant, operating under the Cleveland Target Co. name. The new factory in Findlay was to make some traps and all clay pigeons, plus a fishing reel of which little is known. At Findlay, they would operate under the Chamberlin name.

Contracts were let August 21, 1889, for a factory to be built at the southeastern edge of Findlay, a brick building two stories high. The factory would employ fifty people and turn out 24,000,000 clay targets the first year.

It was soon found there was not enough capacity, and so additions were added in 1890. They also found it necessary to double the size of the steam engine to run the factory, and by this time they were using additional gas from several wells found on their own land. They had added two more target presses, bringing the total to eight, and were turning out 150-160 barrels of targets per day, each barrel containing 600 targets, with cut straw being used for packing material.

The first targets were made from a mixture of coal tar pitch and ground clay, and the company held a patent on the mixture. They went to court a number of times to prevent others from using the same formula.

At first, "Shoot Blue Rocks" was not merely a suggestion but a command; clubs that leased the machines had to agree to use only Blue Rock targets.

SHOOT BLUE ROCKS.

Use Expert Traps and Electric Pulls.

TRY OUR

E. C. SNUFF 'EM OUT CARTRIDGES.

The Best. Quickest and most Reliable Cartridges loaded. Better than hand-loaded because more regular. Send for List.

The Chamberlin Cartridge and Target Co.,
CLEVELAND, O.

The coal pitch was shipped to the factory in boxcars and unloaded into a pitch bin. Clay was dug from shallow pits on their own land. The clay gang could only dig in summer and enough was stored in clay sheds to last during the winter. It was dug by hand with shovels and spades and hauled by mule team to the sheds. From there it was taken to the drying furnace and spread on the top of firebrick to a depth of six inches. After drying, it was shoveled from the beds into grinders, which were simply converted flour grist mills of the type using large round millstones.

The pitch and clay mixture, known around the factory as "dope," was melted together in small kettles, ladled out by a long-handled iron dipper into molds. Because of the speed needed in this operation to prevent the mixture from cooling, dipping was considered an art and entrusted only to older employees.

Once the formula was in the mold, it passed under a plunger to give it its shape. The target cooled enough to be removed by hand from the mold by a "knock-out" man. With the target out of the mold, it was passed to the workmen on the "rubbing-off" stone where any rough edges on the disk were ground off. From here, the targets were carried to the "girls' room" to be painted and packed into barrels ready for shipment.

Targets were shipped from the factory in carload lots only, a standard boxcar holding 200 barrels. Barrels continued to be used until 1926, at which time the targets were packed into cartons of the same type used today.

The old target presses continued in operation until they were replaced by automatic presses in 1935. While the shape and size of the target remained the same, the composition used many formulas until about 1940, when clay gave way to pulverized limestone, and the coal tar pitch was replaced by a crude-oil derivative.

The first Blue Rocks sold for $7.00 per 1000. Pressmen were paid 5¼¢ per barrel—averaging about $1.80 for a 10-hour day. No wonder trapshooting was a less expensive sport in the old days.

The first traps made at the new Findlay factory were the Expert and Extension. The large traps continued to be manufactured at the Cleveland shop until 1921, when all steel-working machinery was shipped to Findlay, including the cartridge-loading machines, which were never reassembled.

Around 1898 the company produced the Magautrap. It was the first truly automatic trap and created quite a furor in the world of trapshooting. Built on a bicycle-like frame and run by pedals, it threw target after target in a smooth and steady way. It was introduced to the American sporting scene at a special shoot in New York City's Madison Square Garden, although Paul North had introduced it in England a month before.

Company ads proclaimed, "The Magautrap is a success." By November of 1898, there were 295 in use throughout the country. Starting with trap #292, they were rigged to operate electrically instead of by pedal power. This ended the shooters' complaint that the operator could slow down the target by pedaling less, thereby favoring certain shooters.

The trap was not for sale. It was leased to clubs guaranteeing to throw only Blue Rock brand targets. This agreement, and a warning of violation thereof, was cast into the metal trap base and frame of each unit. This, too, led to litigation. The company won several small suits, but finally lost a big one when the court decided the notice and warning had to be removed from each trap. They were recalled, some 350 in all, to the Findlay factory, dismantled, and the lettering was ground off. Many of them were eventually sold back to the clubs that had formerly leased them.

Following the Magautrap was a model called the Ideal-Leggett, a very successful design which, in spite of its weight of some 300 pounds, became the standard target-throwing mechanism of its day. Other designs of traps followed until the company was purchased by Remington.

Success or failure of a company depends in a large degree upon

A later-model Magautrap, electrically powered. The first 291 Magautraps were pedal-powered, which permitted some variation in the speed of the targets.

the quality of its leaders. Of the half-dozen talented and capable men connected with the Cleveland and Chamberlin companies, Paul North was probably the most outstanding. He started as a salesman on the road, and, in the American tradition, wound up owning the company.

North's influence was felt throughout trapshooting. A high-average shooter himself, he was highly regarded by fellow gunners—so much so that in 1901 when we sent our All-American trap team to England, it was managed by Paul North. He had also worked hard and long promoting the trip, and personally raised a good share of the $4,000 needed to support the team, which returned undefeated.

He promoted and managed many of the Chamberlin annual tournaments, which in their time were equivalent to our Grand American now. To the historian, the sequence of these tournaments is confusing, because in 1894 they had their "First Annual Tournament," but this was actually preceded by three or four Chamberlin and Cleveland tournaments, not called "annuals." The Atlantic Ammunition

Co. also sponsored shoots. The money, gold watches, and guns were donated from Cleveland Target Co. funds.

North originated the North system of handicapping and prize money distribution for use in the Chamberlin tournaments he ran. Prior to these tournaments, it was every man for himself, winner take all, and quite discouraging to the average shooter who came up to face such men as Rolla Heikes or Fred Gilbert, and knowing he had to beat them for the money. But at the suggestion of A. C. Dick, of Cincinnati, North instigated a handicap system that could assign a percentage to any shooter after a given number of targets, and place him in a similar group of shooters with averages of 60, 70, 80, and 90 percent.

Up to this time, the professional was in direct competition with the "Sunday shooter." It did not endear Paul North to the pro group when he split "their" money into amateur hands. The pros' complaints were loud and clear. They even banded together to boycott any Chamberlin shoot.

This led Paul North to write, "In the old days when Cleveland Target Co. gave tournaments year after year, adding large amounts of money to the purses, three-quarters of which was won by the professional shooters, then Blue Rock Targets and trap and Paul North were all right in their eyes; but since, for a change, the Cleveland Target Co. decided to let the amateurs have a chance at the money the professionals had grown to consider all their own, and not to employ these professionals to sing the praises of our goods, suddenly there is a great change. The Blue Rock Target is not as it was, the Magautrap is an abomination, and poor Paul North stands as an outcast, without friends and alone. It is sad. Let us weep. There is a ray of sunshine however. Not everyone knows how bad we are over here and we may sell a few Blue Rocks and traps yet."

North's electric trap release, a revolutionary development, was first patented in May of 1891. His brother, Charles, improved upon it and patented the improvement in his own name in 1894.

Fred Damm, however, was the main inventor of traps manufactured by the company. He had turned five patents in his own name over to Chamberlin, one of these being for a glass-ball trap which was, of course, never used. Unfortunately, Damm left Chamberlin in 1891 to form the United States Pigeon Co., of Cleveland. Chamberlin immediately sued him for patent infringements, won the case, and put the newly formed company out of business before any significant number of targets could be made and sold.

Frank Chamberlin apparently was not interested in the design of traps or targets, and other than his acting in an official capacity for the company, his name is little mentioned after the firm ceased producing shotshell loading machinery. Al Barton remained with the company for thirty-four years and contributed much to its success. Charles North remained at the Findlay, Ohio, factory for a short time after the Remington purchase, then joined their sales force.

The Cleveland Target Co. and the Chamberlin Cartridge & Target Co. were in business for a half century. Their products were new, original, much needed, and in widespread distribution. The company leaders were well thought of and justly famous in their field. It is strange indeed that shooting literature has seemingly passed them by until this writing.

Gun Control

ARNOLD JEFFCOAT

Arnold Jeffcoat got his first taste of the shooting sports as a small boy on his parents' small farm in Anderson County, Texas, near Palestine. The long East Texas squirrel seasons provided his first hunting experiences. While still in high school, he joined the Texas National Guard and competed in interunit smallbore and highpower rifle contests. Now thirty-seven, Jeffcoat is News Editor of Gun Week *(published weekly by the Sidney Printing and Publishing Co., in Sidney, Ohio), and is equally at home on the legislative firing line and the trapshooting line. He carries an ATA Class A singles average and a 26-yard handicap. He is the father of two up-and-coming trapshooters, Pamela, fourteen, and Alan, thirteen.*

SINCE THE BEGINNING of man's life on earth, some men have coveted each other's possessions. Those who coveted far beyond their ability to resist found methods of depriving owners of their possessions. Some used cunning, while others resorted to force and weapons. But long before man began robbing and killing his enemies with firearms, he used clubs, knives, bows and arrows, and a thousand other implements of violence. And he's still using all of them.

In more recent years, for a variety of reasons, some people have decided that the way to end crime and violence is to eliminate the instruments of violence. They would abolish the manufacture, private possession, and use of firearms. It makes little difference that the firearms themselves are not the culprits; sometimes it seems they would abolish them for the mere sake of abolishment.

Several studies have shown that restrictive control on firearms actually result in an increase in the crime rate, although some politicians and law-enforcement officers would have the American public believe that just the reverse is true. However, it is only logical to believe that if the law-abiding citizenry is disarmed, then the criminal is bolder, because he can reasonably assume that his victim is unarmed. But this is not always the case.

In many instances, an otherwise law-abiding citizen simply will not obey restrictive laws that prevent him from owning a firearm legally. In New York City, for example, city ordinances and the state's notorious Sullivan Law prevent citizens from owning handguns in their homes or places of business without first obtaining a seldom-issued handgun permit. In fact, in New York City, with a population of eight million, less than 20,000 handgun permits have been issued, and most of them are in the hands of security guards, night watchmen, etc. About 3,000 permits have been issued for personal protection and target-shooting.

But every year, thousands of New Yorkers who have committed no other crime are arrested for possessing handguns without a permit. Ironically, many of these victims of illogical gun-control laws are arrested for using handguns to protect their homes or places of business from armed intruders. A situation has developed in New York, and a few other places in this country, where the victim of a crime, if he uses a firearm to protect himself, is in more trouble than his attacker.

Obviously, man's will to survive outweighs his respect for ill-conceived laws that he knows are not in his best interest. It makes little sense to the average citizen to pass laws that will not be obeyed by the criminals the law is intended to control. He knows there are laws on the books against violent crimes such as robbery, murder, and armed assault, but he also knows that hardened criminals use firearms during the commission of these crimes every day. Therefore, to maintain the balance of firepower, the average citizen wants a firearm for protection in his home or place of business.

Despite the average citizen's expressed need of a firearm for personal protection or because he merely wants one for use in a wholesome target-shooting sport, many politicians, law-enforcement officials, and misguided do-gooders have begun to cry for more restrictive gun controls, including registration of individual guns, licensing of their owners, and even confiscation of handguns from private citizens.

On the other hand, those involved in the fight to protect the individual's right to keep and bear arms for legal purposes constantly remind the antigunners that some 20,000 firearms-related laws already are on the books at the federal, state, and local levels, but the current laws are not being enforced. The progunners see absolutely no need for passage of additional laws that will keep a law-abiding citizen from having and using firearms for hunting, target shooting, and self-defense when current laws are not being used against the hardened criminals.

"Enforce the current laws swiftly and surely" is the battle cry of those who cherish the right to own and use firearms in lawful pursuits. But their arguments fall on deaf ears, and the antigun lawmakers continue merrily along in their attempts to enact additional gun controls at all levels of government.

The Gun-Control Act—A First Step

Shortly after the Gun Control Act of 1968 was enacted, amid the hysterical, emotion-charged atmosphere that prevailed following the assassinations of Martin Luther King and Robert F. Kennedy, gunowners got their first taste of things to come. When the legislation went into effect on December 16, 1968, the Federal Government embarked on a headlong course to restrict further the sporting activities of millions. By interpretative fiat, the enforcement agency of the new law, the Treasury Department's Alcohol, Tobacco and Firearms Division, accomplished what the U.S. Congress itself had been unable to do: it provided for the de facto registration of all firearms sold by federally licensed dealers after December 16, 1968.

The ATFD had accomplished by a back-door approach what the antigun lawmakers had failed to accomplish through the front door of the Congress, and when the ATFD's enforcement regulations were unveiled early in 1969 there was no question that registration of firearms was a reality.

While it is true that total registration did not come about with the passage of the Gun Control Act, there is every reason to believe that the antigunners have not given up on the idea of eventually requiring total registration and other controls in the future. In fact, during the Congressional debates of the mid and late 1960's, several of the antigun lawmakers, notably the late Senator Thomas Dodd of Connecticut, and his Senate cohorts Edward Kennedy and Joe Tydings, readily admitted that the Gun Control Act was only "a first step" toward additional, more repressive controls.

But the Gun Control Act itself was too repressive in the estimation of millions of American sportsmen and knowledgeable citizens who viewed the Act as simply another misdirected Federal Government encroachment on individual freedom. The provisions of the new law they most resented were those that made it illegal for them to obtain firearms in interstate commerce. These citizens resent being punished with needless controls because of the activities of a very small percentage of criminals who obtain and use firearms illegally.

Nevertheless, when the Gun Control Act went into effect it no longer was legal for an individual in one state to buy a firearm from anyone who resided in another state. It no longer was legal to obtain a firearm by mail order. It no longer was legal to import certain types of firearms from abroad. The list goes on and on, but despite the restrictions, criminals seem to have little trouble getting guns to use in their crimes.

No Rules, but We Must Play

Another problem that has confronted gun-owners since the Gun Control Act is the continued refusal of the ATFD to define exactly what constitutes engaging in the business of a firearms dealer. Although the Act forbids dealing in guns without a license, with a possible fine of $5,000 and five years imprisonment for violators, the agency has steadfastly refused to set down clear guidelines so that a gun-trading sportsman can know if he's violating the law or not. Making the situation doubly precarious is the fact that some ATFD agents have been known to entice gun-owners into selling them guns; the agents then arrested the seller for "engaging in the business of a firearms dealer without a license."

Back in November, 1969, *Gun Week* brought this problem to the attention of the ATFD, asking for a ruling and a clear-cut definition of exactly what constitutes "engaging in the business" so that our readers could determine for themselves whether their gun-trading activities were within the law. We were told by the ATFD director:

> Unlike most of the terms used in the [Gun Control] Act, that phrase is not susceptible to rigid definition. The facts of each case must be considered to determine if one is engaged in the business. While there is nothing in the law which prohibits an unlicensed individual from selling his personal firearms if the purchaser is from the same State as the seller, that individual is in the best position to know if he is engaged in the business of a firearms dealer.

In effect, the ATFD was saying: "We won't make any definite rules—but you've got to abide by them." What a way to run a law-enforcement agency! But ATFD officials say the situation is not of their making, because Congress failed to define "engaging in the business" in the Act, and it is Congress' responsibility to solve the problem with new legislation.

Meanwhile, countless gun-traders in this country are prone to arrest if their activity comes to the attention of an ATFD agent and the agent arbitrarily determines that the trader has swapped or sold "one too many" guns. How many is "one too many?" No one knows, because the ATFD won't say!

The Law That Caused a Tragedy

At about sundown on the evening of June 7, 1971, Kenyon F. Ballew, a twenty-seven-year-old Silver Spring, Maryland, gun collector, Boy Scout leader, and life member of the National Rifle Association, was taking a bath. His wife, Saraluise, had already bathed and was preparing for bed.

Unknown to Ballew, an apprentice pressman for a Washington, D.C., newspaper, events then occurring outside his apartment in the next few minutes would cripple him for the rest of his life and make him a martyr to gun fanciers everywhere. For as Ballew soaked in the bathtub a 28-member raiding party led by ATFD agents was preparing to break into his home in search of evidence of a violation of the Gun Control Act of 1968.

According to evidence in the case, an "informant" had told a Montgomery County police officer, who told an ATFD agent, that Ballew had a quantity of illegal hand grenades in his apartment. It did not matter to the ATFD agent, Marcus Davis, that the "information" came from a seventeen-year-old burglary suspect who was attempting to divert the heat away from himself; even a rumor of a Gun Control Act violation was enough for Agent Davis to obtain a search warrant for Ballew's apartment.

With their plans made, and ATFD agents and members of the Montgomery County Police Department covering both exits of the Quebec Terrace apartment, the raiders went into action.

"Federal agents. . . . Open up!" called out one of the ATFD agents as he knocked on the door of the apartment. They waited a few seconds, knocked again, and then used an 85-pound battering ram to break open the door.

First inside the apartment, according to a subsequent Treasury Department investigation, was ATFD agent William H. Seals, who was followed closely by Montgomery County Police officers Royce Hibbs and Louis Ciamillo, all of whom were in plain clothes. Another Montgomery County officer, who was in uniform, remained outside.

"When the door opened, I entered the apartment and as I did, I saw a man who was later identified to me as Kenyon F. Ballew in the hallway leading to the bedrooms. At the time I first saw him, he was aiming a revolver at me," Agent Seals said in a report to superiors on the night of the shooting, according to the Treasury investigation.

However, in a subsequent report, made two days later, Seals contradicted his first report: "At that time [after entering the apartment], I heard a shot. I looked toward the rear of the apartment where I saw Kenyon F. Ballew aiming a revolver at me. At that time I drew my sidearm and fired at Ballew."

During the early stages of the investigation, the ATFD agents involved and their superiors indicated that Ballew had fired the first shot at the officers and they had returned the fire.

But Ballew's attorney, John T. Bonner of Silver Spring, Maryland, who called the Treasury investigation "whitewash," charged that the ATFD agents had illegally broken their way into the apartment and shot Ballew in the head without justification. Bonner also charged that the raiders had not properly identified themselves to the apartment's occupants before battering down the door. The warrant on which they entered was faulty because it was based on third-hand hearsay information, and Ballew's apartment contained no illegal hand grenades.

What the ATFD raiders did find in the apartment were several inert, dummy practice grenades, one of which was used as a toy by one of the Ballew children, along with several antique and replica muzzle-loading firearms and accessories, including powder, primers, and percussion caps. Since Ballew was an avid shooter of muzzle loaders, and an occasional user of modern firearms for which he reloaded, it was not unusual for him to have reloading powders, primers, and percussion caps in his home. But the Treasury Department saw it differently:

> An examination of the hand grenades seized from the Ballew apartment by ATFD firearms experts disclosed that three of the hand grenades were functional with the addition of black or smokeless powder to two

of the grenades and only a plug made of wood, paper, wax, lead, or a similar substance, and powder to the third grenade. Since all of the necessary materials were readily at hand, these grenades, according to Government Counsel, constitute "destructive devices" as defined in the Gun Control Act of 1968.

Treasury's interpretation that the possession of the component parts of a destructive device constituted violation of the Gun Control Act immediately sent shock waves throughout the ranks of the nation's sportsmen who handload their own small-arms ammunition. But, apparently, this interpretation has been reserved exclusively for use in the Ballew Case, where the ATFD found itself needing some "hard evidence" with which to justify the raid. I say "apparently" because, to my knowledge, no one else has been charged with possession of a destructive device because he possessed reloading powders and primers as component parts of one.

If such were the case, it would mean the end of home ammunition reloading, because anyone possessing reloading powders, primers, and a piece of lead pipe would have the necessary ingredients for a destructive device under Treasury's interpretation in the Ballew Case.

Maybe the Treasury report on the Ballew shooting didn't say what everyone thought it said, speculated Frank Barnyak, president of Firearms And Equal Rights (FAIR), a California sportsmen's group. He decided to inquire further. The reply he got in a letter from ATFD Director Rex D. Davis, said:

> A person who is a reloader of ammunition could conceivably be in possession of enough parts to assemble a destructive device, if he has black powder, a container and the ability to improvise a fuse train through the use of pistol primers. If it is his intent to use those parts to make a destructive device, then he could be charged under the act. The reloader who has powder and primers, and uses them for reloading purposes only, is well within the confines of the law and has nothing to fear if he has the proper storage facilities for his powder and is buying his ingredients in accordance with the law.

Awestruck by Davis' answer, Barnyak fumed, "Who the hell defines 'intent'? Are these people mind readers?"

Obviously, the ATFD agents aren't mind readers, else they would have known Ballew was not a militant bomber, and the shooting could have been prevented. But the agents, described as "Gestapo" by Michigan Congressman John D. Dingell, do carry a lot of weight in firearms circles, and the opportunity for the misuse of authority is widespread. As evidenced by the Ballew shooting, under certain circumstances (even if the circumstances have to be manufactured later by the agents themselves), they can work their will against law-abiding gun owners under the guise of law enforcement.

Don't get me wrong. I realize there are many conscientious, hard-working ATFD agents who would not knowingly take liberties with the rights of American gun owners. But others, for various reasons, will take advantage of every opportunity to make it as rough as they can for law-abiding gun owners. In many cases, the same goes for state and local law-enforcement officers, as well.

However, two recent developments relating to the ATFD may have some bearing on the agent's enforcement tactics in the near future. One is the $5,000,000 damage suit filed in the U.S. District Court in Baltimore on March 21, 1972, in behalf of Ballew, charging negligence on the part of the agents who took part in the raid. The second is the transfer of the ATFD from under the Internal Revenue Service, which went into effect on July 1, 1972.

Although a court decision on the Ballew damage suit probably won't be forthcoming for two or three years, it stands to reason that the ATFD officials will want as little criticism of the agency as possible to reach the public during the interim. This may prompt ATFD agents to be a little more cautious and reasonable in carrying out their responsibilities, at least for a few years.

Additionally, moving the ATFD out from under the control of the IRS has made the ATFD directly responsible to top-level officials in the Treasury Department, thus removing a complete layer of bureaucratic hierarchy. However, this could eventually turn out to be a tragedy in disguise, if the Treasury Department is ever taken over by a Treasury Secretary with antigun tendencies and the desire to use his authority over the ATFD.

But no matter what the outcome of the Ballew damage suit, and no matter whether the ATFD "mellows" in its respect for the rights of private citizens, millions of gun owners will remember only that the Gun Control Act caused a tragic shooting, which left a law-abiding gun collector mentally incapacitated and paralyzed for the rest of his life. Many will realize that under similar circumstances it could have been they who were the tragic victims instead of, or in addition to, Ballew.

A New Dilemma for Sportsmen

Only in the last two or three years has a rift developed in the ranks of sportsmen over the merits of attempting to prevent the enactment of additional handgun controls at the various levels of government. Some gun owners, including many who do not own handguns, feel that the movement to require registration-licensing, and even confiscation, of handguns is only the next step in the anti-gunners' plan to eventually eliminate all firearms. Others, including some handgun owners, feel that handguns are used too frequently in crimes of violence and a reduction in their numbers or an improvement in their quality would help reduce the crime rate.

For the most part, those unconcerned about the new push to impose restrictive controls on handguns don't own a handgun. The same thing happens when explosives-control bills calling for stiff restrictions on the use of black powder are proposed. Users of muzzle loaders stand up and fight, but other shooters simply don't care because their shooting sport is not involved. And that's where the dilemma lies!

No matter what shooting sport is involved, there should be only one criteria of concern for *all* gun owners, whether the proposed legislation is *beneficial* to *all* sportsmen who use any type of firearms. If the legislation is beneficial to the majority, but detrimental to only a few, then it should be opposed by *all* gun-owners, unless it can be amended to make it acceptable to everyone.

For example, the Ohio General Assembly recently was considering an explosives-control bill that would have limited handloaders to fifteen pounds of smokeless powder. If he needed more than fifteen pounds, the handloader could obtain a one-time, $10 permit. An annual permit would have cost $250.

As any handloader knows, fifteen pounds is not much powder to a trap or skeet shooter who shoots several thousand targets a year. It's not too much to a target-shooting and hunting rifleman, either, but most pistol reloaders probably would find the quantity sufficient.

During a conversation with a "friendly" legislator, who also is an avid trapshooter, I asked how the fifteen-pound limit got into the bill in the first place. I was astonished at his reply. He said: "I recommended it. I thought fifteen pounds would be enough for anybody."

Later, he conceded that although he shot trap, and an occasional round of skeet, he did not reload any of his own shells. Just another example of some of our friends being more dangerous than our enemies, because of a lack of knowledge and not enough time to ask a few simple questions.

But, it's not simply a minor mistake that can be rectified with an amendment, in most cases. The antagonistic lawmakers who have resolved to do away with the citizen's right to keep and bear arms are not simply lacking in information. They know what they are out to do—and they will do it by using whatever tactics are necessary, including chicanery, lying to the public, and other assorted deceits.

In the handgun-control controversy, for example, the antigun lawmakers have stilted and stacked the statistics to make the general public believe that handguns are the most dangerous things in our society. It makes no difference to them that only a minute part of 1 percent of all handguns are ever used in crime. They continually pump away at the fact that in 1970, 52 percent of all murders and non-negligent manslaughters were committed with handguns. At every opportunity, they stress that 466 of the 633 policemen murdered between 1961 and 1970 were killed with handguns. Or that 73 of the 100 policemen murdered in the line of duty in 1970 were killed with handguns.

But the antigunners, in their efforts to misinform the public, conveniently forget to mention anything about the people who shot down the law-enforcement officers. They forget to mention that 71 percent of those arrested for police killings had prior arrests on criminal charges and 57 percent had prior convictions. They also don't mention that 38 percent had prior arrests for violent types of crime, such as murder, rape, armed robbery, aggravated assault, etc. Sixty-seven percent of those who had previously been convicted on criminal charges had been granted leniency in the form of parole or probation. In fact, 23 percent of the offenders were on parole or probation when they were involved with the murder of an officer.

No, the general public never hears about the criminal background of police-killers. Instead of studying methods to keep repeating criminals off the streets, such as cracking down in the courts, the misguided, antigun lawmakers bellow that controlling or confiscating handguns is the answer.

If that were so, New York State, with its sixty-year-old Sullivan

Law, should be the safest state in the country with respect to handgun crime. It isn't! In fact, it is one of the most dangerous, because the law-abiding citizens cannot legally own a handgun with which to protect themselves.

In 1968, Alan S. Krug, former research director for the National Shooting Sports Foundation, conducted a study on the firearms crime patterns in New York State. He found that in 1966, New York ranged second in the rate of serious crime among the fifty states. Although the Sullivan Law had been in effect since 1911, in 1966 unlicensed handguns were used in 83.4 per cent of all firearms crimes. Zip guns were used in another 9.4 per cent. Krug said:

> These patterns of firearms misuse were much the same for New York City. In 1966, 2.85 per cent of all the serious crime in New York City was committed with the aid of firearms. Unlicensed handguns accounted for 87.16 per cent of the firearms crimes. No licensed handguns were used in the commission of any criminal homicide, aggravated assault or robbery. The Sullivan Law has not resulted in a substitution of rifles and shotguns for pistols by the criminal element.

Despite these data, and others, too lengthy for listing here, an alarming number of American gun owners have accepted the idea that additional handgun controls will, somehow, prevent the antigun lawmakers from continuing into the realm of rifles and shotguns. The name of the game is compromise, although the antigunners always end up getting more than they give. Acceptance of such attitudes would have been unthinkable among gun owners only a few years ago, but the selling job done by the "ban-the-gun" faction in recent years apparently has had its effect. The big lie technique is taking its toll.

"The only purpose for which handguns are made is to kill people" is a statement made often by the likes of former Illinois Congressman Abner Mikva and Senator Philip Hart of Michigan, who have the distinction of being the first federal lawmakers in their respective houses to sponsor legislation calling for the confiscation of privately owned handguns. Obviously, these people are unconcerned that many handguns are designed exclusively to punch holes in paper targets. They also conveniently overlook the fact that more than 99.99 per cent of an estimated 25 million handguns in this country are *not* used in the commission of *any* crimes, much less to kill people.

In answer to Mikva and Hart, we would simply point out that there is no inherent criminality in any firearm. Criminality is fostered in the minds of men—not in an inanimate object made of steel, wood, and plastic.

Where Do We Go From Here?

There comes a time in the life of every human being when he feels compelled to take an active part in the solution of some problem confronting mankind. This should be that time for all gun owners. Unless we can reverse the trend and overcome the misconceptions about the shooting sports that have been planted in the minds of the nonshooting public for so many years, the end of the shooting sports may be at hand!

If the shooting sports and the right of individual citizens to keep and bear arms are to be preserved, every gun owner in the United States is going to have to set two primary goals for himself. He must become politically active against the antigun politicians who would deprive him of his rights, and he must become a public-relations spokesman for the shooting sports.

I am not suggesting that every gun owner must run for political office, but he must make his presence felt in the political arena. He must support candidates who will work—and work diligently—to preserve the right of firearms ownership for law-abiding citizens. On the other hand, he must work for the defeat of the antigunners at all levels of government.

To counter the downright lies spread about guns and gun owners in the recent past, the general public must be accurately informed about the wholesome atmosphere that surrounds all phases of the shooting sports. Shooting sportsmen are going to have to get their friends and neighbors out to the shooting ranges so they can see for themselves that we are not a blood-thirsty band intent on shooting up the countryside. In other words, we must serve as missionaries and carry the gospel of shooting to those who have been denied the true message.

But, in the final analysis, it will take the efforts of all concerned gun owners, working in unison, to drive the beast of antigunnism from our door.

Gun Fit

PETE KUHLHOFF

This is Pete Kuhlhoff's last piece. He was a towering figure in any gun writers' get-together—partly because he was a big man, six feet eight, and partly because after a convivial evening of gun talk he was apt to be the only one present who could get to his feet, but most of all just because he was someone to look up to. He died on February 10, 1972, at the age of seventy.

Pete was brought up in Oklahoma, where his family made the land rush in 1889. He was a veteran shooter and hunter by the time he reached his teens. He maintained that because of a regular diet of sowbelly and greens, *he had "gun fit" problems before he was twelve. After studying art in Chicago, he moved to New York and became a magazine illustrator. He was still a dedicated gun buff and managed to get in his share of hunting, and for about ten years he wrote a monthly gun column. He was painting illustrations for* Argosy *when the magazine's president and publisher, Harry Steeger, asked him to organize a gun and shooting department as a monthly feature, and for the next thirty years, until his death, Pete was* Argosy's *Gun Editor. His column was read by millions.*

Both the writing and the man will be sorely missed.

MORE THAN ONCE you may have missed what appeared an easy shot on pheasant or quail in the uplands or on waterfowl when in the marsh or along the shore. Chances are high that such misses were caused by imperfect mounting of the piece to the shooting position owing to poor gun fit!

Also, I have seen an expert trap shooter, using a field shotgun, miss a pheasant on a straightaway shot, empty the gun and watch a deliciously eatable bird fly into a wide extent of space. This same fellow, when shooting trap, will clobber clay targets, one after another for long runs, perhaps into the hundreds. Naturally such an experience ends with a lot of cussing.

I have seen an expert skeet shooter get into the middle of a covey of quail, blast several shots at a particular bird, and see nary a

Pete Kuhlhoff.

feather. This same chap will go through twenty-five targets on the skeet field and smoke them all!

How come?

In most instances, faulty gun fit.

For instance, the first shooter was using a field gun instead of his favorite trap gun, with its straight stock. Actually, he fired successive shots under the rising bird until the gun was empty. The gun simply did not fit him for field use. Using his old reliable target gun mounted in the shooting position, as on the trap field, he would have nailed the pheasant with the first shot.

How about the skeet shooter?

This friend was using his favorite skeet gun. "Ridiculous!" you say. "How could an experienced skeet shooter miss quail with shots similar to those on a skeet field?"

The answer is obvious. This fellow is a stylized skeet shooter. Before calling for a target, he mounts his gun and gets all lined up and set for the clay target as it zooms out of either the high or low house at opposite ends of the half circle on which the first seven shooting stations are located for the game of skeet. Unfortunately, he can't walk the uplands with his gun mounted and ready to shoot!

Mounting the gun before calling for a target is contrary to the original idea of skeet shooting, which had its beginning in 1926. The aim was to simulate field shooting, with targets taken at all angles as in the field with game birds. When the shooter called for a target, the gun had to be in the low position, not mounted and ready to shoot as today. In other words, in the widespread effort to make better scores, skeet today defeats its original purpose.

When my friend had to mount the gun, probably from an awkward position in the field, he was almost helpless as far as hitting the target was concerned. On further investigation, and to add insult to injury, we found that his favorite and time-tried skeet gun did not fit him! When he mounted the gun quickly, it did not point where he looked. Yet he made excellent scores shooting clay targets.

International skeet is a horse of a different color and far more difficult than the game normally shot in the United States and Canada. Instead of a target travel of about 55 yards from the high house and low house, the international target has to go about 65 meters, or approximately 71 yards. Thus, initial speed of the target is much faster. In the ready position the gun must be held with both hands so that the butt touches the hip and is visible below the elbow, and the gun must be held in this position until the target appears. Also, the international target is not instantaneous as in American skeet, but may be thrown at any time three seconds after it is called for. To make things even more difficult, the international target is heavier and harder, but not as high or thick, which reduces its cross-sectional area. The 12-gauge is used exclusively in international skeet. Many shooters prefer No. 8 shot, most always with more choke than cylinder bore.

Actually, there is no reason why a person can't shoot American skeet with the gun in the low position when calling for a target. He may not cream as many clay targets, but chances are he will develop into a better field shot.

The majority of shooters probably go through their gunning life without realizing that there is such a thing as gun fit. The reason is that most are of average or near average build. If that sounds like an enigma, let's take a look at the facts.

The stocks of standard shotguns and rifles are designed and produced to measurements that, in mounting to the shooting position, fit the largest number of people. In other words, the measurements are a compromise, a configuration to fit the "average" individual's physical proportions. A not too apt analogy of the situation would be to produce all suits or hats in one particular size in an effort to fit everyone.

Common dimensions for field shotguns are: near 14-inch length of pull (distance from the front of the trigger to the center of the buttplate); near 1½-inch drop at comb (vertical distance between a rearward extension of the line of sight or top of the barrel and the forward end of the stock's comb); near 2½-inch drop at heel (vertical distance between the line of sight and the top edge of the buttplate or stock's heel). Rifle stock dimensions usually are somewhat similar, sometimes slightly less in each instance. There are other stock dimensions, such as "pitch down," "cast-off" and "cast-on," which we will get to in a few minutes.

Many knowledgeable shooters maintain that precise individualized stock dimensions are more important for the rifleman than for the shotgun enthusiast. My opinion is that they are equally important.

Many years ago, a fairly short and very husky friend blasted out with the comment, "All long guns are designed for seven-foot-tall, rawboned hillbillies."

I am six feet eight inches tall, have long arms, and weigh around 240 pounds—a horrible sight. So my answer was, "On the contrary, all long guns are designed for little bitty and quite fat midgets."

While long guns made with the standard-dimension stocks do fit a lot of people perfectly, they no doubt fit a smaller number of shooters less perfectly. And a hardcore minority of really outsize or undersize shooters, ninety-nine times out of a hundred, never shoot a long gun that even remotely fits.

But the astonishing thing is that most anyone, huge, medium, or small, can almost always adapt himself to the standard-dimension guns and do some excellent shooting.

If that is true, why a hullabaloo about gun fit? Because the majority of gunners can do better with guns that really fit them, and in most instances, very slight changes in a stock may do the job. So, if you are dissatisfied and unhappy with your long-gun shooting, perhaps it is a matter of fit.

In order to really understand long-gun fit, particularly with the shotgun, some shooting experience is necessary. A point to be emphasized: when a shooter finds a gun that fits him perfectly, there is no absolute guarantee that he will suddenly become a deadeye. Some practice may be necessary, if only to overcome habits developed with an ill-fitting gun. In order to get the idea over, let's quickly take a gander at elements that are important in hitting moving targets with either the rifle or shotgun.

First, let's consider position or stance. The body should be loose, with no strain, the knees slightly bent so that the shooter can lean a bit in the direction he intends to shoot. He can then swing freely to follow, overtake, and pass the target for the proper lead to make a hit with the bullet or shot column from his gun. The feet should be suitably close together, depending on the underfooting, with the left foot a little forward toward the target for the right-hand shooter, to be able to shift weight and pivot the body with the gun swing.

There are a couple of things to remember and practice in bringing the gun to the proper position for shooting. In mounting, the gun should be swung out and slightly away from the body, in a sort of arc, and brought back with the butt solidly against the shoulder and comb up to the face. When so mounted, if the gun fits the shooter, the eye is looking straight along the center of the top of the barrel or its rib with a shotgun, or with the sights lined up with a rifle. The out-and-back motion allows for different clothing thickness and avoids hangup at the shoulder.

Most beginners at shooting make the mistake of bringing the gun to the shoulder and then lowering the head so the cheek of the face is against the comb and side of the stock. First, this tilts the head with the eyes at an angle in relation to the top of the barrel, so that the target is not seen properly with both eyes open. Second, bringing the head down to the gun breeds haphazard form because the position of the head varies in relation to the barrel. If the eye is too high or too low with the rifle, the sights are not lined up. If the eye is too high above the barrel of the shotgun, the shot charge is delivered above the target; if too low, the shot pattern is under the target.

When a shooter gets to the point where he mounts the gun correctly and with both eyes open (to facilitate wide field of vision and ability to judge distance by depth perception), he concentrates or focuses his eyes on the target and points the shotgun—not aims it, as when shooting the rifle. Many shotgunners maintain that they do not see the barrel, sight bead, or beads when pointing a shotgun at a target. However, it has been proved, at least to my satisfaction, by a long series of experiments that the experienced shotgun handler, either consciously or subconsciously, sees the top of the barrel or rib when shooting.

After an individual has used a shotgun enough to more or less groove the mounting technique, he can make an accurate check to determine if the gun really fits him. This is easy to do by dry-firing. (A note of warning: in some instances, dry-firing with double- or over/under-barrel guns may damage the firing mechanism unless snap-caps or dummy shells made for this purpose are used for its protection. Snap-caps are made in various shotgun gauges and double-rifle cartridge sizes with a contained cushion or spring-loaded nylon plug in place of the primer to absorb the shock of the falling firing pin.) The procedure is quickly to mount the gun to the firing position while looking at an instantly selected object and pulling the trigger. If the gun is aligned, with the eye looking down the middle of the barrel or rib at the object, at the instant the trigger is pulled, there probably is nothing much wrong with the gun fit. This routine of mounting the gun and pulling the trigger should be tried on objects at various heights.

Another way of checking is to close the eyes and bring the gun to the shooting position. If the gun points exactly where you look when you open your eyes, and your line of eyesight is down the center of the barrel, you are in business and can give a try at moving objects such as clay targets thrown from a practice trap or from a hand trap.

Shooting at moving targets with the shotgun can be a little confusing for the beginner. If he is practicing by himself, with the aid of a hand trap or practice trap, quite often it is impossible to determine where the shot charge went with a miss. So, if practical, it is best to have an experienced shotgun handler observe, while another friend does the target throwing. Such an observer usually can tell exactly why the miss—under or over shooting, in front of or behind an angling target.

It certainly is true that most misses on crossing targets, be they clay or game birds, are due to lack of lead and shooting behind. Actually, it is best to overlead slightly on moving targets, because the pellets of a shot charge not only spread out in flight but string for quite some length, somewhat like a stream of water from a hose, and there is a chance of the target moving into the shot string. If, however, the shot charge is behind the target, all is lost!

Of course, the idea is to put the shot charge into the air so that it arrives at a point where the target has moved and intercepts it. This is not a piece about how to shoot a shotgun, but perhaps I'd better mention the three basic ways of putting the shot charge on the moving target.

One method of getting lead is to start with the bead on or near the target, then quickly pull out ahead of it until the correct lead is obtained, shoot, and follow through. This probably could be called spot-shooting. It is difficult because the timing has to be exactly right. However, it may work well on a fast flushing bird, say a ruffed grouse, when it is about to vanish in heavy brush.

Pointing-out, or maintained-lead, is where the gunner tries to estimate the necessary lead, swings the gun, and maintains this lead until after the gun is fired with a continued follow-through. Many shooters prefer this system, but with the many variables—angle of the target, speed, distance, and amount of lead—it can be quite complicated.

The swing-through method is, in my estimation, the simplest form of shooting for many types of upland birds, and it is used throughout the world. The shooter starts the swing of the gun from behind the moving target, fires as the barrel passes through the target, and continues to follow through. Here's the way it works. The average person's reaction time—the time it takes to will a shot and the physical action of pulling the trigger—is about a fifth of a second. With the speed of the gun swing being determined by the speed of the moving target and moving faster than it, there is about a fifth of a second built-in lead. With this method many shooters believe that they shoot directly at the target.

Some hunters, when using the rifle, have the idea that not much lead is necessary on a running target. Several years ago, we were fooling around with a running deer target that moved around 25 to 30 miles per hour. We found that with .30/30 cartridges, used at

50 yards, we had to aim the rifle almost two feet forward of the chest line, with maintained lead, in order to place the bullet in the heart-lung area. To do such shooting the gun has to fit the shooter fairly well. And the spot-shot, ahead of the target, often is used successfully on fast-moving big game with crossing or angling shots at near distances.

As I mentioned earlier, the majority of our long guns are fashioned to fit the average man. Just what is the "average" man? Say we take a number of average-sized fellows, all of exactly the same height and weight. Are their faces the same in fullness and in height of cheekbone? Are their shoulders, necks, and arms the same width and length? Are their hands the same size? When we look at the situation from this standpoint, it is evident that very few shooters have over-the-counter long guns that exactly fit them. However, most everyone can adapt himself to the standard-dimension gun and, with practice, do fair to excellent shooting with it. Chances are, better shooting can be done with a better-fitting gun!

Several minor adjustments to the gun stock may do the job and mean the difference between poor shooting and excellent shooting, or good shooting and better shooting.

Before making any changes in a shotgun stock, it is important to shoot the gun on paper as in patterning. I use newsprint (obtained as end-rolls from our local newspaper) and shoot on a 12-by-14-inch brown spot on a 4-foot-square piece of paper at a distance of 35 to 40 yards. The brown spot represents the overall size of many smaller game birds.

The idea is to mount the gun quickly and point and shoot immediately, imitating field shooting conditions as closely as possible, even to the detail of wearing clothes usually used in the uplands. The purpose of the whole operation is defeated with deliberate shooting. After shooting several targets, say at least a half dozen, an opinion probably can be formed.

If the shot patterns are consistently high or edging above, with but few pellets on the brown spot, the comb of the stock probably is too high. Sometimes, high shooting may be caused by the heel of the stock being too short compared to the toe, not enough pitch down. The reverse may be true if the shots are consistently low—too much drop at the comb, or perhaps too much pitch down. Incidentally, pitch is controlled by the angle of the buttplate when compared to the axis of the barrel. Pitch down may be measured by placing the butt of the gun on a horizontal surface, such as the floor, and moving it against a vertical surface, as a wall, until contact is made in the receiver area. The distance, in inches, between the gun muzzle and vertical surface is pitch down. If a shotgun shoots low, it is said to have a long toe or smaller amount of pitch down. Thus, the point of pellet impact may be raised or lowered by altering the slant of the butt.

If your patterns are consistently to one side or the other, with fast pointing and shooting, the chances are that the length of pull is not correct for you. To the left, with a right-hand shooter, often indicates that the stock is too long; to the right often indicates a too short stock. Cast can also be the problem. Cast-off is where the vertical plane through the stock slants to the right of a vertical plane through the rib; the stock bent to the other side is called cast-on. More often than not, the right-handed shooter requires cast-off and the left-handed shooter cast-on. Sometimes, shooters with very thin faces need zero cast.

One thing to check for, when the shot pattern does not go where you look, is a bent barrel. Several years ago, a friend and I were checking a number of shotguns. We came to one that neither of us could hit a thing with. When checked by shooting patterns on paper, we found that it shot to the left in all instances. Well, we checked that gun for everything we could think of, including cast. We figured that it should shoot perfectly. Finally, when glancing down the barrel, I noticed that it was slightly bent to the left. Once seen, the bend was obvious. I'll never know why we hadn't noticed it earlier. With a slight straightening job, the gun shot where we looked.

Actually, the very best method of determining an individual's stock measurements for a shotgun, be he big or small or just having trouble putting the pattern on the target, is to have a fitting with a try gun by someone who really knows his business. A try gun has a fully adjustable stock, one that can be adjusted for length of pull, drop at comb and heel, as well as for cast and pitch, as used by custom stock makers for exactly ascertaining the stock measurements required by a customer.

I have been measured several times by fellows skilled in this field. In all but two instances, these measurements varied very slightly,

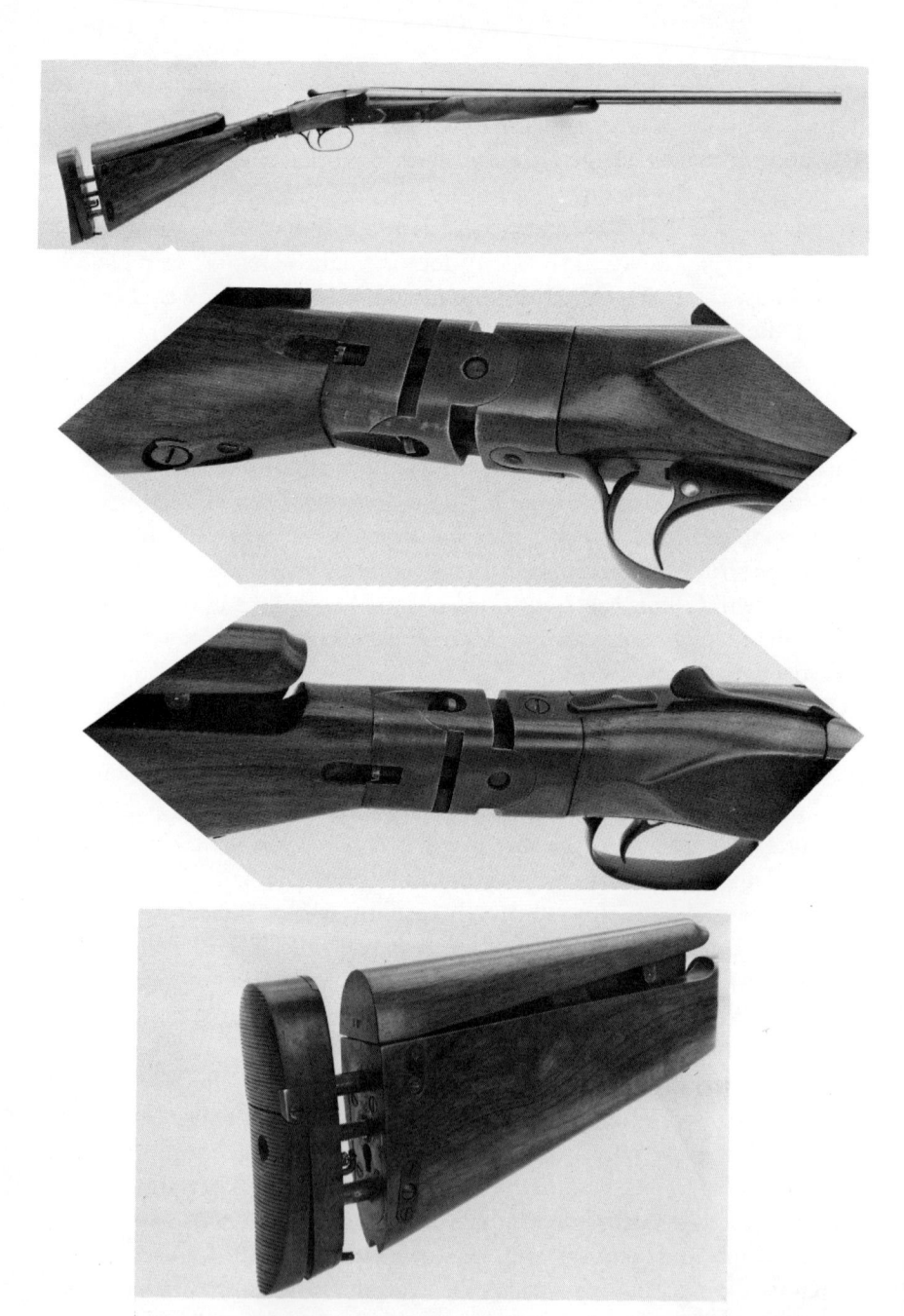

A try gun is the best method of determining the individual's optimal stock measurements. It can be adjusted for length of pull, drop at comb and heel, and cast and pitch.

probably due to difference in clothing. Only once have I fired a shotgun that really fit me (among other things, I take a 16-inch pull, about 2 inches longer than standard) and that was with a field version try gun that was shootable. I used that gun for a whole day on practically all kinds of moving clay targets from tower to quail walk and skeet. What a pleasure! Someday I'm going to get Len Brownell to make a stock to my measurements. As a matter of fact, that is the best bet: give the job to a competent stock maker, one who knows his business, and let him do the worrying. The hell of it is, that can run into money.

In the meantime, a number of adjustments can be made without too much trouble. A note of warning: be absolutely sure that changes are necessary before doing any cutting or gouging or making additions!

It is a cinch when the problem is length of pull. If too long, try the gun with the buttplate or recoil pad removed. If still too long, some cutting will have to be done, a very little at a time, until the correct length is obtained.

When the stock is too short, a slip-on recoil pad, such as the Pachmayr, which comes in several sizes, may be added very quickly for trial, without doing anything to the stock. Cardboard shims may be added inside the pad for further lengthening.

Another way of lengthening the pull for trial is to put a few washers on the two screws between the buttplate and stock. Only about a quarter of an inch can be added without obtaining longer screws. Changes in pitch can be obtained by this washer method. Pitch down can be decreased by adding washers to the bottom screw, and vice-versa.

Drop at comp and heel can be decreased by adding material to the length of the upper edge of the stock, in sort of Monte Carlo fashion. Thin strips of leather can be held in place with friction tape for trial. I am almost certain that most shooters have too low a comb, that is for the uplands and at skeet. And I also believe that too low a comb is less favorable than a slightly too high comb.

Once the correct dimensions are determined—length of pull, drop at comb and heel, pitch, and cast—it is a good idea to turn the job of adjustment over to a good stock maker. He usually can do the task by adding or removing, eliminating the cost of making a new stock.

Handguns Are for Anything and Everything

MAJ. GEORGE C. NONTE, JR.

George Nonte retired from the U. S. Army Ordnance Corps in 1964 after a twenty-year career in weapons training and maintenance. Presently Technical Editor of Shooting Times, he annually publishes approximately 150 magazine articles and is a regular contributor to most gun and shooting publications. Since 1961, when his first book was published, he has written twelve others, and currently is working on three more.

In his extensive travels, Maj. Nonte has hunted most of North America, Europe, and much of the Near East and visited arms manufacturers throughout the western world as an arms consultant for his firm, George C. Nonte and Associates. For several years he has competed regularly in registered pistol matches, including top military competitions and National Matches at Camp Perry, Ohio. Maj. Nonte lives in Peoria, Illinois.

THE MOST COMMON questions I'm asked about handguns—by aficionado and neophyte alike—center around the best guns for particular purposes, with a fair amount of curiosity about the reasons for my personal selections.

Why, for instance, even use a handgun for anything? To any confirmed pistolero that may seem a rather silly question, but even an ardent rifle or shotgun shooter—without experience or feel for handguns—considers this a very valid question. An affinity for handguns is like a taste for scotch whisky or far-out poetry: it can't be reduced to a simple explanation easily understood by anyone. A certain rapport and knowledge of the subject is necessary to begin to understand why people like and use handguns. The aficionado knows what you're talking about, but getting the message across to someone with no knowledge of or interest in the subject seems almost impossible.

Part of a handgun's appeal is as an art form or an object of beauty in the eyes of the beholder. And the aesthetics can't be pinned down or defined, for there are those who find the angular bulk of a .45 Colt auto fully as pleasing to the eye as the graceful flowing lines of the traditional SAA revolver, or the more modern appeal of Smith & Wesson double-action revolvers. People like to associate with beautiful things, and if a handgun possesses beauty in a man's eyes, he wants to own it—to look at it, to care for it, to fondle it with the same almost sensual pleasure women get from diamonds and other precious gems. Many people own handguns only for their beauty and wouldn't think of shooting them. Possession is their bag, not shooting. An old gentleman once told me that pride of ownership was the best reason he'd found for owning anything.

Then there is the factor of a handgun's excellence as a mechanism or as an example of modern production processes. The engineer, the mechanic, and people in similar fields often prize handguns for this reason. A superb old Smith & Wesson New Century Triple-Lock revolver is as fine an example as can be found of hand-fitted and finished production work of the early 1900's.

There is also the collector instinct, usually based on a strong historical bent, but also including goodly portions of the reasons already given. The collector needs no genuine *gun* interest to hold handguns; their historical significance alone justifies collecting them. And it is significant that handgun collecting goes hand-in-hand with other collecting interests. A high percentage of gun collectors also collect other items: stamps, coins, antiques, Indian artifacts, and so forth. Many collectors gather and hold handguns for purely economic reasons, speculating that they will increase greatly in value and thus help build a substantial estate.

So, many people own or want to own handguns for reasons that don't even involve shooting.

Of course, many other reasons do involve shooting to some degree; ranging from the once-in-a-lifetime incident, where a gun may be fired in defense of self or home, on through all levels to the consumption of thousands of rounds annually in weekly or daily firing sessions.

The defensive gun owner probably fires, at most, a few dozen rounds when the gun is purchased. He may not even *like* shooting. He owns a gun to defend his home and family, and shooting per se is actually a more-or-less undesirable secondary consideration. He *hopes* the gun will never be fired.

At the other end of the scale is the shooting enthusiast, whose main goal is the consumption of large amounts of ammunition. Here, shooting is the primary reason for ownership, and the guns proper are actually secondary, just a vehicle. I've known several individuals who shot 1,000 or more rounds monthly, but had no particular interest in the individual guns. Their only concern was that the guns shoot accurately and reliably, without regard to make, model, type, or appearance.

In between those extremes we find the bulk of shooting handgun owners to whom both the gun and the shooting are equally important—or nearly so. These people appreciate handguns for their aesthetic appeal, their mechanical excellence, their social and industrial-historical significance, for their usefulness as defensive weapons, and for their shooting capability.

One other class of handgun owners, whose numbers approach one million men and women, are the people whose professions and duties require them to be personally armed most of the time. Generally, we regard them as law-enforcement officers, though, in fact, many of them are not active as *enforcers* of the law. They carry handguns primarily to defend themselves against the hazards to which they are exposed, rather than for active, offensive use in support of the law. Naturally, among this big group we find all classes of handgun owners. Yet, in the main, they regard their handguns purely as tools—as much a professional tool or instrument as the carpenter's saw or plane, or the surgeon's forceps or scapel. Many of them don't even *like* handguns, and their selection is likely to be based mostly on departmental or employer regulations, price, and reliability.

It is worth noting, though, that many people to whom a handgun begins as a tool eventually come to appreciate and like it for several or all of the reasons we've already described. Many a young man whose first association with handguns is in training at a police academy soon becomes a collector or a shooter. The handgun's other endearing qualities often become more apparent with familiarity.

There are your reasons for wanting or owning handguns: aesthetic, mechanical, historical, engineering, safety, recreation, support of the law—and a few dozen others any reasonable man can produce with very little effort.

Probably the question asked most often is: "What kind of handgun is best to keep around the house for defense?" There's no simple answer, no cut-and-dried recitation of make, model, and caliber, nor even of type. The trouble with choosing a "house gun" is that most people in the market for one haven't the knowledge or experience with guns to recognize or understand the factors involved. Worse yet, they often have preconceived notions that lead them to a poor choice. Generally, they want—or think they want—a small gun that doesn't cost much. And those characteristics aren't compatible with the basic requirements for a house gun.

A house gun must first of all be utterly dependable, able to lie loaded and neglected in a bureau drawer for months or years—gathering lint and dust and the aroma of milady's underthings—and then respond to a frenzied grab in the night with absolute certainty of fire. The one time in life when you may need a gun will not approach gradually with plenty of time for checking and preparation. This kind of reliability is not compatible with very small size, nor with low initial cost, nor with designs that keep heavy springs compressed in order to achieve readiness.

Simple readiness requires that it be possible to fire the gun with a minimum of movement and effort—without the necessity to cock a hammer, retract a slide, disengage a safety, or any other action except *grasp* and *squeeze*. And that requirement cannot be met by single-action guns of any sort: revolver, auto, single-shot, derringer, et al.

Power and accuracy are not terribly important in a house gun. In fact, too much power and accuracy may well result in a gun difficult to handle and actually less suitable than a more modest choice. Little accuracy is required to hit an intruder already in the same room with you. At such a range, assuming the gun is reasonably well aimed, even a smoothbore barrel of common pipe will direct a bullet well enough to hit. Power of the Magnum sort will mostly insure that when the time to fire does come, the bullet will whip right on through the walls of your house, and into the unsuspecting neighborhood. Not a very pleasant situation. As for effect on an intruder, any hole you put in him—even with the lowly .22 rimfire—will cause him to get the hell out, if he's still able.

With all this in mind, what does make a really good housegun?

For utter reliability, choose a modern, solid-frame, swing-out, double-action revolver; for readiness, the same choice; for the same reason, and for ease of operation by even a small woman, make it of medium size, no smaller than the S & W .32 caliber frame and no larger than the .38 caliber. For adequate accuracy without the control problems of the ultrashort gun, a barrel no shorter than three inches, no longer than four, is good.

Caliber? Anything from .22 Long Rifle, upward through .38 Special—but stick to low-velocity loads in the latter.

Sights? Don't worry about them. In-house gun work is strictly a point-and-shoot proposition. If you take time to use sights in the accepted fashion, your adversary may knock out your teeth with the gun and add it to his loot.

How about a second choice? Well, I figure the only acceptable substitute for a good double-action revolver is a medium-size, double-action autoloader similar to the Walther PP/PPKS series. Loaded, with a round in the chamber, hammer down, and safety *disengaged,* these small autos are *very nearly* as reliable for the first shot after a long rest as a good DA revolver. The big, full-bore, military style double-action autos are generally too powerful and are difficult to handle without a good deal of experience.

If I were to choose a specific house gun for a favored relative or good friend who was *not* a handgun enthusiast and who possessed only the basic knowledge? Well, I'd give him (her?) a Smith & Wesson Model 36 (Chief's Special) with three-inch barrel, and loaded with .38 Special 148-grain wadcutter ammunition. As a second choice, I'd make it a .380 Walther Model PP and standard factory ammunition.

If the party thought these calibers were too big or placed him at a psychological disadvantage, I'd replace the first with a S & W Model 34 Kit gun loaded with .22 Long Rifles; the second with its .22 LR version.

Of course, the genuinely experienced handgun enthusiast need not be bound by any such restrictions. If he's honest with himself, he knows what gun he can handle best. Someone who has hunted for years with a single-action Colt certainly needn't buy a different gun for his own use in the house, though it might be prudent to do so for wife or kids. Neither does a fellow who regularly shoots a .45 automatic need to swap it off for a Chief's Special to keep in the house.

In the end, the experienced handgunner is best armed at home with the gun he handles best afield.

Handguns Are for Anything and Everything

Probably more handguns are actually *used* for plinking than anything else. Handgun hunters and serious competitors would only make a patch on the number that simply shoot for fun.

It's hard to say what makes a good plinking gun, simply because there aren't any specific requirements for the game. Within the bounds of safety, plinking is whatever the individual wants it to be. It can be double-action or semi-auto blasting of empty beer cans at six feet, knocking pine cones off forty feet directly overhead, or even busting rocks on a hillside 200 or 300 yards away.

The first sport might appeal mightily with a pocket-size .22 short auto or revolver of the most rudimentary sort, while the last virtually demands a big, heavy, target-sized six-gun chambered for a Magnum cartridge.

Generally, though, plinking is a game for .22 rimfires. It's a fast game, and the amount of ammunition consumed usually rules out expensive centerfires. It's easy to plink away 200 rounds or more on a Sunday afternoon in the country, and that much heavy-caliber ammo will run as much as $40 to $50. Five bucks will buy the same number of .22 Long Rifles!

Many people feel that a revolver is the *safest* plinking handgun because it is never "hot" except when the hammer is cocked or the trigger is pulled through double-action, both deliberate actions, not likely to occur inadvertently. Some revolver fans feel the single-action type is even safer, since it cannot be fired unless deliberately cocked first. Autoloaders are certainly more hazardous in the hands of neophytes, since every shot leaves the gun cocked and susceptible to a careless trigger finger. Sure, the safety can be applied or the hammer lowered, but those are extra actions the shooter must remember, and just might be overlooked.

So, at least in the beginning, a .22 revolver seems the best choice. Though the single-action has a theoretical edge in safety, the double-action is just as good for all practical purposes. And the double-action lends itself to more varieties of shooting, as well as being more convenient of reloading, than the single-action.

Though you'll do a lot of close-in plinking, you're sure to yield to the temptation to take faraway targets now and then—or maybe you'll just want to try real small targets, like aspirin tablets or candy mints at ten feet or so. And that means something better than the rough fixed notch and blade found on most low-priced revolvers and autos. Ideal, of course, are full-house target sights. They aren't really necessary, though, so long as some means of adjustment is available to allow correct initial zeroing.

Plinking is an informal kind of shooting where it isn't really so very important that the sights be zeroed precisely at 37½ yards with lot number CO384X of a particular load, the way the serious paper-punchers do it.

Accuracy requirements aren't very high. Again, it depends on you. The average domestic, and most foreign, revolvers and autos are more than adequate with mill-run ammunition to hit anything that needs hitting. Serious inaccuracy in any modern .22 handgun costing over about $40 is usually the result of damage or excessive wear. Any of them in proper shape will shoot a lot closer than you can usually hold.

A plinking gun shouldn't be too small. Probably the smallest revolver that lends itself to good handling is the Smith & Wesson .22/32 Kit gun. Barrel length isn't too important, but the average plinker will obtain more gratifying results with a four-inch or longer tube. The stubby three- and two-inch guns are lots of fun, but the very short sight radii will handicap the average shooter. Again, it's all in what pleases you most. After all, the name of the game is fun; there aren't any fancy trophies or great battles at stake.

Shooters with a little experience won't be wrong in choosing a good autoloader for plinking. It isn't quite as versatile as a double-action revolver, but it has the advantage of large magazine capacity and often lower cost for comparable quality. And if you're a rapid-fire fan, an auto is far, far ahead of any revolver ever made. It's particularly good when you're trying for multiple hits on unbreakable aerial targets. To my way of thinking, no shooting is more fun than bouncing a tin can across the sky with rapid shots.

What is the best plinking gun? Well, it's been said that the best target gun you can afford is the best plinker. Technically, I suppose that is true, but top-grade target guns are usually too specialized, too bulky, too heavy, too difficult to handle for enjoyable informal plinking. On top of that, they are expensive. If you've got one, OK, but it would be a mistake to buy one just for fun shooting. Of the currently aavilable models, S & W's .22/32 Kit gun and .22 Combat Masterpiece, or Colt's .22 Diamondback are tops among revolvers. In autos, the low-to-medium price Colt and High Standards are fine.

My own favorites agree with this only in part. My pet wheelgun plinker is a 3½-inch S & W Kit gun, while the auto I reach for most often is an old and well-worn Walther PP chambered for the .22 LR, and fitted with a fully adjustable rear sight. Sure, there are plenty of other fine plinkers available, but these two suit me best, and remember, that is the major requirement.

But maybe a hunting handgun is what you want. Again, the answer isn't really simple—it depends on whether you want to knock off small game for the pot, or big game for trophies and big chunks of meat, or undesirable varmints at long range.

Small game for the pot requires no great amount of power or gilt-edge accuracy. The game is small and easily killed, and usually taken at short ranges, thirty yards or less. In fact, too much power is bad in that it will spoil half your meat. With this in mind, putting the cart out front this time, the .22 LR is a fine cartridge choice. It will neatly and quietly dispatch cottontails, squirrels, and anything else small and edible without spoiling so much as an ounce of meat. It makes so little noise you'll not disturb others or game.

It's pretty much a toss-up between revolver and auto for pot-shooting. If you're addicted to sitting shots, then either a double- or single-action revolver will do nicely, because really rapid fire won't be required. For this reason, many people prefer the medium-size single-action revolvers such as the Colt Scout or Ruger Single Six.

On the other hand, an autoloader offers a decided advantage of speed on running shots. Mighty quick shots—sometimes several—are often required on running cottontails or bushytails. The auto allows faster follow-up shots and offers more shots before reloading than a revolver. Some fellows who like to do it the hard way prefer single-shot pistols for small game. I can't go along with that, because a cripple can get away before you reload for a finishing shot.

Again, it might sound like a first-rate target gun would be the best small-game choice. But their weight and bulk interfere with hunting handling. Smaller and lighter guns work better and, incidentally, usually cost less.

Regardless of type, the gun should be of medium weight and barrel length, and have sights sufficiently adjustable for precise zeroing. In this respect, revolvers on .32-size or larger frames, with four-inch or longer barrel, and target sights are to be preferred.

Actually, though, I prefer the autoloader. Fully as accurate and convenient as a revolver, it repeats faster, shoots more between reloadings, and is immeasurably faster to reload if you carry a spare magazine. If I were to go looking for a new small-game handgun today, I'd think it a toss-up between the Colt and High Standard medium-price autos with adjustable rear sight. They are efficient, compact, not too heavy, finely accurate, and handle as if they were made for the game—which they are!

Varmint-busting is another game entirely. It requires the most accurate long-range gun/sight/cartridge combination you can afford and carry about without a wheelbarrow. Shooting will often be required at one hundred yards or more, and that rules out traditional handgun cartridges; they just don't shoot flat enough. And it rules out the typical revolver and autoloader; they won't handle the cartridges required.

Sticking to factory cartridges, only one really suits this need—the .22 Remington Fireball. There are nothing but single-shot pistols capable of handling this load, yet readily available. Just two of them, in fact: the Thompson-Center Contender, and the Remington XP-100.

The latter is really an ultrashort bolt-action rifle, and the former a breaktop job that allows quick barrel interchange. The Remington might be just a tad more accurate, but the Contender is by far the most versatile, and much more in keeping with traditional styling. No problem here in choosing gun and cartridge.

As for sights, nothing less than a top-quality, low-magnification scope will allow full advantage to be taken of the gun. Not many are available: the Thompson-Center Puma, the Hutson, and the Bushnell Phantom. All are good and will do the job, so any choice is best made on price and availability.

Bagging big game requires the most power you can wring out of a handgun. That doesn't mean you can't knock off a nice whitetail with your trusty .38 Special. But it does mean that the most *powerful* handgun you can find puts out less energy than the *weakest* of modern deer rifles. In other words, there's no surplus power in *any* handgun cartridge when it comes to taking big game. Consequently, cartridge choice is a simple mater: take the biggest you can handle *well* in a gun of best quality.

This doesn't necessarily mean the man-eating .44 Magnum. Too many eager pistoleros can't handle it well enough to hit an automobile at ten yards, much less a buck's rib cage at fifty. The drill is to try them all, then pick the most potent you can shoot well enough to hit an eight-inch plate a fifty yards. If the .357 Magnum is the biggest you can do this with, then choose it.

With one notable exception—the .44 Automag self loader—only revolvers are chambered for the more powerful cartridges. Conventional autos are out unless you figure the .45 ACP and .38 Super are potent enough. Of course, single-shots are out: multiple hits are often necessary, and they are too slow in this department. Also, only Smith & Wesson offers good double-action revolvers in the heaviest calibers—the big N-frame guns in .41 and .44 Magnums. Ruger offers its Super Black Hawk single-action in the same calibers. That simplifies choosing a good bit. Both are supplied with excellent target sights, and both are superbly accurate. Consequently, with just the two guns available, your choice depends mostly on whether you prefer single- or double-action wheelguns.

Where our most powerful cartridges are involved, the big single-action can be as quick for follow-up shots as the double-action. There's plenty of time to ear the hammer back during recoil and recovery. A second *accurate* shot is thereby just as fast as with the double-action.

A short barrel is no advantage in a big-game handgun. The longer the tube, the more velocity and power you'll get, and the resultant longer sight-radius helps hit where you want. If you think a 7½-inch or 8¾-inch barrel is too long to handle, just remember how much longer (and heavier) the shortest practical rifle would be. To be blunt, the longest barrel you can get won't be too long, especially when you're blowing at the top of a rough climb like a run-out pony, and the muzzle waves all over the landscape while you're trying to draw a close bead. Extra weight out front helps keep the jumps down and makes hitting easier. It also reduces recoil and muzzle jump. Pick the one that feels best in your hand, and you can't go wrong.

What other kind of handgun might you need? A pure target gun? Telling a man what target gun is best is like advising him in selection of a mistress or wife: whatever you tell him is bound to turn out wrong, sooner or later. Needless to say, the very best in accuracy is required, as is maximum ease of rapid fire. Those two requirements exclude revolvers and make autos the only practical choice.

Among centerfires only two production guns are offered. Both are excellent, offering a choice in .38, but only a Colt can be had in .45. Not much room to play. Where .22's are concerned, at least a half-dozen makes and models are available, and generally, the best you can afford is none too good. On the other hand, it would be devilishly hard to improve upon the S & W M41 at even the much higher prices of comparable foreign models.

Of course, there are the specialized handguns for international competition, but anyone skilled enough to have such aspirations is already sufficiently educated to evaluate everything available for himself.

As we said in the beginning, whether it's simply to possess, or for shooting, handguns are for everything. There isn't any type of gun need that can't be met to some degree with shortguns—and they can do lots of things no long gun can ever do.

That in itself is reason enough for me to keep a bushel of them.

Some Notes on Big-Game Cartridges

JACK O'CONNOR

Jack O'Connor has been hunting since he was old enough to handle a rifle, and writing about hunting and guns for almost as long. He was Arms and Ammunition Editor of Outdoor Life from 1941 until Spring 1972; he is now Hunting Editor. He has written a number of books, including two novels and an autobiographical account of the Arizona of his youth as well as books on hunting and shooting. O'Connor's advice on cartridges for the big ones is well worth listening to: he was one of the first hunters to collect specimens of all four varieties of North American wild sheep and has hunted all over the continent; he has made eight safaris, collecting the Big Five and such rarities as addax, Barbary sheep, and Limpopo bushbuck; he has shot tigers and other Indian game on two shikars; he has hunted red sheep, urial, and ibex in the mountains of Iran. How does he manage to get in so much time in the field? Well, for one thing, his wife, Eleanor, is his favorite hunting companion and no mean shot herself.

FUNNY HOW QUICKLY time passes. I can remember myself as a twelve-year-old kid with hair bleached white and hide burned dark brown by the Arizona sun lining up an old .30/40 Krag on my first desert mule deer. I can remember this same guy, older now but still inclined to the shakes, blowing his first chance at desert sheep because he got the buck. I can likewise remember how when older this guy managed to control his tendency to jitter and shake so he performed creditably on his first bighorn, his first moose, and his first tiger.

As I write this my old head has been silvered by the snows of seventy winters. This does not make me worth listening to or reading, because, as anyone knows, the world is full of old fools, and from what I have been told, an old fool is the very worst kind. However, I fancy myself a reasonably intelligent guy, fairly well educated according to the antique standards of my day, and I have been banging away at game animals of various shapes and sizes and in various places for lo these many years. I have kept my eyes and (I hope) my mind open and my notions have changed as the years have gone on.

As an enthusiastic kid along about the time of the First World War, I was an ardent believer in high velocity—the higher the better. I read and swallowed the material in the seductive catalogs put out by the late Charles Newton, the Roy Weatherby of the pre-World War I United States. Newton, who designed the .22 High Power and the .250/3000 Savage cartridges and the .256, the .30, and the .35 Newton cartridges, as well as some which did not go into production, and who manufactured two versions of the Newton rifle, was as sold on high velocity as Weatherby was thirty years later. I also read in various magazines the stuff of Captain (then Lieutenant) E. C. "Ned" Crossman, who was a high-velocity enthusiast (as high velocity went in those days—around 3,000 f.p.s) as well as an entertaining and instructive writer. So, in spite of the fact that I knew little about it, I became a real 24-carat believer in fast-stepping bullets. I read Ned Crossman's sneers about what he called the "Thutty-Thutty," and I was just as convinced that the .30/30 was at its best only a fair deer cartridge and no elk cartridge at all as Elmer Keith is convinced that it is impossible to kill an elk with a .270. By grinding economy and horrible toil at the jobs kids did in those days before the Turbulent Twenties, I managed to accumulate about $50. With this I bought a deluxe grade .256 Newton with what was alleged to be a French walnut stock with a cheekpiece, a checkered bolt knob, a little engraving, Lyman 1-A cocking-piece peep sight, a sling strap, and 100 rounds of factory ammunition. I don't know exactly what I expected when I shot a deer with this outfit, but I suppose I wanted the poor deer to explode with a hell of a bang or something. I was somewhat disappointed when the deer simply ran about 30 or 40 yards and fell down dead.

In the summer of 1919 I had the job of shooting enough small whitetail deer in Sinaloa to feed the Mexican hands who worked on a relative's peckerwood sawmill. I had an old .30/30 Model 94 Winchester and a Model 94 Winchester carbine in .30/30. Both cartridges were adequate, but I noticed that the quick expansion of the fast little 87-grain .250/3000 bullet gave quicker kills than did

Some Notes on Big-Game Cartridges

the heavier and slower 170-grain .30/30 soft-point. Score again in my opinion for high velocity.

I sold my Newton at a time when I was (a) broke and (b) there was no factory ammunition on the market for it. I have always regretted doing so. What hunting I did in the early 1920's was with a revamped Model 1903 Springfield in .30/06. In the fall of 1925, not long out of college, I got a Winchester Model 54 in the new .270 WCF. I shot some deer and a couple of antelope with it. I liked the flat trajectory, the relatively light recoil, the adequate killing power. I also acquired not long after that a .30/06 Springfield NRA sporter. This was a rifle turned out at the Springfield arsenal with a rather bulbous and ungainly sporter stock and a Lyman No. 48 receiver sight. These NRA sporters were very accurate. However, they were also pretty heavy. I had mine lightened up a bit and restocked by R. D. Tait, a good California stockmaker who has long since passed to his reward.

Came the Depression, along with some family illness. The O'Connors had to hock some guns and were down to my restocked .30/06, a Winchester Model 75 bolt-action .22, my wife's Model 30 Remington in .25 Remington caliber, and a couple of double-barreled 20-gauge shotguns. We had been through a bank failure and things were at their blackest when I discovered that magazines were willing to pay me cash money for putting words on paper. I had a chance to buy from Bill Sukalle, the barrelmaker and gunsmith who was then located in Tucson, a beautiful little 7x57 Mauser. I put a Noske 4X scope on it. I traded off my Tait-stocked .30/06. Later I had Bill Sukalle put a light 22-inch barrel on a Springfield action. I had the stock made by Adolph G. Minar, a genius who lived in a Colorado mountain village and who died long before his time. He was one of the finest stock makers ever to practice the trade. This was the first custom rifle I had ever had made up from scratch. Because I described and pictured this Minar stock in articles, it has had, particularly in the area of comb and pistol grip, considerable effect on design of American classic stocks.

In 1937 I got my second .270. In Sukalle's shop one day I noticed a nicely contoured .270 24-inch barrel with ramp front sight fitted to a flat-bolt Mauser action. Bill must have been pretty hard up for cash at the time, because he told me I could have the barreled action for $35. Since Bill at that time charged $30 for a barrel fitted, contoured, and blued, I got the action for $5! I had him fit a 2½X Noske scope with a Noske side mount and then sent it to that old genius, the late Alvin Linden, for a stock of European walnut. This .270 and the Minar .30/06 formed the battery with which I have shot more North American big game than with any other two rifles I have ever owned. I carried them from Sonora to the Yukon. With them I have shot all varieties of North American sheep, elk, moose, grizzlies, goats, caribou, and whatnot.

The native Merriam elk of Arizona were exterminated by meat hunters in the 1890's. Transplanted elk from Wyoming did well after they were put down on the high Mogollon Rim about 1912, and in 1935 Arizona had its first elk season. I put a couple of 150-grain Remington bronze-point bullets into the ribs of a bull that ran by me about 125 to 150 yards away. I could not track him over volcanic rock, and I didn't find the carcass until after I had shot another bull a couple of days later. I decided on this one exceptional experience that I needed more bullet weight for elk. It didn't occur to me at the time that the reason that bull was hard to bring down was that another hunter about a quarter of a mile away had smoked him up and scared hell out of him. I also didn't stop to think that I had not looked for the bull long enough or hard enough. I was sort of hurting for another rifle anyway, so I had a .35 Whelen made.

The .35 Whelen wasn't the smartest investment I ever made, as I really had nothing I needed to use it on. I loaded the old 250-grain soft-point bullet designed for the .35 Winchester and constructed to leave the muzzle at 2,200 f.p.s. Loaded to around 2,450, these bullets were bombs. I shot a couple of mule deer with them and they just about blew the far side off. Boosting the impact velocity to 200–300 f.p.s. made that rather soft, thin-jacketed bullet expand rapidly even on an animal the size of a deer.

In the 1930's I lived most of the time in Tucson. There were javelinas and mule deer in the lowland deserts and whitetail deer in the mountains. I used to make from three to five hunting trips a year into Sonora for whitetails, desert mule deer, desert bighorn. I used a 7 x 57, a .30/06, and a .270. The whitetails particularly were often shot on the run at from 200 to 300 yards. My wife, who is one of the best game shots I have ever hunted with, graduated from the .25 Remington to a .257 Roberts. I can't remember her ever

Some Notes on Big-Game Cartridges

losing an animal. I decided that I liked the .270 with 120 Barnes bullets loaded to about 3,200 and 130-grain bullets a little better than anything else. It shot flatter than the .30/06, kicked a bit less, and I fancied it gave me a slightly higher percentage of instantaneous kills.

On my first trip to the Canadian Rockies in 1943 I took a .30/06

O'Connor with good Stone ram shot in 1946 above the Prophet River in northern British Columbia.

with handloads driving a 200-grain bullet at about 2,600 f.p.s. With this I planned to knock off my grizzly and my moose. The grizzly cooperated, but when my chance came for a moose I had the .270 in my hand, loaded with 130-grain Winchester Silvertip bullets, no less. I jumped the bull where it had been lying down in heavy cover, drove the 130-grain Silvertip up through the paunch from the left and in line with the right shoulder. The bull ran 30 or 40 yards and fell. As I walked up to it the bull wobbled to its feet and started off. I shot it through the lungs as it ran. It went down dead after running perhaps 50 to 75 yards. It dawned on me then that if a bullet got inside the vitals of an animal it didn't make too much difference what it weighed and what caliber it was, but that sufficient penetration is absolutely necessary. All hunters are to some extent superstitious. Since then the .270 has always been my lucky moose caliber. I have shot exactly twelve bulls with the .270, all with the 130-grain bullet.

On the other hand, the .30/06 is my lucky grizzly caliber. I have shot ten grizzlies with my old Sukalle-Minar Springfield .30/06, two with a .270, and one with a .300 Weatherby Magnum. Most of the caribou and elk I have taken have been with the .270. Others have shot more of both species than I have, but I have shot enough to know something about them. Just as it isn't necessary to read a whole book manuscript to know it is lousy or to eat a whole egg to know it is rotten, it isn't necessary to shoot one hundred elk with a rifle of a certain caliber to know that it is adequate.

In the years since 1943 I have made many trips into the Yukon, British Columbia, and Alberta. I have hunted elk in Wyoming and Idaho, black and Alaska brown bears in Alaska. On these hunts I have done most of my shooting with the .270 and the .30/06, but I have also used a 7 x 57 and a 7-mm. Remington Magnum, a .300 Weatherby, a .338 Winchester Magnum, and a .275 Holland & Holland Magnum. In Alaska I used a .375 on a couple of brown bears.

Such experience as I had in North America convinced me that if a bullet were well placed, expanded enough to cause hemorrhage and tissue destruction, and yet penetrated deep enough to get into the vitals, the weight, the diameter, and even the velocity did not make too much difference. *But it had to be put in the right place.*

I made my first African safari in 1953. I landed in Nairobi with two Texans, Herb Klein and Red Earley, about the middle of June

Eleanor O'Connor with a very fine Angola lion shot with a .375 in 1962.

and left just before Labor Day. Since Herb and I were both gun nuts of the worst kind, we took a staggering amount of armament. At the time I thought this would be my last as well as my first safari, but as I write this, I have been on nine more. My wife, who likes to hunt but who is no gun nut, went on her first safari in 1959. She took one rifle, a 7 x 57 Mauser, and shot eland and sable as well as the smaller antelope.

In 1962 we shot in Mozambique. My wife still had her little 7-mm. Our white hunter was Harry Manners, who has shot over 1,000 elephants and no end of other game. He was unhappy because he was afraid my wife's 7-mm. lacked killing power. My wife killed 17 head of big game with 19 shots—and three of the 19 were in a big bull kudu that didn't know it was dead when the first shot went

O'Connor and Dave Christensen with an Idaho bull elk taken about 1964.

Eleanor O'Connor with a tigress she shot in India in 1965. This was a one-shot kill with the 180-grain bullet in a .30/06 Winchester Model 70. The tigress didn't even grunt, but following Indian custom with tigers Mrs. O'Connor put a second "finisher" beside the first. Note the bullet placement—the classic shoulder shot.

through his heart. By the end of the first week he was calling her One-Shot Eleanor.

My wife, who is not enamored of recoil and not afraid to admit it, would not be caught dead shooting a .375, the recommended tiger medicine, but she did agree to use a .30/06 when we went to India in 1965. Prince Abdul Quayum, our gentleman shikari, was a tiger hunter of great skill and experience. He was very unhappy about the .30/06 and was absolutely certain that her using it meant trouble. She used the 180-grain bullets to kill two tigers very dead, and Quayum's notions changed a bit.

I suppose it is human nature to want to seek and believe in the magical, the sensational, the spectacular. Hunters are no exception. They want rifles so deadly that a hit on an animal anywhere from head to hock results in an instantaneous kill and shooting so flat that no holdover is necessary up to 600 yards. If they don't go for ultrahigh velocity, they go to the other extreme and seek the magical effect with large, heavy bullets. A True Believer in heavy bullets who published a book on African hunting after having made a couple of safaris tells how he shot a nyala in the hind leg with the 300-grain bullet in a .338 Winchester. He and his white hunter tracked the nyala up and found it lying down. He said that spoke well of the shocking power of the heavy bullet. I find such wide-eyed belief in magic incredibly touching!

I have always set considerable store by what I see myself. I remember one occasion on my first trip to Africa I took a shot at a running Thomson's gazelle, which weighs 35 to 40 pounds on the hoof. I was using a blown-out .300 Magnum that gave a 180-grain bullet an advertised velocity of 3,300 but which was actually about 3,120. Anyway, the little Tommy was only about 80 yards away and the bullet was still traveling right along when it struck. I didn't lead enough. The bullet struck too far back and blew his guts over the surrounding countryside. I had to chase the poor little creature down and shoot it again. This experience reinforced my conviction that where game was hit was more important than what it was hit with.

Over the years I have learned to take most testimonial evidence with a large helping of salt. I have heard of and have read about too many spectacular shots, too many incredible kills. Some stand out in my mind. A couple were by a writer who now unhappily has become an angel in Heaven. In one tale he bounced a galloping ram at 600 yards and in yet another he rolled over a fleeing glacier bear at exactly the same distance. I also remember the tale of a writer who bumped off a mule deer at 600 yards with a .44 Magnum pistol.

I have also heard of animals that escaped wounded when according to my fairly extensive experience they should be very dead. One writer has told how he saw a half dozen elk shot squarely through the lungs with 130-grain .270 bullets only to run off. This has struck me as odd, because I have shot a good many elk in the same place

Some Notes on Big-Game Cartridges

with the same bullets and have yet to see one get away. This same writer has told the same tales about the .30/06 and the .264, neither of which he likes.

Yet another writer told how tough caribou were and how even the 250-grain bullet in the .338 was not enough. This struck me as strange indeed, because I have shot a considerable number of caribou and have found them the easiest large animal to kill in his tracks I have ever encountered.

Anyone has to go large by his own experience. I have read statements by writers with more African experience than I have had that lions are easier to kill than the large antelope like kudu, sable, eland, and roan. My own very limited experience on five lions and two tigers is that the big cats are easy to knock down but hard to kill with one shot. On the other hand I have seen many of the large antelope killed with one shot, and with rifles as small as the 7 x 57.

There are people with enough experience, knowledge, and objectivity so that I will believe them. One of these was the late Colonel Townsend Whelen. His stuff always made sense to me and checked with my own experience. Another guy I always take seriously is Les Bowman, who has had a more extensive and more varied North American hunting experience than anyone I know of, including myself.

Following is the list of the calibers I have taken on various safaris and shikars:

Tanzania and Kenya, 1953: .257 Weatherby, .270, .300 Weatherby, .375, and .450 Watts. I only shot one head of game with the .270. It was not my rifle. I took it along because a scope manufacturer pressed it on me. I didn't care for that particular rifle. The .450 Watts was the wildcat predecessor of the .458 Winchester, the .375 case necked up to .45 and *not* shortened.

India, 1955: .270 and .375. I used the .270 on boar and antlered and horned game with 130- and 150-grain bullets. I used the .375 only on tiger.

Iran, 1955: .270 on wild sheep, ibex, and boar.

Chad, 1958: .270 and .375. The .270 with 130-grain bullets was used on Barbary sheep, white oryx, addax, desert gazelles in the Sahara, the .375 on lion and antelope in the bush country north of Fort Archambault.

Two safaris in Tanzania, 1959: one with Syd Downey in the

This excellent gemsbuck was taken with one 130-grain bullet in the Kalahari Desert of Botswana in 1969. The rifle is a battered old Model 70 Winchester Featherweight in .270 caliber, restocked by Al Biesen. Scope is a 4X Leupold.

north and one with John Kingsley-Heath and Dave Williams in the far south for lion, eland, greater kudu, sable, puku, etc. I used a .375 on lion, leopard, and eland, the .30/06 on everything else, my wife a 7 x 57.

Iran, 1959: .270 borrowed from Prince Abdorreza Pahlavi on urial (wild sheep) and ibex.

Mozambique, 1962: My wife used a 7 x 57, I a 7-mm. Magnum, a .375, and a .416 Rigby. The .416 was used only on one buffalo.

Angola, 1962: My wife used a 7 x 57, I a 7-mm. Magnum and a .375. The .375 was used only on lion.

India, 1965: My wife shot two tigers and horned and antlered game with a .30/06. I used a .375 on one tiger, a 7-mm. Remington Magnum on horned game.

Botswana, 1966: My wife used a .30/06, I a .270, a .375, and a .450/.400 Jeffery double rifle.

Zambia, 1969: My wife took only a .30/06, shot a lion and various antelope with the 180-grain Remington round-nose soft-point Core-Lokt bullet, and made a one-shot kill on an elephant with a 220-grain solid. Because I had heard Zambia was very brushy, I took along a .338 as a "light" rifle, a .416 Rigby as a "heavy." I shot an elephant (frontal brain shot) with the .416 factory solid and a buffalo with the same bullet. I cracked a magnificent lion with a handload of 93 grains of No. 4350 and a 300-grain Winchester .375 caliber Silvertip swaged up to .416.

Much to my surprise the 250-grain Silvertip bullet used in the .338 didn't get through brush any better than the 180-grain .30/06 bullets my wife used. Both of us missed standing shots through fairly heavy brush at magnificent sable. The sable I shot at was dimly outlined through brush and only about 125 yards away. I had a rest over the limb of a tree. The sable my wife missed was only about 40 yards away but likewise behind thick brush. Neither of us touched the sable.

On the other hand, our son Bradford was forced to do all of his shooting with a .375 since someone had liberated his .270 en route. He had no trouble with brush. I might add also that he killed three buffalo with three shots using the 300-grain Western solid. My own reaction to the .338 was that with the same shot placement it killed no better than the .30/06, the .270, or the 7-mm. Magnum, all of which I had used extensively on safari.

In 1972 my wife, my son Bradford, and I made safaris in South West Africa and Rhodesia. For "light" rifles my wife and I took two 7x57s, hers a custom-made rifle on a Mauser action, mine a Model 70 Winchester remodeled and restocked by Al Biesen of Spokane, Wash. In case I decided to shoot a buffalo or an elephant I had in addition a Model 70 Winchester in .375. Bradford took a Ruger bolt-action .30/06 and a restocked Winchester Model 70 in .375.

My wife used a handload with the 160-gr. Nosler bullet, I a handload with the 140-grain Nosler. Between us we shot kudu, sable, mountain zebra, gemsbuck, and other antelope with the two 7-mm's. Most were killed in their tracks with a single shot. Bradford used his .30/06 on everything except one elephant.

I shot my first deer in 1914 when I was twelve years old, my last in 1971 when I was sixty-nine. In between I have hunted from southern Mexico to Alaska and from Idaho and Washington to India and Botswana. I have never kept track of the girls I held hands with when I was in the hand-holding stage or the number of big-game animals I have shot. Let it be said, however, that I have held not a few hands and have bowled over a fair number of game animals of assorted sizes. I try to draw conclusions from my experience and to write about them as honestly as I can.

One Man's African Rifles

WARREN PAGE

Warren Page, Shooting Editor of Field & Stream for nearly a quarter century, has done some African shooting: he has made thirteen separate safaris and has sought specific game not only in Kenya and Tanzania but also in Ethiopia, Uganda, the pygmy jungles of what was once French Equatorial Africa, the Congo, the Luangwa regions of Zambia and Mozambique. Some of these safaris were without the benefit of the usual professional guidance. Holder of the Weatherby Game Trophy, he has also hunted widely elsewhere—Asia, Alaska, Europe, South America, New Zealand, and virtually every Canadian province and U. S. state. All told, some 30 of his trophies have made the various world-record listings. Page is also a competitive shooter—winner of nine national bench rest championships and a member of the Bench Rest Hall of Fame—and an experimenter; he was directly involved in the development of several commercial cartridges and often serves as a technical consultant to manufacturers. His book The Accurate Rifle *is a bible for both competition shooter and hunter.*

Page is also well known as a conservationist. He was the founder and is currently President of the National Shooting Sports Foundation, an association of more than 100 manufacturers involved in the shooting and hunting industries. The NSSF is one of the strongest voices in the country for practical conservation—the sort that recognizes the importance of skilled game management and the significance of hunting as a management tool.

MORE YEARS AGO than I care to admit, at the entrance to the NRA Convention exhibit hall, I encountered a firearms writer of considerable renown. Skipping any greeting and throwing all restraint aside, he announced, "I'm going to Africa!" Since I knew that a safari had always been his dream—as indeed it must be of every hunter worth his salt—I bent an ear. He then detailed how he had tuned up his .475 No. 2 and his .470 and his .577 and his $4.98 and so on and on, listing a collection of elephant-busters well calculated to give this nation's orthopedic surgeons a year's work on recoil-bent shoulders. "Fine," said I, "but what are you going to take over to do your shooting with?"

And there's the whole problem in a nutshell. Every one of us, whether we're adherents of the big-bore or of the high-speed bullet, somehow seems to connect Africa, land of the elephant, rhino, and buffalo, only with shoulder cannons. We seem to forget, in discussing the African arsenal, that for every bullet we blow at behemoth, we'll get off a dozen into beasts not significantly bigger or tougher than a healthy deer. Our big-bullet friend is not the only one who falls into that trap.

Very probably such glamour comes to the fat calibers because they are unfamiliar to the American shooting scene. The fine .458 Winchester Magnum, or any of the British-devised large-slug calibers that preceded it, whose ballistics the .458 duplicates in a more modern bolt-action package, is in all honesty about as useful on the North American continent as a four-ton truck to a housewife on a shopping tour. I won't even grant the necessity of this breed of cartridge on Alaskan brown bear, though it may be worlds of fun for gun nuts to cook up forms of the .45/70 that end up like lever-action .458's, or reduced-caliber .458's that end up as cousins to the .375 H & H or the .416 Rigby. This does not knock the .458 or rap its British brethren, though why any U.S. hunter raised on bolt-action game rifles would want to handicap himself with a totally unfamiliar side-by-side double that doesn't shoot very well anyway, I dunno. Kenya law, for example, requires a caliber over .40 for the hardskins, and while other areas of Africa, probably because the British predilection for thinking of power solely in size of the muzzle hole hasn't spread everywhere, may not demand the big ones, the 500-grain ball does have its uses on the biggest game. For elephant, anyway.

Nobody gets to hunt rhino much any more for one thing. The close-permit systems applicable in, for example, Zambia and Tanzania are slowly but correctly spreading everywhere, and in many ways the .375 makes a better buffalo caliber than the .458, because more people can shoot better with a .375, and with buffalo, bullet-placement is more important than brute wallop. I once banged a buffalo square up the schnozzola with a .460 Weatherby from about fifteen feet, and while four tons of energy must've given him a helluva headache, he didn't even stagger that we could observe.

So the .458 and its cousins are really essentially for elephant. Superb solids are available in the caliber, and with the velocity down at the 2,200 mark, the 500-grain steel-jacket will punch into the X-place on an elephant just fine. Of nine elephants so far taken, I used the .460 on two, the .458 on two. With well over 100 grains of powder, the .460 Weatherby, even if deliberately slammed into a corner of an elephant's bean at such an angle that it can't possibly make the brain, will tend to stun the bull for a few seconds. A .458 into the same spot won't necessarily do that. On shots *properly* lined up, I can't see that the 8,000 foot-pounds of energy of the Weatherby item has any major advantage over the 5,000 foot-pounds of the Winchester. On elephant, it's placement plus penetration of all proper aiming points that counts.

Note that four from nine leaves five elephants unaccounted for. We'll get back to that later.

Were I to become involved in a knock-down, drag-out fight with any of the big and tough ones, however, I frankly would rather have in hand a rifle of mine that, after thirteen safaris, is so thoroughly worn that the barrel holds blue only in a few spots up around the front sight. The stock has a patina and a smoothness on those carved sections that pass for checkering, so it obviously has been toted thousands of miles in grimy gunbearer fists. The reason for the preference has not one damned thing to do with ballistics, even though this rifle clocks the 300-grain bullet at 2,775 and so churns up some 5,000 foot-pounds, albeit with zip rather than weight. The reason has to do with reliance.

That elderly rifle, chambered .375 Weatherby, a soup-up of the standard .375 H & H that Roy doesn't even chamber anymore, has indeed been in my hands on not one but several occasions when facing high-tempered beasts of weight and power, ranging from an irate 450-pound boar, bound and determined to give me an appendectomy with his 12-inch tushes, on up to an elephant with many years, 75 pounds of ivory, and some thought of squashing Mrs. Page's boy into hamburger. Probably the first custom rifle ever put up on the Remington 721 or later 700 action, it has never bobbled, and with Hornady's true solids, which do not deform in the hardest elephant skull, it has for me killed elephants at least as decisively as the larger calibers.

I recall one situation in the Belgian Congo when it did far better. A .458-toting Swiss friend named Tommy Aman and I, without benefit of professional, had stalked a pair of feeding bulls to a position where from a slight bank we could await their moving into head-shot range. That means fairly close, since the target, to reach the breadloaf-small brain either from the side or the front, is roughly palm size. One bull carried typical Kenya bush-elephant tusks, curved and stout; the other, the long and straight stabbers of the jungle *tembo* of Africa's more westerly regions. The weight of either bull, as closely as we could guess, seemed much the same at 75 pounds per tooth.

It was agreed that Tommy should take the left-hand animal, I the right, and when we fired they were broadside, about 40 yards from us. My bull went down poleaxed, but Tommy's, probably because the shot was slightly off line, staggered and then took out for Mozambique. The Swiss hit the bull with the rest of his magazine, but

Page's faithful .375 Weatherby Magnum took the elephant bull at 20 feet after he had started a charge, and the record Zambia lion at 275 yards. Page doesn't recommend a large-caliber rifle for such a range, but in a pinch the flat-shooting .375, squirting a 300-grain bullet at 2,775, will do the job, and a .458 or .460 cannon won't.

it was still shuffling off at an angle when a solid from the reliable .375 Weatherby oldster clipped the head halfway down, behind the flapping ear, and the bull dropped instantly. Evidently that bullet had driven into his brain. The point here is not that 300 grains at 2,775 is a better elephant choice than 500 grains at 2,200, but rather that it's easier to shoot quickly and accurately.

The argument is even stronger if we stretch ranges a bit. The recoil of 300-grain bullets permits use of a 2½ or even 4X scope as the normal sight. That obviously helps on, for example, a buffalo at 150 yards or a lion at 200 or better, both of which constitute really long shots for such game. The last lion I took, a Zambian whopper, had to be shot from some 275 paces or be passed up completely, and while I agree that any such yardage on lions puts

The trophy black rhino bull (28½-inch horn) was taken with one shot from the .375 Weatherby Magnum, but Page uses a rock of much larger caliber to make sure the animal is dead.

the shot way over onto the chancy side, trying it with a .458 would have been asinine indeed. With the old Weatherby-improved .375, its trajectory as flat as that of the .30/06 with 180-grain bullet, it was not really that difficult.

So for this one man, as the larger rifle in my own African battery I have been happy indeed with a heated-up .375, and while I can appreciate the virtues of the .458 clan in some circumstances, I'll probably be lugging that old mesquite-handled job back on the next trip. And the Kenya authorities won't say a thing about it, I betcha.

Back in the dear days of the 1920's and '30's, the classic African battery was a three-rifle group, with a scattergun added for birds, but that was when most safarists traveled by ship, or at least forwarded their firearms by sea, and total weight was of no importance. Times have changed. We now go in a Boeing 707 or equivalent, and it is very easy to acquire a fair-sized chunk of that airplane by offering the counter clerk too many guns. The excess baggage mounts up faster than a New York taxi meter!

Therefore, today the one-gun hunt is quite common. That can mean a personal rifle of any caliber toted over, and a .458, big double, or a .375 rented there. The rates aren't bad, about a buck a day. Some one-gunners take their own .375 H & H or a .338 Winchester and make it do everything. An apple-growing buddy of mine, hunting in Zambia, an area where the ill-founded British big-hole rule doesn't apply, took all there was, including elephant, with his handloaded .338. I think he wasted two rounds or mebbe three in collecting twenty-six trophies. But me, as a conservative, I like to take a two-rifle battery.

Where the earlier concept called for a big'un, a medium (by which the British meant a .375 or some Germanic equivalent), and a light rifle (on the order of a .318 Westley Richards, an 8-mm., or most probably the ubiquitous .30/06), I've generally operated with two. These were the .375 Winchester Magnum mentioned above (usually without any heavier musket along) and a 7-mm. Magnum of one persuasion or another. And frankly, within my experience with the big 7 clan, which is possibly the largest experience in the world, since it is highly probable that I have taken more game with a big 7 than any man, surely well over 500 head, any real difference between the Weatherby version, the Remington version, the Mashburn version, or any of the other large-cased 7-mm. Magnums, you can put in your eye and never feel the scratch! I do think the largest Mashburn case makes a bit more speed possible with 175-grain Nosler bullets. I *think* so. The game critters have never commented one way or another.

My reason for sticking by the 7-mm. Magnum in Africa, for general multi-purpose use, is simply that it does a good job at either end of the game scale. Presumably it's way too much rifle for a gerenuk or a Thomson gazelle, for example, and theoretically it's too light for a massive eland or a heavy-maned lion, but it does a

The 7-mm. Mashburn Magnum, Page's general-purpose and long-range choice for years, felled the Tanzania sable (45-inch horns) and the 450-pound record-quality bull bongo. Page has probably taken more game with a big 7 than anyone else in the world.

really superb job on all the middle-sized items, impalla, zebra, kudu, hartebeeste, wildebeest, puku, kob, and such that make up the bulk of our African shooting.

A story that I have told before bears retelling because it makes a clear point. In Mozambique with Jose Simoes, before he quit the hunting game, we were checking out a sizable waterhole for evidence of lion. As we searched the edges, one of the trackers spotted the dove-gray and light browns of a bunch of eland a quarter mile up in the scattered bush. There seemed to be at least one bull, so I sneaked closer, to a point where a down tree offered both a hide for me and a rest for the rifle. The bull finally showed clear, long in the horn and by all odds the heaviest eland I had ever laid eyes on, his neck and dewlaps fully six feet around. The 7-mm. Mashburn was in my hands. Anything heavier—and most professionals talk about the .375 H & H for eland—was unreachable, back at the car. Before the breeze could betray me, I had to shoot. With 175 grains behind his foreleg the bull jumped once, ran a half dozen steps and piled up.

Now, it is quite possible that an identical hit with a lesser round than the big-cased 7 would have dropped the eland, but I'd have been loath to try the shot. After all, on an earlier safari I had chased a bull eland halfway across East Africa after he had been hit with too little steam.

As a matter of fact, while I have never essayed taking a buffalo with a 7-mm. Magnum, I have little doubt it can be done by a reasonable shot. The cartridge will handle a lion seemingly as well as one of the large-bodied .30's, as I know from personal experience. The lion in question went fifteen yards under a bush and passed away. I don't recommend it for lion, however, even though the heaviest of these cats won't beat 500 pounds with a bellyful of zebra. And on leopard it works fine. Better than a bigger caliber, I suspect, because it's easier to shoot—and on a leopard crouched along a branch, the target area can be pretty small and you get only the one try. It has taken care of everything save the hardskins in both Africa and Asia. If there's a better round for urial and the ovis beasts or the assorted Asiatic goats it can only be the .300 Weatherby, which does, alas, whack me around a trifle much, and I know that from experience. It was in Asia, after all, in Baluchistan in fact, that a blue-eyed mountain man offered me fifty fat-tailed sheep and his second wife for a 7-mm. Magnum he'd seen performing on markhor that afternoon. He must've been impressed, though I also suspect he had a blood feud to settle with some gents over on the Afghan side!

Of course, having the energy of a big 7 and the penetration of a good 175-grain bullet does not cure all ills. I recall a Zambian zebra that, probably out of pure carelessness, because it was truly an easy shot, I hit a shade high in the withers. It went down as if stunned, recovered, and then led us all over the Luangwa Valley in a hopeless chase. The same day my chum Art McGreevy had potted his second zebra hide with a .243 and no problem at all. But all this means is that he put his little bullet in the right place, and I didn't.

I do not, however, recall any failure with the big 7 with any other African animal of antelope size, and in the case of sable or kudu that means upwards of 400 pounds on the hoof and a very great desire to remain among the living. There has been much debate about the relative durability of African and North American game, and I must confess that I have during my hunting lifetime swung back and forth. Finally, however, I came to the conclusion that the larger antelope—after all, you cannot compare an 80-pound impalla and a 300-pound mule deer—that are the subject of attack from the big carnivores of Africa do seem to fight harder for life, do seem better able to resist the effect of anything but a very precisely placed bullet. I see that as a strong reason for picking a 7-mm. Magnum over a .30/06 or the like as a light or "standard-use" rifle.

I do recall a roan bull that had no intention of giving up. These antelope, with their tufted ears and horns back-sweeping like a sable's but shorter, are said by the locals to fight off lions with some success. They are certainly brave. This one roan, when by all the rules he should've passed away, did his damnedest to get at me, to hang me on those stickers like a butterfly on a pin. The big 7 was only just enough for him.

And on the really fragile but highly edible African beasts, the Tommie, the gerenuk, and various forms of gazelle, while the idea of 175-grain bullets and energies in the 3,600 foot-pounds class may seem utterly absurd, you may be overgunned but not wastefully so. With the right bullet, which is to say the Remington PCL, the Nosler, or the Bitterroot, the 7-mm. Magnum does *not* devastate the entire animal. On so fragile a frame the bullet expansion actually may take place *beyond* the far side of the animal, so that minimal ruination of chops and steaks occurs. Sometimes it's almost like using a large-caliber solid on one of these delicate speedsters.

What all this amounts to is that for over thirteen safaris I have been well pleased indeed to have had in my hands during walkabout, or chamber empty and muzzle down when we were batting around in a vehicle, the 7-mm. Magnum as the general purpose rifle. The larger caliber stays back with a gunbearer unless it is obviously going to be needed, and that is mighty seldom. After all, even in Africa, while all the glamor may accrue to the great blasters with their big bullets and impressive ballistics, it's the small piece that gets all the shooting.

A fair percentage of the world's trophy hunters are not much interested in guns *per se*. They seem to regard them as tools and are satisfied with the adequate. Fortunately for the bull sessions that go on at African Safari Club dinners, gatherings of Game Coin and the like, there are always a few in the gun nut division who have pronounced opinions about what constitutes a reasonable battery. The range of thinking is infinite, it would seem. But in every case, if the opinion is worth registering it is based on personal experience, out of which has grown an affection—call it love if you wish, because it goes beyond what men ordinarily feel for objects of wood and metal—for one or two rifles. These are the numbers that have made the long shots, the lucky shots, the shots when only a bullet stood between hunter and absolute destruction. All questions of ballistic mathematics or logic go down before such a relationship. And that's precisely the why of my choice of a personal African battery, probably why there are two rifles on my rack you couldn't pry from me for all the gold in Fort Knox. Well, most of it, anyway.

When Your Rifle Goes Sour

BOB STEINDLER

Bob Steindler began shooting and handling guns before he was ten, and as a youngster he hunted some of the finest game areas in Austria and Czechoslovakia. He has been a professional gun writer and editor for the past thirteen years; he has written four books and is a regular contributor to many of the gun magazines, including several foreign ones. Steindler also operates a firearms consulting service, and he is Consulting Firearms Examiner for the Illinois Crime Laboratories and Firearms Examiner for the City and County of Peoria. A reloader and wildcatter, he has his own indoor and outdoor range, complete with high-speed photographic equipment. As well as being an expert on equipment, Steindler is an avid and accomplished hunter who has taken game in the States from Alaska to New Hampshire and in most of the Canadian Provinces.

IN SOME RESPECTS, rifles and cars are very much alike. They are mass-produced, within the financial reach of most of us, and they go sour—sometimes within a week or two after you get them.

If that new car stutters and knocks like an old Model T, or the engine falls out, you simply take her back to the dealer and let him worry about tinkering it back into operating condition. While most of the factory guns are under some sort of warranty, if your shiny new rifle doesn't deliver bench-rest accuracy, taking the gun back to the dealer won't help one bit. It's either fix it yourself or pay a gunsmith to do the job.

Why should a brand-new rifle fail to deliver reasonably good groups? The first thing that most shooters blame is the barrel—it's bent, crooked, rough as a cob, the rifling is too deep or too shallow, the barrel vibrates, the barrel doesn't vibrate, it's improperly crowned, or maybe the guy who drilled the hole into that solid steel rod had indigestion the morning he did the job.

Before worrying about your rifle, be it brand new or last year's model, let's be sure we're talking about the same thing—accuracy. Webster's Unabridged Dictionary, customarily considered the final authority, says: "Accuracy . . . b: conformity to . . . some standard or model . . . the [accuracy] of a firearm is its ability to deliver a close group of hits on target." Sounds great and very erudite, doesn't it? Unfortunately, it doesn't define accuracy, since it doesn't define the term "close group."

Accuracy is a very subjective and relative term. Bench-rest shooters are looking for rifles that will deliver five .22 caliber bullets into one .22 caliber hole at 100 and 200 yards. Then there are fellows who feel that a varmint rifle or even a big-game rifle should consistently deliver groups that measure no more than, or perhaps a shade under, one inch—that famed MOA, or minute of angle, group.

Every once in a while, you'll find some typewriter-pounding gun sage stating that so-and-so gun gave him something he calls "hunting accuracy." Unfortunately, this could mean a headshot at a squirrel at 25 feet, a brainshot at a chuck out there at the 350-yard marker, or breaking the shoulder of a charging rhino at five feet. So let's say, for the sake of the argument, that a hunting rifle should deliver groups no larger than 1½ MOA at the customary 100 yards.

As a devout target and bench-rest shooter, I will spend hours fiddling around with my hunting rifles until most of them will deliver a degree of accuracy I can live with. I'm reasonably well satisfied if I can tune a hunting rifle to deliver three shots into a group measuring not more than 1¼ inches at 100 yards from the bench, though I'd like the rifle even better if it shot MOA groups.

Contrary to popular belief, the test guns shipped to gun editors have not been hand-picked for accuracy, finish, appearance, or inletting. The big gun makers simply don't have the manpower to hand-pick guns for the writers, and the importers have only a limited number of guns that they can afford to have converted from "new" to "used" status. Hence, we shoot what is being shipped to us and report on the accuracy of the gun as it comes from the shipping carton. Sometimes, if time permits and we are so inclined, we'll tinker with a rifle in order to squeeze the groups down a bit more.

One other point about test-guns and accuracy is often forgotten. Most gun writers spend a fair bit of time on the range, and we develop shooting habits that are conducive to wringing the last shred of accuracy potential from a gun. The average shooter or hunter, at best, spends one or two afternoons a month on the range.

Numerous times another shooter, trying his best to get some reasonable accuracy from his rifle, turns to me for help. With the same ammo, from the same bench, and on the same target, I'll shrink the fellow's 2 MOA group to 1¼ or some such figure. Even shooting from a solid rest with a properly focused scope requires a certain amount of skill and coordination. Add to this breath control and an educated trigger finger, and groups are bound to differ from shooter to shooter.

Can a barrel wear enough after 100 rounds to lose accuracy drastically? That's a question asked quite frequently. Even some of our hot factory Magnums don't wear out barrels that fast. Most of these hot calibers now come with stainless-steel barrels, and they'll last for at least several thousand rounds before losing their gilt-edged accuracy. I'll bet my battered Stetson that most accuracy troubles can be traced to one of three sources: barrel bedding, action bedding, and sight troubles.

The most frequent reason for accuracy failures is the third and last group—sight troubles. And don't think for a minute that a scope installed by a gunsmith cannot be at fault! Aside from actual scope trouble—and here fogging is the number one trouble spot—loose scope rings can allow the scope to wiggle like a puppy's tail or to slide back and forth; the scope can be canted or turned in the rings; or maybe the scope was mounted in rings with some residual packing grease left on them. And, as unlikely as it sounds, there's a chance that you may have the wrong size rings wrapped around your scope tube.

To add to your woes, the scope mounts or blocks may not be the right ones for your rifle; the screws lashing the block to the action may have worked loose; or one or the other block may need shimming to give you the correct alignment between sight and bore. Don't exclude from your "suspect" list the holes in the receiver of the rifle: they may not be lined up properly, thus preventing the scope bases from lining up with each other and with the bore.

With the exception of a bum scope and improperly drilled holes in the receiver, all of the above troubles can be cured easily. But before attempting any gun tinkering, be sure that your screwdrivers fit the slots in the screwheads. If you do happen to louse up the head of a screw, either replace it with a new one or dress down the damaged head. This is best done with some fine Swiss files. The slot can be restored to usefulness by means of a screwhead file. These

One screwhead damaged, the other completely ruined. If a screwhead is damaged to this extent, it is best to have a gunsmith drill out the old screw and replace it with a larger one.

narrow files cut only on the edge, come in various sizes, and are worth their weight in gold!

Once the slot has been cleaned out, the surface of the head dressed down smooth, and any grease that might have accumulated removed, then use a good touch-up bluing. Properly done, it will be almost impossible to tell that the head of the screw was once mutilated. Tools for tinkering with your guns can be obtained from a number of gunsmith's supply houses, such as Brownell's, Inc.

One question often puzzles shooters-turned-amateur-gunsmith. How tight should you pull a screw? Most gun screws are specially hardened, but it can happen that too much torque on a screw will shear off the head. Here is a tip about scope-mounting screws. Tighten all screws with a fitting screwdriver until you can't feel any more play in the screw as you bring pressure to bear on the screwdriver. Then give the handle of the screwdriver a healthy whack with a rawhide mallet. This will allow you to tighten up the screw as much as a quarter turn, and that should do it.

Before you start feeding scope screws into the holes in the mounts and receiver, apply one or two drops of a product called Loctite to the threads of each screw. This sealant, bought in any hardware store, sets up a tight bond between male and female parts of the thread, and there's little chance that a screw seated in this way will ever work loose. A drop of shellac or varnish can be used, but Loctite is better, since it doesn't tend to dry out in the tube, is easier to handle, and a tube will last you a long time.

Scope slippage in the rings is due to residual packing grease. To

When Your Rifle Goes Sour

forestall any slipping troubles, degrease bases, rings, and don't forget the screws and the surface of the receiver. Degreasing is best done with denatured alcohol, since it has a minimum of toxic fumes. Reinstall bases and rings, and don't forget the Loctite on the screws and a whack on the handle of the screwdriver.

Here is a suggestion that will make such home gunsmithing jobs a lot easier. If you don't have a bench vise, build yourself a wooden box about 20 inches long and anywhere from 6 to 10 inches wide. Cut matching notches into the narrow ends, pad these notches with hunks of tanned deer hide and some soft material like Turkish toweling. Put the box on your workbench, and to stop it from shifting around, weigh it down with a bag or two of shot. This will hold your rifle in a nontilting rest as you work on it, and the box is a good place to stash the parts that you take off or out of the gun. Trying to find a 3/16-inch screw in the usual bench clutter can be a harrowing experience.

If you do have a vise, make a pair of jaw protectors from scrap hardboard, then glue fitting pieces of heavy felt on them to protect

After applying Loctite and cinching down screw, give the end of the screwdriver a whack with a rawhide mallet, then tighten another quarter turn.

the stock finish. If you do use a vise, be sure never to tighten it too much—the area of the magazine well on the average stock has little wood, and too much pressure can crack the wood. I built an adjustable stand with a padded rest that I shove under the fore-end of the gun. With the gun held gently in the vise and the fore-end supported this way, there's little danger of the gun working loose from its perch.

If the scope appears canted, first make sure that your bench and vise are really level. While you have the level in your hand, also see if the gun is held level in the vise or bench box. If the scope still appears canted and everything else is level, loosen the screws that hold the rings tight, then rotate the scope until the cross hairs no longer appear canted. Now retighten the screws just enough so that the scope can't turn as you lift the rifle out of the box or vise. Bring the rifle to your shoulder and see if the cross hairs now appear level. If you do cant your rifle and habitually make corrections for it in setting the scope askew, do your scope rotating before you cinch down the ring screws again.

Sometimes it is difficult to get on target with a newly mounted scope. After using a collimator, or bore-sighting, you may find that there is neither enough windage or elevation adjustment in your scope to permit you to adjust the scope to your needs. Usually a shim under one or the other block will help, but this is best done by a gunsmith who has the shimming material and knows what he is doing.

Little can be done about the mount screw holes that are out of alignment. In some fifteen years of gun tinkering, I have seen this only once on a factory rifle, but it is not too uncommon if the scope-base installation was left to some hammer mechanic. If the job is quite a bit out of alignment, it may be possible to plug the holes and start anew. In any case, take the gun to a competent gunsmith. Perhaps he can hack, shave, and file some sort of Rube Goldberg base that will do the trick. You can always tell your friends that you use only custom scope bases!

It's hard to realize that wood is tougher and more powerful than steel, but a fore-end pushing against a barrel will give the barrel a dandy curve. Some ten years ago, when a new big-game caliber was being introduced, I was asked to take a rifle chambered for this round on a projected grizzly hunt, a sort of off-the-record field test.

When Your Rifle Goes Sour

The gun arrived in plenty of time, and whenever I had a couple of hours, I worked up handloads, checked them for accuracy, and ran chronograph tests. By the end of July I had several choice handloads, but all of them had been checked out only on the 100-yard range. I wanted to run accuracy and drop tests on the 200-, 250- and 300-yard range before heading into the boondocks.

We had the wettest August on record, and I never did get back to the range until the weekend before leaving for the hunt. With about 100 carefully assembled handloads, I settled at the bench to check the 100-yard accuracy of each load for the third or fourth time. Surprise! The three bullet holes formed a neat four-foot pattern, yet a month before, those same loads had given me excellent accuracy.

Even at the shooting bench, I could see how the fore-end had warped and was pushing the slender barrel upward. Although well inletted, the moisture had gone into the wood, and when I took the barreled action out of the stock, it became obvious that the barrel channel had not been protected in any way, thus allowing the wood to soak up moisture like a thirsty pup drinks water. Since warpage is always uneven, every shot fired moved the barrel in the channel differently, thus the four-foot pattern rather than the customary tight group.

After that experience I learned to take each of my newly acquired rifles out of the stock and do my thing with it. First I make sure that steel and wood make contact where they are supposed to make contact. If the barrel channel has not been waterproofed, I give it a couple of coats of marine spar varnish or wash coats of shellac.

Gunsmiths use a blue gunk, commonly called inletting blue, to see where wood and metal make contact. Depending on where they want metal to bear against the wood, or where they suspect contact when there should be none, they apply a thin layer of inletting blue to the steel. Seating the barreled action in the stock and tightening the stock screws transfers the die to the wood at the contact points. From then on it's scrape and fit until adequate wood is removed.

In the case of the warped fore-end of the Magnum rifle, I used inletting blue to indicate the pressure points. Then, with a special barrel channel rasp, I removed the wood gradually, constantly checking my work with the barreled action, applying fresh inletting blue when needed. Since the barrel was originally free-floated (that

A spot of inletting blue indicates where wood and steel bind. The channel rasp removes small amounts of wood. The work must be checked constantly so that not too much wood is removed.

merely means that the fore-end makes no contact with the barrel), I decided to free-float the barrel again. Once the gun delivered its shots to the same point of impact again, I treated the barrel channel as outlined above.

Loose action or bedding screws affect a rifle's performance. Some actions have two bedding screws, others have three. Surplus Mauser rifles frequently have two large bedding or action screws, plus two smaller ones, right next to the two big screws, with cut-outs in the edge. These small screws act as locking devices for the large ones, and the small screw has to be turned in or out so that the cut-out allows the large screw to pass.

Before going into the matter of action bedding, let's turn to a few other sources of accuracy trouble. Assume you have sighted your rifle properly on the range, then decide to fire a few rounds from the sitting position with a tight sling. If your rifle is a light sporter model, the pull you exert on the sling can alter the point of bullet impact. Similarly, resting the rifle barrel on a limb or across some other sort of rest will alter the point of impact, since you are actually pushing the barrel upward.

If you fall heir to a double rifle, or drilling, before shooting your new treasure, ascertain for what load and bullet weight the barrel or barrels were regulated. In one drilling with a .30/06 barrel, the tube had been regulated for the 180-grain bullet. The owner of the gun didn't know that, tried the 150-grain bullet in the barrel, and accuracy was not in the bragging class. The fellow almost broke my heart with his sad tale at the range. I took the gun apart, checked the markings on the barrels, selected five 180-grain rounds from my ammo box, and shot an MOA group. I still can't figure out why the guy almost cried—frustration or relief?

Every so often you'll read or hear about a fellow "shooting his rifle in." Or you may read where some guy fired a couple of hundred rounds to "settle his rifle." In essence, both shooters are doing the same thing. Even the most painstaking inspection of a barrel, either visually or by means of such precision toys as air gauges, can often miss a tiny burr in the barrel. This may be a small shaving that was not knocked loose from the edge of the land, a minute roughness that was not polished by the finishing reamer. Wood gives under recoil, and even a slight trace of moisture in the bedding area can

Military Mauser actions have two small screws that lock the bedding screws into place.

bind the action, the magazine, and even the safety. Thus, this "shooting in" helps to settle the gun in the stock, and jacketed bullets will burnish the bore. This is especially true of the small-caliber, high-velocity centerfire numbers that will give better accuracy after several hundred rounds.

A few years ago I acquired a custom bench-rest rifle and with it came a target shot by the gunsmith who built the rifle. On it he noted that the shots represented rounds 100 to 120, and that by the time I poured another 100 or so rounds through the barrel, accuracy should further improve. I did and it did!

Some time ago I had a test rifle that shot extremely well for a factory rifle. Suddenly, the gun lost much of its gilt-edged accuracy, and checking on the bedding screws revealed a loose one. I tightened both of them, but then the safety bound and it required a major effort to get the safety off. Too much pressure on the bedding screws and a poor inletting job caused that problem. The bottom of the receiver should bear evenly against the wood. If there is binding, it is possible to spring the action or twist it, depending on the type of action.

This brings us to action bedding, a topic often discussed and relatively little understood.

Some of the areas where the metal of the action or magazine make contact with the wood have a direct relationship with the accuracy potential of your gun. One such area is the recoil lug. Wood and steel must make perfect contact there, with the recoil abutment of the stock squarely fitting the recoil lug area. An improper fit there on a large-caliber rifle that develops a fair amount of recoil will lead to a splintered stock. If the recoil lug bears unevenly, that is, more pressure on one side than the other, the barrel will whip in the opposite direction from the point where it bears harder. If you ever have sudden dispersion of your shots in a horizontal direction, this may well be the reason for such erratic behavior on the part of your rifle. Use inletting blue to check the bearing of the recoil lug against the recoil abutment.

Another possible trouble area, this one quite visible, is the bedding of the rear tang of the action. Poor bedding or inletting can lead to a prematurely split stock. This sort of splitting occurs most frequently on shotgun stocks, especially the 10-gauge guns that have a very narrow wrist. Here it is a question of the recoil affecting the wood, and too many stocks have not been waterproofed in the tang area.

Wood is a contrary material. Some years ago a custom stocker showed me two stock blanks that he had sawed from the same hunk of wood. One blank had been kept in the warm shop, the other in the loft where he dried most of his wood before placing it in the kiln. The divergent direction of the warpage and twist in the two blanks was hard to believe. Wood, even when glassbedded, will take on a certain amount of moisture, but not at the same rate of speed or in the same area.

The bedding screws that hold the action in the stock should never make contact with the stock wood anywhere. If the recoil lug and the recoil abutment don't meet properly, or if an area of the inletting is compressed during recoil, the bedding screws can be forced rearward during recoil. Thus, the screw will make contact with the rear of the screw hole. This can spring the action, and eventually there will not only be accuracy loss, but the stock will split.

The bolt handle should not make contact with the cut-out in the stock. In some rifles, especially Mausers, the rear of the top tang should be inletted with just a bit of space showing between tang and the edge of the wood. Customarily, the companies selling factory-inletted semifinished stocks don't inlet the tang completely, since the various Mauser actions have tangs of varying sizes. Stock makers leave extra wood in the tang area that should be removed during the bedding operation. Mausers stocked by inexperienced men often show splitting of the inletting simply because not enough attention was paid to the vagaries of some of these actions.

Another source for possible inaccuracy lies in the method of barrel-bedding. Some of the sporter barrels do best if they are free-floated. Others require varying amounts of upward pressure near the fore-end. But just because your buddy gets surprising accuracy from his rifle by shoving a hunk of matchbook cover under the forward end of the barrel, don't be too hasty in copying him. It may well be that your barrel needs to have more or less pressure, and not even the direction from which pressure must come can be guessed at. It's a question of trying varying amounts of fore-end tension and a fair bit of shooting. Lateral or side pressure is almost sure to affect accuracy, since the lightweight sporter tubes tend to shoot away from any such source of pressure.

If there is upward pressure on the barrel channel, try this experiment before you get out the rasp. Remove the barreled action from the stock and insert a thin piece of cardboard; a double thickness of file card will do very nicely. Place the cardboard under the receiver, directly behind the recoil lug. Now tighten the rear bedding screw first so that when you tighten the front screw you won't tip the action. Take the rifle to the range and see if three or four groups don't show an improvement in accuracy. If there's a noted improvement in accuracy, your barrel will do its thing when free-floated. Get out the barrel rasp and go to it! And don't forget to give the raw wood a coat or two of marine spar varnish.

Up to now we have considered only new or relatively new rifles. What about a tube that has seen considerable service? What about fouling and leading? If you have reason to suspect that the fault may really be in the barrel of your rifle, the first step is a thorough cleaning. Use a good powder solvent and a wire bristle brush. After pushing and pulling the brush through the barrel five or six times, apply some J-B Bore Cleaning Compound to a patch and give the barrel another thorough scrubbing.

Be careful how you handle the cleaning rod and avoid scraping it against the lands, either near the muzzle or the chamber. The J-B stuff is excellent and is used widely by bench-rest shooters, but don't get carried away with it. It is after all an abrasive, and thus some caution must be exercised when using it. After polishing the bore with J-B, use liberal amounts of solvent and lots of patches. Wipe the bore until the patches come out clean. If the lands and grooves are still sharp and the barrel shines brightly, you may have cured an inaccuracy caused by fouling.

The sad truth is that eventually everything wears out. I have a pet Magnum rifle that has had better than 4,000 rounds through it. After six or seven years of hard service, the rifle now barely shoots 1½ MOA groups where some years ago, with factory ammo, ¾ MOA was not at all unusual. The bore, or rather the throat, is badly worn and the tube is literally shot out. The only answer in this case is a new barrel. But if not too many rounds have gone through the barrel and accuracy suddenly drops off, you may have a simple case of fouling.

Most shooters have heard about some of the old black-powder numbers like the .30/40 Krag and the .45/70. Between the black powder in the cartridges and the lead bullets, keeping a gun clean was danged near a full-time job. Our ammo makers today extol the virtues of their noncorrosive priming mixes, hard bullet jackets that supposedly leave no residue during their hot travel through the barrel, and the clean burning powders. All of this is true—but you still have to clean barrels. Remember that those accuracy nuts, the bench-rest shooters, clean their barrels after every relay. They spend as much time cleaning one barrel as they do in making up five or ten precision handloads!

If barrel-channel tinkering and action-bedding sounds like a lot of work, you'll probably want to consider glassbedding. There are some very definite advantages to glassbedding, but it is not a cure-all for poor stock work, nor will it make a tack-driving bench-rest gun out of some old clunker. Most of the custom stockers will bed a tube tightly. That means that the action, the recoil lug, and the full length of the barrel is in close contact with the wood. This is accomplished by careful scraping and fitting, scraping and fitting, and so on. There's a lot of skill, labor, and time involved in the job.

It is also true that you can fit the whole shebang loosely, then glassbed so that the glassbedding compound takes the place of the tightly fitted wood. While this is a convenient way out, it doesn't take into account the fact already mentioned about barrel pressure. If your barrel requires some upward pressure, the full-length glassbedding will nullify the advantages that can be gained by the upward pressure. It is true that glassbedding will make the stock moisture-proof, that glassbedding will correct a lot of careless chisel and rasp work, but the tendency to glassbed every single gun stock seems to me nothing more than a poor excuse for sloppy stock work.

There is one other way to wring the last bit of potential accuracy from your rifle. A good crisp trigger pull can do wonders for your shooting. Two-stage military triggers are nonadjustable, but a skilled gunsmith can work miracles with a carefully applied stone. Best, of course, is to have him install one of the commercial triggers, and then have him set the trigger to your liking. The great majority of today's factory rifles have adjustable triggers, and quite a few of them can be tuned without too much trouble.

Tuning a rifle is really not difficult. A few basic tools and a few hours at your workbench and on the range can turn that mediocre rifle into a gun that will deliver consistent varmint accuracy.

Black Powder: Fundamentals for Field Use

HAL SWIGGETT

Hal Swiggett was started on the road to shooting pleasures at the age of six by a very understanding grandfather. Within two years he was roaming the woods and streams of southeastern Kansas alone, except for his faithful .22 rimfire rifle.

Swiggett has hunted over most of North America and has been writing about it for publication since 1947. Although he writes here on the use of black powder, a subject he is thoroughly familiar with as it pertains to field use, his specialty is undoubtedly handgun shooting and hunting. He spends most of his free time seeking furry targets for his scoped handguns.

Currently Swiggett is Shooting Editor of Gunsport. He is active in Ducks door Times and is Black Powder Editor of Gunsport. He is active in Ducks Unlimited, a past president of the Texas Outdoor Writers Association, and currently on the Board of Directors of the Outdoor Writers Association of America.

I ONCE HEARD a fellow say that if bows and arrows were any good the Indians would still have this country. That's not exactly true, because it was black powder that caused the downfall of the bow, and whether modern shooters choose to admit it or not, some mighty powerful shooting can be done with black powder. Be it handgun, rifle, or shotgun, black powder stuffed in chambers of front loaders or brass cases can produce some awe-inspiring results.

I got interested in the stuff a decade or more ago and have done a good deal of hunting with all three types of guns. My use has been field straight down the line. Targets are used only to sight in rifles, check points of impact for handguns, and on occasion to pattern a shotgun. I'm not in the least interested in how tight a group can be shot at 100 yards under any given set of conditions. I am interested in how many jackrabbits I can kill with a given number of shots at varying distances encountered in the field.

Most of my handgun grouping is done on tin cans or cactus leaves. The majority of smoothbore patterning is done on cactus leaves. If a pear (cactus) leaf gets itself thoroughly perforated at 15 or 20 steps, I try again at 25. Soon as those pellet holes dwindle to maybe one every inch and a half, I consider that my maximum distance for bird shooting. I don't know about percentages. My interest is in killing birds, cottontails, and the like.

Same goes for shooting balls. I'd a lot rather see how many holes I can put in a No. 2 can at 40 yards than plant my posterior on a bench using sandbags and a spotting scope and try for one-hole groups at any distance. My experience has been that if I can hit those No. 2 cans at 40 or 50 yards, I can also hit cottontails or jack rabbits at the same distance. If a ball can be plunked through the can consistently at 60 or 70 yards, then I feel free to use that same gun on rabbits at those ranges.

Handguns, front-loading handguns of most makes (meaning replicas, because nobody in his right mind would shoot an original), can be relied on to put their balls in a rabbit-sized can at 20 steps. Some of them, those with the rifling cut deep, will do far better. In fact I've known a couple that will put modern revolvers to a rugged test to stay in a shootfest where a couple of men shoot at the same can and keep it rolling until someone misses. Just because black powder is used as the propellant doesn't mean the gun isn't accurate.

The Hopkins & Allen Boot Pistol does an excellent job and is possibly more accurate than revolvers because a patched ball is used, just as in a rifle. This one is .45 caliber. Swiggett's homemade ramrod combines the short starter and ramrod in one unit.

I'm not going to bore you with how black powder is manufactured, when it came to be, specifics on how it was used in any era or stuffy data on how some modern "experts" think the stuff is to be used.

I realize there is a picture-book use for each of the guns. I also know for a fact those picture-book situations couldn't possibly have been available to the majority of hunters, Indian fighters, and frontiersmen back when black powder replaced bows and arrows.

My methods are field inspired, field used, and produce field results. Which means with a bit of the same "try this and if it doesn't work for you, try something a little bit different" approach you can kill quail, ducks, and geese with your shotgun; rabbits and squirrels with your handguns and rifles; and big game such as deer and on up with the big-bore rifles, especially those utilizing minié balls.

Let's start off with handguns. Most of those available today are made in Italy or Belgium. Most are adequate. You can somewhat go by the price. If the gun is being sold ridiculously low-priced, your chances are more than even that you are getting a gun of lower quality.

Barrel accuracy is controlled by how deep, up to a point, the rifling is cut. There has to be ample depth for the ball to be grabbed and sent spiraling on its way. Other than that, a little observation will tell you whether the gun you are looking at is one you want to own or not. I've mentioned this depth of rifling because at least one importer of black-powder "cap-and-ball" guns has some that border on smoothbores. They are fine to look at and even fun to shoot so long as shooting is the object. Hitting something is another ball game.

Most of the handguns are in either .36 or .44 caliber. Plinking and tin-can puncturing are fine for the tiny little .36-caliber guns, but if your plans include a try at small game, by all means get the larger caliber. The reason being the .36 caliber balls weigh only slightly over 82 grains on the average. Most of the replica .36 caliber reproductions have a .375 chamber and use balls of .376 to .380.

The .44 caliber handguns shoot .45 balls that average out at about 128 grains. This added weight makes killing small game more certain.

This might be a good time to point out a confusing fact about fodder for front-loading guns. As I mentioned, .44 cap-and-ball revolvers shoot .45 balls. The reverse is true with rifles. Balls for

.45 rifles are .44 caliber. This is simply because handguns fire balls without patching material. The ball is jammed into the chamber with the aid of a ram, and it fits so tight it will actually remove a ring of lead as it is seated.

Val Forgett of the Service Armament Co. (Navy Arms) loads his cap and ball revolver during the Outdoor Writers Association Conference at Pensacola. Val wears full Civil War regalia.

In rifles, on the other hand, the ball is seated by hand. As a result, the ball has to be of a smaller diameter than the bore in order to get it down against the powder. This extra space is filled with patching material, which not only makes the ball a tight fit in the barrel but also should be of a thickness to fill the grooves. This is what gives the rifle ball its spin, hence its accuracy.

But back on handguns. You'll probably be reading more on black powder if for no other reason than to try and disprove my methods, so as I said before, I'm not going into methods prescribed in most books. Mine are safe, believe me, as I still have two eyes, two arms, two hands and, let me see, one, two, three—yep, I still have ten fingers also.

Basically, black-powder handguns shoot FFFg powder. What is FFFg powder? Black powder comes in four granulations. Fg is the coarsest and is used in cannons and I guess maybe 10-gauge shotguns on occasion. FFg is used in all the shotguns I've ever shot and all rifles I've used except once in a while when I would stuff in FFFg, the finer-grain powder, to see what would happen. FFFg is intended for handguns. FFFFg is practically dust and is used for priming flintlocks. It is also handy to have around for the times when a ball gets rammed down a barrel and just as it hits bottom you realize you forgot the powder. On these "rare" occasions, sometimes enough FFFFg dust can be trickled through the nipple to get the ball out of the barrel without having to resort to worms or removing the barrel plug.

What is a worm? That's a gadget similar to a corkscrew. It's a very necessary item when for one reason or another a powder charge fails to fire or was never dropped in the barrel. Any brass screw fastened firmly to either a brass or wooden ramrod will do.

Handguns, basically, require their chambers filled with enough FFFg powder to allow the ball to be seated firmly against it and still be slightly below the cylinder mouth so it can be turned freely. Many will tell you that the lightest possible charge of powder to get the ball to the target will give better accuracy. This is probably true, but like I said earlier, I'm a field shooter. I much prefer a load stiff enough to punch holes in tin cans and kill rabbits or other small game. That's why I say the charge should fill the chamber allowing seating room for the ball. This same feeling carries over to rifles and shotguns.

Piddling loads might be fine for piddling purposes, but my shooting might be one chamber at a cactus leaf, another for a running lizard that I know I can't hit but have to try for, a cottontail for lunch or maybe a knot on a post. I never know for sure, so I load 'em full and I'm ready.

Cap-and-ball revolvers have a bad habit of setting off adjoining chambers when one is fired *unless* some grease is used to cover the balls and seal off each chamber. This grease also serves to soften residue left in the barrel, which in turn makes them shoot better longer, meaning without cleaning. It also makes the guns easier to clean.

There are commercial products. Probably the best known is Beare Grease. It is good and I use it when I'm hunting or when I don't know exactly how long the gun is going to be loaded. For plinking where shots are fired rather rapidly after loading or when the weather is cool, I usually use either Crisco or Vaseline. Both do the job. Old-time shooters, I've heard, used axle grease. Waterpump grease also does an excellent job. Whatever you use will reduce the chances of a chain-fire situation, and that's the idea.

How accurate are front-loading handguns? I can't really say because I'm not that good a shot, but I do know it is possible to put all six balls in a playing card at 20 steps.

I seem to have better luck with .44's than I do with .36's for some reason, but can't believe it's the guns. It is probably because I'm a .44–.45 funatic (that's what I mean—funatic). I've shot big-bore handguns nearly all my life and can work up little enthusiasm for anything smaller. Which could very well be the reason I don't do better with the smaller-caliber handguns.

What sort of lead ball is used? Where muzzle loaders are concerned, use nothing but absolutely pure lead. No mixture of any sort. Most of the time when handguns or rifles are purchased there will be a mold with the gun, or at least made available so it can be bought to use with the gun. These are designed for round balls, usually, and the intent is for a pure, soft lead product.

If none came with the gun and you aren't supplied with the precise bore measurement, then you'll have to slug the barrel to find what size mold to buy. This is done by pushing a soft lead ball through the bore. Measure the product of your efforts and order a mold or balls of this diameter. I've oversimplified the procedure.

Never underrate the power of a .44 black-powder handgun. A 28-grain charge easily penetrated a San Antonio telephone directory.

The ball has to be smaller than the bore in rifles in order to get it patched and still pushed snugly against the powder. Your slug tells the dimension of the barrel. As a starter, try a half caliber smaller. Sometimes a full caliber below does better. This is where the do-it-yourself part comes in.

Handguns require a snugly fitting ball. Many times, in fact most of the time, I am far too lazy to cast balls for my handguns. I've found over the years that Lawrence Brand .44 and .45 balls do an excellent job in my front-loading short guns. So they aren't perfectly round; they become that way immediately on being rammed into the chamber. A perfectly cast ball is turned into the same misshapen mess, so why bother. I say "mess," because the ball is no longer round, except in one dimension. It is definitely longer than wide because it was forced into the chamber. This disregards the fact that if the ball is really the right size for the gun, it is large enough that a tiny ring of lead will be removed as it enters the chamber. So, again, why bother with perfectly cast round balls?

All this malarkey about "sprue up" is so much balderwash so far as handguns are concerned. Rifles, it makes a difference, but handguns no, absolutely no.

The revolver I use most is Navy Arms Model 60 in .44 caliber. Twenty-eight grains of FFFg and a Lawrence Brand .45 ball topped off with either Crisco, Vaseline, or water pump grease has done in cactus leaves, knots, lizards, cottontails, jackrabbits, a couple of squirrels, and more rattlesnakes than most people knew existed.

It isn't at all uncommon to put a cylinder of charges into one of those aforementioned playing cards at twenty steps. That's as good as I can shoot any handgun. And there's nothing tricky or special

Jackrabbits are sporting targets because the shots are usually longer. This shoulder shot connected at 46 steps after the first shot, at about 35 steps, missed. The jack stopped again, and it was his last mistake.

about it. Just load up and fire. Do it enough times and you'll do the same thing and chances are a lot sooner than I did.

One thing about black-powder handguns though. I feel jackrabbit killing punch is limited to about 40 yards, 50 if you can keep your shots in the chest, but I prefer the shorter range.

Jackrabbits are tough. I've never seen one give up. They have to be killed, and a round ball spurted out of a short barrel with only 28 grains or so of powder isn't exactly a bear killer.

I know of one Remington replica that's done in a rather large amount of crippled deer. Whitetails. This on a Texas ranch where a good deal of commercial hunting is done. Dogs are used to catch deer that have succeeded in evading the hunter, even though many times they aren't far away at the time. These dogs are trained to trail blood. Naturally, the man running those dogs is the first one on the scene, so he disposes of the deer immediately. And as I said, this one Remington replica has more than taken its share.

Unfortunately, I can't recommend shooting a healthy animal the size of a deer with a black-powder handgun. I'm sure it's been done, and will be done again, but not by me on either count.

Rifles—well now, that's something else. There isn't anything on the face of this earth that can't be killed with a muzzle-loading rifle. That's a mighty definite statement, but it's also mighty true.

The biggest animal I personally have taken with black powder is an American buffalo, bison if you prefer. He wasn't a giant of the species but did weigh about 800 pounds, and it was no contest so far as his getting far or doing much after coming in contact with a 505-grain minié ball.

But let's start off with more common shooting and definitely smaller rifles. Muzzle-loading long guns can be had in about anything from .38's on up to .68's but most popular are the .40's, .44's, .45's, .50's, and .58's. Squirrel rifles, as they were termed, were usually .38 and .40 caliber guns. In my opinion nothing smaller than .45 should be used on small game, other than squirrels and rabbits, and nothing smaller than .50 on deer-sized and up animals.

This is where formalities have to be followed if proficient results are to be achieved. This is where those perfectly molded round balls come into play. This is where "sprue up" means something.

Black-powder rifles, meaning muzzle loaders in this instance, aren't overly particular as to the amounts of powder used for hunting accuracy, but are extremely particular as to how the ball fits and the thickness of patching material employed. The ball goes out of the barrel spinning, or at least it should go out spinning, yet it never touches the rifling. That's what the patch is for.

Shallow-cut barrels utilize thinner patch material than do those cut with deep rifling. In extreme cases it's necessary to go up or down a size or two with the diameter of the ball in order to find the combination of patch material thickness and ball diameter best suited to a given barrel.

I've seen everything from shirt tails to Hoppes cleaning patches used and know one .45 caliber rifle that's killed several head of game using nothing but those Hoppes patches.

What you are looking for here is a patch that fits the ball to the bore so snugly it has to be forced down the barrel. Retrieved patches should not have a hole burned in the center, which means they weren't thick enough; nor should they be in a near black condition, which means they still aren't thick enough but are darned close.

The perfect patch, so I'm told, should have a cross showing where it bore against the rifling. This part should be black, or nearly so. The rest of the patch should be of the original color.

I have to say "I'm told" where this is concerned, because as I said in the beginning, I'm a field shooter and don't go in for some of these finer points. I get the best fit I can out of whatever material is available at the time and don't let it worry me. I figure when I shoot at an animal he's worried, and there is no sense in both of us doing the same thing at the same time.

The patch should be cut round. The aim here is for it to protect the ball from the bore. Lead should touch no place. On the other hand there should be no sloppiness with the cut, as excess material draped over the front of the ball will hinder accuracy, at least a little.

By setting the patched ball only very slightly below the muzzle, then cutting the material with a sharp knife, you'll get a perfect-sized patch every time.

Should you use a dry patch? No! Shooting on a range or plinking where the gun is fired rather rapidly with no great time lapse between shots, do nothing more than wet the material in your mouth, not to a dripping condition but thoroughly moistened. If hunting or loading up when the rifle isn't apt to be fired for a lengthy period, use tallow or one of several commercial products available for this chore. I've often used precut patches soaked in melted beeswax. It works perfectly for me.

In seating balls against the powder at least two steps are necessary. I normally use three. First there is the very short starter. This is merely an extremely short length of dowel, same diameter as the ramrod, imbedded in a square block of wood so that about one quarter inch or a bit less protrudes. Its sole aim is to set the patched ball slightly below the muzzle for patch-cutting purposes.

Next use a four- or five-inch length of the same dowel imbedded in another side of the same block of wood. The purpose of this short starter is to get the ball down in the barrel so the ramrod can be used. From here, seat the ball with a firm motion without ramming it against the powder so hard as to crush granules. Most often it will take two efforts to get the ball seated, but do it in a single motion if possible.

Now, and I think all muzzle loader shooters agree on this point, permanently mark the ramrod at the edge of the muzzle. Do this with the ball seated firmly against the powder. Every time the rifle is loaded, from that point on, refer to this fully seated mark. If it isn't flush with the muzzle you know the ball isn't all the way down and is in a dangerous position. The ball *has* to be seated against the powder firmly to be safe.

Almost as important, though not at all dangerous in any manner, the marked ramrod tells when powder has failed to be poured in ahead of the ball. If the mark disappears down the gullet of the barrel it immediately shows another problem is at hand.

Without any powder under the ball, it is there to stay until brought out forcibly by hand *except* when a man makes the effort to slowly and painstakingly dribble dust from the bottom of his flask, or better yet a little FFFFg, through the tiny nipple hole. Sometimes it's necessary to remove the nipple for this. Most of the time enough powder can be sneaked in behind the ball to shove it out the barrel. If not, the gun either has to be dismantled so the ball can be pushed on through or a worm used to pull it out from the front.

One note of caution here. If the small amount of powder dribbled in through the nipple doesn't get the ball out and you want to try again, go ahead. Add more powder for this second attempt then *push the ball down against the powder again before firing.* If you don't do this, a burst barrel will surely occur and maybe even injury to yourself. Take no chances. Make sure the ball is firmly seated against the powder before attempting to fire.

How much powder should be used? Ask half a dozen guys and get half a dozen answers. Several old formulas exist. One said to load one grain of powder for each caliber. This was primarily squirrel, or Kentucky, rifle data. It means 40 grains of powder for a .40 caliber rifle.

Percussion rifles in the .44 class and up should be loaded, according to some writings, with the lightest load that will get the ball to the target. Others said to put a ball on the palm of the hand and cover it with powder. The proper charge would barely cover the ball. Still others—and it's to this school of thought I subscribe—say there ought to be enough powder in the charge to make the gun "crack" when it is fired.

Paper-punchers might do all right with extremely light loads, loads that barely get the ball to the target. Hunters, plinkers, anybody shooting in the field at various and unknown ranges need their rifles to speak with a bit more authority, a good deal more authority in my opinion.

I start off .44 and .45 caliber percussion rifles with 60 or 65 grains of FFg. I say "start" because that's exactly what I mean. I have one .45 that does a beautiful job with 70 grains. Another seems to do as well with 65. None do I ask to perform with less than the mentioned starting figures.

A recommended load for one popular .50 caliber front loader is 65 grains of FFg. Even some paper-punching friends found this too light and upped it 15 grains. Using the same rifle in the field, I ended up going to 110 grains of FFg but finally settled on an even 100-grain load. Using perfectly molded balls that weighed 172 grains, patched with the tail of a khaki shirt, this load will consistently hit football-size targets at 125 measured yards. And it gets there with enough oomph to make any animal hit smart a little.

I'm not recommending overloading. I am recommending shooting full loads, charges that can be depended on to put a ball up to, into, and even through a live target, charges that turn a front-loading rifle into a real hunting arm.

There is nothing dangerous with this approach. Of course, no one in his right mind would set out to attempt such a feat with an original firearm without thoroughly going over the gun to make sure it was in first-class shooting condition. My data, for rifles and handguns, has all been obtained through the use of replicas. I feel, at least in most instances, that replicas are probably stronger than the originals they duplicate.

I tend to go by sound and feel a good deal of the time in arriving at a load for a rifle. If recoil is lacking and a more or less dull, lifeless sound creeps forth from the muzzle, the whole thing leaves me very cold. I want my rifles to snap back against my shoulder and crack like something had just happened and was going to happen again farther out.

A good example is my big .58 caliber Buffalo Hunter. As I recall, accompanying directions mumbled something about 65 grains of FFg under the 505-grain minié. I actually tried a shot loaded that way. One shot. Then I went to 75 grains, 85 grains, 90, 95, 100, 105, and finally 110 grains of FFg. By then the rifle spoke with real authority on both ends. There were also a lot of sparks flying through the billowing cloud of smoke, so by backing off in 10-grain increments, I finally settled on 90 grains as the most efficient load for my use.

Using 505-grain minié's obtained from Dixie Gun Works (I buy nearly all my round balls and all my minié's from them rather than spend time making them myself), this rifle and load has killed Corsican sheep, Japanese sika deer, American bison (buffalo), whitetail deer, and wild hogs. And when I say killed, I mean exactly that. When 505 grains of lead propelled forward by 90 grains of FFg hits bone and flesh, the result is somewhat devastating. I've often made the statement that an animal can only be killed dead, but this big bruiser does even more than that.

I hate reminiscence, mine or someone else's, but I have to go back to one outstanding instance of total devastation. The shot was maybe 60 yards. The target was a big Japanese sika deer. When he and the 505-grain minié got together, it was as if he were a puppet and his handler suddenly jerked his legs out from under him. I mean, it was instantaneous. At the shot, legs went out, deer went down, and by the time I got to him he was already turning cold. Of course this was several seconds later. In nearly half a century of hunting, I have never seen an animal so instantly and thoroughly clobbered.

Let's talk about velocities a bit. Many folks seem to have the idea

A beautiful Japanese sika deer killed with the .58 Buffalo Hunter.

that muzzle loaders are antiques and, as such, are really antiquated in their results. Could be, but it's hard for me to think of a modern steel rifle or handgun being an "antique" just because it is a replica of a bygone era.

As to antiquated results, did you know 60 grains of FFg under a

.44 caliber rifle ball gets that projectile moving out of the muzzle at over 1,700 feet per second?

I've never made any effort to chronograph black-powder loads, but the trajectory of .50 caliber round balls out of my Thompson/Center Hawken indicates there is a muzzle velocity of around 2,100 to 2,200 feet per second. This is with a round ball weighing 172 grains and 100 grains of FFg. A .30/30 Winchester firing 170-grain bullets starts out at 2,200 feet per second. Need I say more?

Load your rifle until it has a real nice, rather sharp report. When this happens it will also recoil with a bit of a snap, not the usual shove normally associated with muzzle-loading guns. At this stage, unless something is abnormally out of kilter, your rifle will group within six inches at 100 yards. If that isn't hunting accuracy, I'd like to know what is.

Sure I know all about light loads barely getting to the target grouping in two and three inches. Personally I'd much rather double the group, still be within hunting requirements, and have the ball get there the same day I squeeze the trigger.

There is one phase of black-powder muzzle loader shooting that is very neglected. Why is it so few shoot shotguns? These guns can be used even if they are ancient. Have a competent gunsmith, preferably one familiar with black-powder guns, go over the shotgun and correct any faults he might find. From that point on it can be shot comfortably, inexpensively, and with rather fascinating results.

Many of the originals, especially English-made guns, are small-gauge shotguns. Though I've shot both quail and dove with little 32-gauge guns, my real enjoyment is to take a full 12-gauge in the field after those birds as well as pheasants, ducks, and geese.

My theories on muzzle-loading shotgun shooting don't conform to the so-called "standards" in many cases. Loads, yes, but how to assemble them, no. Basically, shotguns are loaded with equal volume of shot and powder. Make or obtain a dipper for one ounce of shot or whatever charge you prefer. Fill the same dipper to the same point with FFg powder for the proper powder charge.

Right now might be a good time to point out that charges can be varied in front-loading shotguns to fit any given situation. If your gun happens to be a 12-gauge, that's what I'd recommend if you have a choice. It means you can load it with full-house 12-gauge loads or down to pipsqueak 20-gauge ⅞-ounce loads, and go right on shooting.

My variance with tradition is in the manner those charges are contained. Purists say the powder should be held in place under pressure from properly designed wads, the wad column about the same thickness as the powder charge and shot charge. If the allotted chamber space was divided into thirds, each would get an equal share: Powder, wad, and shot.

Some say the wads should be cut from hard compressed cardboard. Others seem to think it's best to use fiber wads as used in conventional smokeless powder shells. Now everything is plastic. I've gone the entire route. From newspaper to cardboard to lubricated fiber to plastic wad with shot cup to paper towels.

So help me, and this makes dyed-in-the-wool purists cringe, but I can kill just as many birds with paper towels used as both overpowder and over-shot wad as I can with any of the others. This hasn't been a one-time-around affair either. My first double front loader was a 16-gauge. It killed a good many doves, lots of quail, I haven't the vaguest idea how many cottontails, more than a few ducks, and a couple of geese before I knew something other than newspaper was supposed to be used.

Nowadays I usually take a standard sheet of paper towel and tear it in half. One of these is then torn in half. The larger piece is wadded up and stuffed into the muzzle, then tamped down tight against the powder. After dumping in my shot charge, one of the smaller pieces is then wadded up and stuffed in to hold the shot in place. It may not be the prescribed method, but I guarantee that it works fine.

Black-powder shotguns tend to be a bit choosy, more so than their smokeless-powder offspring. This persnicketyness is about shot size. I normally try loads of Nos. 5–6 and No. 7½'s. One of them will definitely pattern better than the others. I've been known to use No. 4's also but try to stick to one of the aforementioned if at all possible.

Most of these muzzle-loading shotguns have no choke in the barrels, so patterns limit the range to 25 or at the most 30 yards for best results. They are cheap to shoot, a heck of a lot of fun, and more than adequate for bagging the restricted limits we're allowed today.

How are black-powder guns handled in the field? How is the powder and shot carried? What about balls and patching material? Percussion caps?

Normally I carry the caps in the container they arrive in when purchased. Round balls, or minié's, are usually carried loose in the pocket. Sometimes shot is dumped in a hunting coat pocket and sometimes it's kept in a wide-topped bag in a pocket. Powder is best carried in the brass flasks available or a plastic bottle. I have a small plastic container that tapers from about two inches across at the bottom to three quarters of an inch wide at the cap and is maybe five inches tall. It's been on hunts all over the country.

Measuring devices are many and varied. The normal method is to cut the spout of the flask to hold a given charge. If you are like me and get involved with all sorts of charges, spouts become a short item. A .45 Colt case holds 42 grains of powder when scraped level full. A .45 ACP case holds 28 grains. A .38 Special case holds 24 grains. It isn't hard to find a measure for any load you desire. Take the 90-grain charges I shoot in my Navy Arms Buffalo Hunter. At the range I simply pour three heaping .45 ACP casefuls down the barrel and fire away. All sorts of variations can be used.

Hunting, well that's a different matter. Shotguns require dipping, and I've found no way to counteract the procedure that's proven any better. Handguns don't gulp a big charge, so cartridge case measures, dippers, or flask spouts all work equally well. Rifles are single shot and there's always the chance a fast second shot might be necessary.

I combat "the hurrieder I go the behinder I get" feeling by carrying preweighed powder charges in small plastic vials. In this little container I put the ball, a piece of dry patching material already cut to size, and a percussion cap. A wad of cotton separates the powder, which is on the bottom, from the other components. Should a hurried second shot be needed, a vial is grabbed from my pocket, the top flipped off, the patch removed and placed in my mouth for soaking, the ball and cap held in the cup of one hand, the cotton flipped out, the powder poured down the barrel, the patch placed over the bore and the ball placed over it. A sharp blow with a knife butt drives the ball in far enough to get the ramrod started. One hard shove, slip the cap on the nipple, grab another out of my vest pocket if I've dropped the one I started with by then, and fire. A

Swiggett dropped this Corsican ram on the YO Ranch with a chest shot from his Hopkins & Allen Buggy Deluxe .45 carbine. The short barrel makes this a very handy hunting rifle.

few caps are carried loose in my vest pocket while hunting for just this emergency.

This sounds complicated but honestly doesn't take near as long to accomplish as it does to tell about. The main thing is to always keep in mind that too fast means not getting it done at all. A much faster overall time is reached with a slightly slower performing pace. This is one time when haste really makes waste.

I believe anyone can load a handgun cylinder, ready to fire, in a minute and a half, even less with practice. Double-barrel shotguns can be charged and shots fired in far less than a minute. My time runs close to 45 seconds if I really apply myself.

Rifles shooting round balls can be easily done in 30 to 40 seconds. (I believe the military requirement during Civil War days was less than half that.) Minié balls in even less time.

The thing to make sure here is that there are no sparks remaining in the barrel before a fresh charge of powder is poured in. Blow through the barrel first to help relieve this possibility.

Never never load with your head, hand, or any part of your body over the muzzle. Hold the ramrod from the side. Pour from the side. That way, if anything does go wrong, the most that happens is maybe burned fingers or a trip to the laundry.

Now that our guns have all been shot and the true meaning of black powder discovered (I don't know of any other way in the world for a man to get dirtier in less time), how are we going to put them away? Not for a while, believe me.

One of the penalties of enjoying muzzle loaders is having to clean them at the end of each shooting session. This is mandatory. Handguns are easiest. Strip them down to the barrel, cylinder, and frame. Dunk both barrel and cylinder in a pan of hot water and swab them thoroughly, inside and out. Rinse off with the hottest water available and set aside to dry. The hot metal, from all that hot water, will dry almost immediately. Wipe off the frame with a damp cloth, then oil the three parts inside and out with a light oil. Actually I use WD40 for this and have ever since it's been on the market.

Most rifles and shotguns are harder to take down, so I usually pour hot water down the barrels, using a funnel, with the gun upside down and tilted so the water runs out the nipple. Removing this nipple makes a faster job, but it isn't absolutely necessary. When the water starts to run clean, swab the bore thoroughly with a patch

Engraving on an original English 32-gauge double from the Dixie Gun Works.

An Italian 12-gauge replica from the Dixie Gun Works and what Swiggett shoots in it. On this particular hunt he was using plastic wads and 1¼ ounces of No. 7½ shot. This is all the paraphernalia necessary to go hunting with a muzzle-loading shotgun.

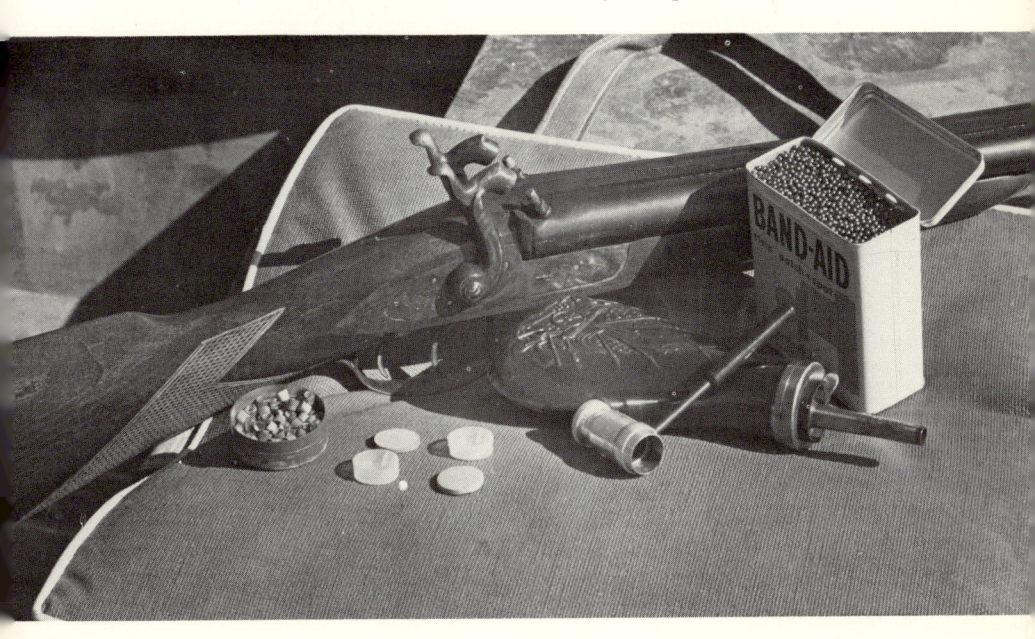

on a cleaning rod. Use several patches and alternate with more hot water. It doesn't take long. Wipe off the outside with a clean, damp cloth. When dry, use WD40 same as on handguns.

I've put guns away cleaned in this manner for months at a time and have had no trouble at all. I check them in a day or so to be sure everything is all right, then forget about it until they are needed again.

Black-powder shooting is a lot of fun, surprisingly inexpensive, and produces rather startling results for the newcomer. Fine sources of information on the subject are available. A book by Major George Nonte entitled *Black Powder* and published as one of the Shooters Bible series can be purchased through any book store. Lyman Reloading Handbooks feature a chapter on front loaders. Probably the best source of all is the Dixie Gun Works, Inc. catalog. Though this publication carries everything Dixie sells and is reissued each year, it is also filled to overflowing with valuable information concerning every phase of black-powder shooting. No shooter of black-powder guns should be without it.

Keep your powder dry and don't wear white shirts while shooting.

40 Yards Is It

KEN WARNER

Ken Warner, Executive Editor of The American Rifleman, *has been writing about guns for twelve years and shooting them for thirty years. In that time he has owned and shot lots of guns and, he says, "written about a few." He has hunted in a dozen states and Canada and has done some shooting in foreign countries, most recently in Finland.*

Warner's thesis in this article was borne out about 100 kilometers from the Arctic Circle in September 1972. Let him tell it: "We were stalking capercaillie when the bird flushed early and gave me a perfect Station 8 shot at 10 yards or so. With my usual class, terrific spotting instinct, and the help of a full-choke pattern, I left that bird to its own pursuits. I know I didn't cut a feather and I am sure I didn't even scare one."

MOST SHOTGUNNERS in the United States throw too much lead too far through too much choke. The fields and marshes are full of 40-yard shooters carrying 50-yard cannons chopping holes in the sky at 60 yards.

And it's all wrong.

We dream the pintail cleanly killed crossing at 50 yards with a tail wind, and we gear up for that job. The thought of reaching that nearly gone pheasant and saving the day with the third shot sells full-choke guns and 12-gauge short Magnum loads.

No matter how good we are—you and I—we tend to short-change ourselves on what really happens. The jumped mallard at 20 yards and the tight-holding pheasant rocketing out at 15 yards should be meat on the table, just one quick shot. It can be done with 281 No. 6 shot bunched up in an 18-inch, 20-yard pattern, but it's a sight better accomplished with a 25-inch circle and 394 No. 7½ shot or even 281 No. 6's spread to 25 inches.

Why is this better? For one, no gunner alive points 'em just right every pop. So if you shoot a combination that slops the pattern wider, you pick up a few points. On days you're dead on with the full choke and the big loads, you pick up a whole lot less bird than you shoot. A really centered tight choke chews up eating meat real bad. An open bore and a moderate load is better.

Reality happens inside 40 yards. Most flying targets taken under sporting conditions fall well inside that magic yardage. That's why shotguns are patterned at that range—it's the normal sporting extreme.

To get to specifics, a calm and rational acceptance of 40 yards as a normal maximum permits a fellow to make comfortable decisions about guns and gauges, loads and shot sizes, and chokes.

Inside 40 yards—and, for normal misjudgments, a little beyond that—the size of the hole in the end of the barrel makes very little difference. The 28 gauge and 410 bore are limiting, it's true. A fellow whose mode of approach or chosen territory consistently gets him more targets beyond 30 yards than closer ought not to shoot the little guns. That's an opinion backed up by simple arithmetic. In practical terms, the numbers seem out favorably whenever the gun will handle an ounce of shot.

There's not much money in arguing about the type of gun, either. For a fellow who started with a Model 97 cornshucker, I'm partial to break-open types, but there are lots of good friends who shoot autoloaders, and for rough and nasty, here-comes-the-salt-spray trips, a pump gun is a comfort to the mind. You know it's going to work, and if it gets a bit battered, you know you're not tearing up $100 bills to prove a point.

A rundown of shotgun types as this writer sees them:

The single shot comes cheap, and it can come high. Whether it's an H & R Topper or a treble-locked engraved European dandy, a break-open single is a joy to carry, offers little recoil problem with sensible cartridges, and is a fast and deadly provider of that first and most important shot. It can be rendered completely and visibly safe at the touch of the top lever. A good single can be made about as pretty as guns get. Taking field chances as they come, a fellow with a single should wind up a season with nearly as many birds in the bag as he would have gathered with a double or repeater.

The double barrel offers all the joys of a single, plus the other shot, and thus considerable added versatility. Depending on the gun, a fellow gets instant choice of chokes or of loads. As a practical matter, two shots handle most situations, though not all.

Whether the barrels are stacked or side by side is a matter of personal taste. There's a case for the over-under as a good choice in double guns for a man raised on repeaters; a fellow's left hand doesn't have to learn a new place to be, and his eyes don't have to get used to a wide-sighting plane. In the field there are some distinct advantages to the side-by-side. It carries more comfortably over the long haul, and its barrels don't need to drop so far to load. No man with lots of experience can call the choice anything but a toss-up or a personal matter.

Either break-open type lets the user change ammunition quickly and quietly. That can be the difference between good and bad in many hunting situations.

The slide action repeater is the All-American shotgun. It was invented here. It is very reliable. In the bad old days, fully loaded slide-actions carrying five rounds or more cut up whole flights of ducks in one long splutter of noise. There are men alive who have seen five mallards taken out of a single bunch on one pass, one shot per duck.

The pump gun requires a certain manual dexterity, best learned early. Some of us work the slide handle on an autoloader, just from habit, disregarding the fact that there is no slide handle! Slide-actions come in all gauges and all flavors, from $80 to expensive. You can have long barrels or short, and in a try for more versatility, you can hang a variable choke device on the barrel.

Slide-actions have some distinct advantages. For instance, they can be carried magazine-loaded without a round in the chamber, yet be ready in a flash. It is fairly simple to render the pump gun completely safe by opening the action part way, a useful arrangement for crossing fences and the like. A fellow can, by dint of *extreme* care, open most loaded slide-action shotguns and change the chambered round without making too much noise. This is nothing like the convenience of the break-open guns, but it can be done.

Above all else, the sound slide-action—at least, any of the big name guns—is reliable. You do your part, and you will get a loud noise each time you pull the trigger.

The autoloader is a joy to them as loves it. Given care, it is reliable. It has to be, or all those skeet shooters are in grievous error. However, it doesn't take an unusual set of circumstances to turn an autoloader into a rather awkward single-shot. A moderate-to-heavy rain often will do it. When remedial action is called for, the auto-

The rewards of staying inside 40 yards—Warner with a banded mallard. Beyond 40 yards he uses the binoculars.

loader offers only a relatively small bolt knob. When loading an empty gun, or unloading a loaded one, that small handle can be stubborn.

Still and all, there has to be a sound reason why the self-shucker is the main game in the shotgun-selling business these days, and there is. The autoloader works as a shooting tool. For someone not raised on a pump gun, it is the only repeater to use. It is a little more expensive, true, but its mechanical operation offers no mysteries to generations that learned the M1, M1 carbine, M14 and M16.

There are two main branches to the autoloader family—recoil-operated and gas-operated. The Browning Auto is the classic recoil machine, while the Remington 1100 is far and away the big gun in the gas-operated ranks. Most recoil-operated guns provide a thump-clack sort of sensation in recoil, while most gaspipes offer a noticeably reduced recoil sensation. A good recoil-operated gun may work better in the rain, but needs some special attention for reliable below-freezing operation. Again, the choice is a toss-up, unless a fellow has a personal taste in the matter.

In the matter of ammunition, the autoloader is the only action that can be called sensitive. All other actions will handle any round of the usual dimension that will slide into the chamber. The autoloader usually has to be set up to handle one or another range of loads. Some models are near universal, and some specimens of any model turn out to be remarkably generous. Most autoloaders insist that reloads, for instance, be neither the slightest bit oversize or very much below a definite power range. You can make any autoloader work at any power range within reason.

With all that said, the autoloader provides three shots while its operator simply points the gun and pulls the trigger. It can be made quite light and responsive. Some states, notably Pennsylvania, legislate against it, but that is only prejudice. The autoloader is another All-American.

So much for guns and gauges. Any safe gun in 12, 16 or 20 gauge will do.

As with most firearms, it's the load that makes the difference. And shotshell loads are pretty confusing. That one 12-gauge shell, a cylinder .80 inch in diameter and about 2½ inches long, comes in an immense array of choices.

Shot load and powder charges are matters of drams and ounces. The dram is a bulk measure once used for black powder. To render smokeless powders intelligible, seventy or more years ago, some ammunition-making genius invented the term "drams equivalent," and it has been used ever since. To render "drams equivalent" intelligible takes a lecture hall and a set of Kodachrome slides, but here goes: When your shotshell says it is loaded with 3¼ drams equivalent, it means that the 20-odd grains (not *granules; grains* is a unit of weight) of smokeless powder in it will produce shot velocities roughly *equivalent* to the velocities 3¼ drams of black powder would produce. For this discussion, we will just say "3-dram" and "3¾ dram." We will speak of the 12-gauge only, the common or garden variety with a 2¾-inch case. We'll try to catch up on the rest before we finish.

Shot comes by the ounce. In the U.S., it comes mostly in over-one-ounce charges.

The 2¾-inch 12-gauge shell you and I purchase—handloads can be anything, of course—comes in powder charges at five levels and shot charges at four levels. However, you can't buy low-pressure loads with heavy charges of shot or high-pressure loads with light charges of shot.

The combinations work out like this in 12 gauge: 2¾ dr.–1⅛ oz.; 3 dr.–1⅛ oz.; 3¼ dr.–1⅛ oz.; 3¼ dr.–1¼ oz.; 3¾ dr.–1¼ oz. Then there's something called "Maximum" variously loaded with 1⅜ oz. or 1½ oz. of shot, or with rifled slugs or buckshot. And sometimes you see 4-dr.–1½ oz. loads, called Magnums—*short* Magnums.

In general, these work out at four levels: Target, Field, High Power, and Short Magnum loads. Target loads have 2¾ or 3 drams of powder. The field load is usually 3¼ drams equivalent and 1⅛ ounces of shot. The loads with 1¼ ounces of shot are the middle ground in the U.S. The fearsome short Magnums are on the high ground at the high prices.

Price gets into this, inevitably. We operate the United States of America under a profit system. The people that load and sell ammunition make profits and they want more. They have found that they go through the same motions to sell a $3.75 box of field loads as a $6.10 box of Magnum duck loads and *it is the motions that cost them money.* Sure, the heavy loads sometimes go into more expensive shell cases, and there is more powder and more shot there. But regardless of its price, every shotshell needs a case, primer, powder charge, wadding, and load of shot. Each, regardless of price, has to be assembled in the same manner. Each must be inspected, counted, packed, and shipped. It costs only a little more to ship the heavy ones. The labor force that does all of this gets the same pay per cartridge, no matter what.

Any red-blooded American capitalist can figure that one out. And at least several did so about four decades ago. For forty years, ammunition makers have been preaching power to the people. The whole campaign has been aimed at increasing the average retail price of those loud and rude noises with which American hunters salute passing legal targets.

Of course, this was all sold as a consumer benefit. Game was getting scarcer and wilder and had to be taken at longer ranges. Packing plenty of punch gradually became part of the game. Of course, 50-yard shooting became the norm. It is true that 50-yard hitting didn't get any more common, but there was plenty of shooting.

This had to be a gradual process at the beginning. Too many men were still alive who knew better. A very common pre-World War I 10-bore load involved 3¼ drams of propellant and 1¼ ounces of shot. Today, you can get nearly that load in a 20-gauge and it is rather low-powered in a 12-gauge. There were many lighter loads for the 10-gauge. And 1⅜ oz. was a big boomer, taking a special heavy gun back at the turn of the century.

Well, on and on it went. We came to believe there is no fun like the 45-to-50-yard clean kill. The joys of a long string of *short-range* clean stops were never touted, except to skeet shooters. And in their tens of thousands, skeet shooters left their skeet guns home when they went hunting. They loaded up with "hunting" shells, too.

There were exceptions. Those who shot over pointing dogs, mostly quail hunters, retained their senses, although there remain, even in the heart of Dixie, gentlemen who wait out a covey rise and get their shots off just as the birds get to the palmetto because they are shooting one barrel marked "Mod" and one marked "Full." One or two worthies of the gun-writing trade admitted early that skeet choking, and skeet loads, worked fine on a wide range of feathered targets. Not many listened.

Overseas, the conservative British didn't change much. Blinded by tradition, they couldn't see that the game was getting harder to kill. They just went right on with their ridiculous 12-bore 2½-inch shell, loaded with a scant 1 1/16 ounce of shot. The game didn't know, either, so the ignorant continued to be killed cleanly by the blind, with lightly loaded guns.

In 1967, at Holland's in London, I stood before a showcase in which secondhand "best" game guns sprouted like weeds, and discussed chamber lengths. Turns out that H & H does not make a practice of opening up 2½-inch chambers to 2¾ inches unless it's a customer's gun. That is, if you buy it, they will, for an additional fee, chamber it longer. But they won't rechamber to sell it to you.

Why not? Well, in the first place, rechambering means a trip to the proof house. In the second place, they can sell about all they have to British who don't want 2¾-inch chambers. In the third place, and very confidentially: "Our standard game load is all you need, you know."

He was right.

Any time we pick up loads heavier than 3 dram–1⅛ ounce, we ought to be expecting some special situations. If it is late in the season, and the cock pheasants are getting up farther out, and heavy coats are getting in the way, a switch to 3¼ dram–1¼ ounce loads will do all any gun can do for the problem. The 3¾ dram–1¼ ounce loads won't add anything, and the short Magnums are ridiculous.

What is a special situation? Much turkey shooting takes a stiff combination. True pass-shooting on ducks and geese is special. Some open-country grouse-shooting combines fairly big birds with only long-range chances at some seasons. Some dove and pigeon shooting is just like pass-shooting wildfowl, except the target is smaller. A lot of sea duck shooting is long-range stuff at physically tough birds. There are others.

Think what that leaves for the inside-40-yards gunner: all wood grouse, woodcock, marsh birds, bobwhite, 90 percent of pheasant hunting, 90 percent of inland duck hunting, and almost all dove shooting. For all of these, an ounce of shot will cut the mustard for anyone willing to admit that a bird 40 yards off and unhit should be left alone.

With this approach, shot selection becomes pretty simple. Anything bigger than No. 5 isn't really necessary, and anything smaller than No. 8 is for special situations, such as early-season quail shot over dogs. Shot size is pretty unimportant in this real world.

I once knew a shotgun, an old Ideal Grade L. C. Smith, that liked No. 1 buck, No. 5, and No. 8 shot. That's all it liked, its owner told me. I patterned it enough to find he was entirely correct. That gun did like No. 1 buck, No. 5 and No. 8 shot, and it did not like the others. In fact, its attitude, as revealed by the patterns, could only be termed stubborn. However, thirty years or so of shooting had not uncovered any weakness in that gun's approach. It was a killer. It killed deer with No. 1 buck, and birds and doves with No. 8's, and everything else with No. 5's. When you missed *you* missed. That gun knew damn well what *it* was doing.

This is by no means an indictment of Nos. 4, 3 and 2 shot, particularly No. 3. There just is no substitute for these sizes on the bigger shotgun game. Personally, I don't think a better gobbler turkey load can be made than one using No. 3 shot. In the right guns, you can make power and pattern come out that will shoot right through a pretty big turkey well beyond 50 yards. The same must be true of big geese, though I have never tried them with No. 3's.

But the point is that for most gunning, smaller shot hit as hard as it takes to get the job done. And the little ones are a whole lot more likely to fill the pattern smoothly.

Mentioning patterns brings up the magic word *choke*. Choke is, after his choice of cartridges, the American gunner's basic mistake. We have learned a great deal, in our one-hundred-year flirtation with choke. You could make a fair case that American gunners have become better shots than they know because of their use of shotguns choked too tightly. If you carry a full-choke gun, you are handicapping yourself, and much gun-pointing that would provide a clean kill with a cylinder bore or improved cylinder choke is a miss or a fringe hit with the full choke.

There's another case to be made concerning this obsession with long-range results: We put together truly remarkable shotshells, both in our factories and at our own reloading benches. We also tailor these to individual gun barrels—and tailor some gun barrels —in remarkable fashion. There really are men in these fifty states who can make shotguns deliver the 85 percent patterns at 40 yards it takes to get 50 percent patterns out at 60 yards.

There are also remarkably fine long-range shots out there. We have all known one or two blue-eyed mountaineer types or farmboys that grew up with one long-barreled, full-choke 12-gauge. Those are the fellows who stop to check the weather when a pheasant gets up, and then, very precisely, pick him off out there at 40-to-50 yards. On ducks, these fellows are deadly beyond belief. They'll give it a go on any target within earshot, it seems, and hit an awful lot of them. More than once, in my own experience, I have fired one shot, even two, at a bird, decided he's gone and begun to bring the gun down, and thereupon watched some galoot finally shoot and kill that out-of-range bird dead as hell.

I knew an old fellow once long past his shooting years. He had given up goose hunting when they made live decoys illegal. He was a great gentleman who had shot one Remington Browning patent autoloader for forty years. It had a trap barrel regulated for No. 7½ and that is all he used. His name was Art Henneman.

I saw him shoot that gun exactly twice—two shots. He was in his seventies, and hadn't done any gunning in ten years or so. We were standing where we could see doves trading around in a grove of citrus trees. They would pop up out of those twenty-foot high trees, get a little height and head for water as only a dove can. We were on a platform maybe five feet high.

We convinced Art he ought to try a shot. We had been patterning his gun out of curiosity. It sure did shoot No. 7½ shot. Art somewhat reluctantly took the gun, and we all stood there, waiting for the right dove. Up he came, a long way out. We were facing south and he was headed west in a hurry. He had just about got up a full head of steam when Art shot and missed. Instantly, Art shot again and the dove tumbled, dead in the air at every bit of 50 yards, and likely more.

Art turned to us and said, in honest wonder, "You know, I shot behind him the first shot. That was darn poor shooting. I'm sorry."

That, gentlemen, is a long-range shooter, and he is a rarer bird than ever he shot. It's time for the rest of us to admit it.

All right. If not a full choke, what? Do we go all the way to basics and a cylinder choke? No choke at all? Or somewhere in between?

Well, cylinder is better than full, but improved cylinder makes a lot of sense. There has been a lot of talk about modified as an all-round choke. But why be half safe? The idea is to get your pattern wide as quick as possible so you won't tear up the target *really* close, and then hold the killing pattern to 40 yards. That's all.

So, you're shooting 1⅛ ounces of shot and you're getting 50 percent at 40 yards. With No. 7½, you get a 30-inch circle with nearly 200 shot in it. With No. 6, the circle holds 125 shot. And No. 5's give you about 100 shot. By the standards worked out by shotgun-wise men, that's enough shot to do the job, reserving the 5's and 6's for the bigger targets. Big loads of big shot are for big birds at big yardage.

There's a bonus in a relatively open bore. It seems obvious enough. If your gun puts 50 percent of its shot load in a 30-inch circle at 40 yards, then it puts 50 percent of the shot *outside* a 30-inch circle at 40 yards. Some of that stays close enough to count on the target. The 30-inch circle is only a convention, an agreed and universal measuring stick. The killing pattern is bigger than 30 inches. Every shotgun pattern fringes out and becomes ineffective around the edges, but the open chokes don't seem to deteriorate so quickly. It is only out toward the edges of the 48-inch paper used in patterning that a good improved cylinder pattern thins to ineffectiveness.

What does a good pattern look like? Smooth. A good full choke —one meant for the long chances—is heavy in the center, and the heavier the better. But an open choke should be uniform, with shot regularly scattered across the whole circle. If your fisted hand can be placed on the circle in six or seven places without hiding some shot holes, you ought to try another load.

Shotguns are immensely variable and often respond to a change of brand, even without a change of load. Going from Remington to Winchester or vice-versa can do the trick. If 3-dram loads don't pattern smoothly, try 2¾-dram loads, and then 3¼ drams.

If you bother to pattern your gun, do a good job. That means big pieces of paper and lots of them. Five shots will only give you an idea about a given load and barrel. Ten are pretty good. Even if you fire twenty patterns, your calculated percentages can be as much as 5 percent off for any one succeeding shot. So it is perhaps as well to shoot five and examine those patterns carefully for smoothness, and calculate the percentages as a rough guide.

There's no point in getting all fussed in the head over patterns. The idea is to kill birds flying, and not blame the gun or the shells when you miss. Shotgunning is more art than science, particularly inside 40 yards. And a 50 percent pattern is a good tool for the work.

There's no point in a treatise here on gun-handling or lead or any of that. The same goes for gun fit. Unless a gun is wildly out of line with factory specifications, the average American can shoot it. He can shoot it better if it fits well, but he can shoot it, almost regardless.

There is much written about gun fit. Fit is a function of pull length, drop at comb and heel, pitch, and the configuration of the stock grip. There is also much discussion of *cast*. *Cast* can be defined by a cynic as *crooked*. It refers to the distance the vertical center line of the buttplate is to the right or left of the center of the barrel or barrels. Cast-*off* means the stock crooks to the right; cast-*on* means it crooks to the left. Right-handers use cast-off; southpaws cast-on.

The British are very big on cast in gunstocks. A showcase full of British game guns looks like a lot of warped wood to an unspoiled American eye. The intended effect of cast, *proper* cast, whatever that may be, is to permit a relatively erect head position while the butt is seated properly in the hollow of the shoulder. It also makes the gun jump funny, and most Americans have to train themselves to use a gun with a cast. A typical right-handed Yankee, even one that drawls, will throw that crooked gun up and find himself looking along the right side of the right barrel.

A proper fitting, British style, includes shooting with a try gun. The fitter watches the fittee, giving him hints on "style" and changing the adjustable try-gun stock until, between the coaching and the dimension changes, the fittee is putting the charge in the right place.

A gun-fitter can, if he tries hard, come very close at the first try. How much of the subsequent fussing is required, and how much is salesmanship, depends on the fitter. It is true that a properly capitalized fellow who simply can't make it to the shooting ground gets fitted in the showroom. After all, if a man with a full lifetime of teaching and fitting experience can't do a fair job without the full-dress rehearsal, he's not been paying attention.

This writer had the showroom fit, once, try gun and all. The fitter was the managing director of a firm that makes best guns. I kept mounting and pointing the gun for him while he changed dimensions. We talked a lot about how I thought I shot and what sort of birds and action I saw. He got the length and drop with one adjustment. One more try and he had the pitch set up properly. Then, rapidly, he adjusted the cast back and forth, seeking the magic crook.

The fitting ended when he said, "Why, you shoot a dead straight gun!"

Damn right. So do most of us. If an American didn't shoot a dead straight gun, he wouldn't shoot. If you start at age twelve with a U.S. product, you start with a dead straight gun. If you shoot dead straight guns for twenty-five years, you are then guaranteed to give the managing director of a London gun maker a fit at your fitting.

And does your shooting suffer? Not a helluva lot. Some of the finest game shots in the world are British, but they're a long way from having a monopoly on shooting class. I remember one tall Southern fellow—he had maybe twenty-five years of Arkansas-Louisiana duck shooting behind him—who was provided with a gun and about seventeen minutes of flighted mallards on an estate over yonder. He killed 38 or 39 ducks with a dead straight gun.

Read a book and fiddle with your gun's pull length, comb height, and pitch and then go out and shoot it plenty with sensible loads at sensible ranges. Give yourself the best break with an open bore. You'll do all right.

Once you discover that this really works, you can get a bonus from an old rule of thumb. Over the generations, a gun weight of 100 times the shot-charge weight has been considered about the minimum for a nonkicking shotgun. If your Betsy runs something like 7½ pounds, as a great many American Betsys do, there's your bonus: she is a pleasure to shoot with 1⅛ oz. of shot.

Now, that works the other way around, too. That is, if you have determined that 1⅛ oz. is the maximum you need, then you can probably get a lighter gun. In fact, you can probably shade 7 pounds by several ounces and still shoot in shirtsleeves.

Where do you get these light loads? All the ammunition makers load them. Skeet loads in No. 8 and No. 9 are available in 2¾ dram–1⅛-ounce and 3 dram–1⅛-ounce charges. Winchester has a series called "Upland," and you can get Nos. 4, 5, 6, and 8 in these 3 dram–1⅛-ounce loadings. There is a 3¼ dram–1⅛-ounce load on the market. Remington-Peters has the same 3 dram–1⅛-ounce loads, and calls them Victor and Shurshot. S & W–Fiocchi have a 3 dram–1-ounce load in Nos. 6 and 8 shot, a sensible selection. And, of course, any loading manual provides directions for assembling similar loads.

That's how those foreigners get away with their skimpy doubles, by the way. If you're not loaded for bear, you don't need a bear gun. The real bonus in gearing up for reality for birds way inside 40 yards is that your poor soft muscles, your old and tired tendons, don't have to carry that big club around any more. The difference between a 7½-pound gun and a 6½-pound gun is about four hours for the average fellow, and as many as six for us real sloths.

All the intelligent and dedicated hunting writers in the world can tell us how to condition our bodies, but the world remains divided into a heavy majority of softies and a minimum of guys in good shape. If you are dedicated, you don't need physical training advice; if you are normal, you won't take it. That means, in practical terms, that a fellow whose legs will carry him, adequately if not joyfully, through a full day in the field has arms that start to protest about 10:00 A.M. By noon, he's in trouble. If he gets some shooting after a mid-day rest, and does well, he might make the end of the day, but chances are he'll be missing shots all afternoon.

The chap taking the lightweight, though, he might very well remain in comfort all day long. If that sounds like a contradiction, consider: We all handle some weight every working day, so we can handle *some* weight all day out in the fields. Then, a gun that goes 7½ pounds carries a lot of that up forward, which means that aside from any problems involved during a shot, all day long a pound or so is being swung around at the end of a 30-inch stick by your wrists and forearms. An engineer can figure that out in foot-pounds, I suppose, but a guy who has been carrying such a gun for six hours or so knows all he needs to know.

It might well be that a 20-gauge or a 16 might be easier to find at the right weight. Remington has lightweight autoloaders and slide-actions in the 20-bore; the good Browning Sweet 16 is around in quantity. A fellow would make a mistake, though, if he tried to make up for the size of these bores by using whopper loads. An ounce of shot really doesn't care what size hole it comes out of, despite the theory.

The Germans, when they get down to serious patterning, do a bang-up job. One of the things they talk about is the "best range," which for a given load and barrel is that range at which the pattern is as big as it gets before the ineffective fringes increase markedly. It almost always works out for open bores at pretty close to 30 meters, or about 33 yards. (And you'd be surprised at how it works out for most full chokes—a good long way short of 50 yards.) The pattern is effective beyond the best range, but it is deteriorating.

O.K., that's about all there is to say. Very few of us, in the bulk of our shotgunning, get enough over-40-yard chances to be good at them, and certainly we shouldn't carry the specialized equipment it takes to be good at them. Most of us kill what we kill inside 30 yards. And for that work, an open bore and a modest charge of No. 5's and up—mostly up—is the best choice.

With that settled, if we want, we can go to lighter guns and get on the birds a little quicker, even at the end of the day. We'll do better on the close ones, too.

It all rests firmly on a proposition U.S. shooters are determined to deny: the shotgun is a short-range gun. That's worth repeating: *the shotgun is a short-range gun.* Treat yours as such an arm, and figure that 40 yards is it, and you can find gunning satisfaction quicker than by any other route.

Shooting the Old Winchesters and Marlins

KEN WATERS

As a boy on a New York State farm and in a Connecticut small town Ken Waters was brought up on guns, and he has managed to keep shooting, hunting, and collecting central to his life ever since. His marksmanship earned him a sniper assignment during World War II, and after the war he devoted ten years of intensive study to just about all phases of shooting, especially ballistics and the reloading of metallic cartridges. He has been a competitor and instructor in both rifle and pistol shooting, and currently he captains an active auxiliary police unit—his men are required to be armed when on duty, and they know how to use their weapons.

Having been a writer of technical articles for various publications, it was only natural that Waters would eventually come to writing about his favorite subjects. He considers his mentors in the shooting-writing game to be Maj. Ned Roberts and Col. Townsend Whelen, and he and Roberts co-authored the book The Breech-Loading Single Shot Match Rifle. For many years his hobby has been the collecting —and shooting—of the older cartridge rifles, especially the 1870-1910 single-shots and lever-actions (he still owns the big octagonal-barreled 1886 Winchester .45/70 that bagged him his first deer). Waters is "Pet Loads" Editor of The Handloader.

GUN COLLECTORS and shooters need not be separate entities. Depending upon the type and condition of firearms collected, a hobbyist can often materially increase the enjoyment of his collection by getting out and shooting the old pieces. By using modern ammunition components, this can be done safely without detracting from the value of a specimen.

Of course, whether a collection piece is suitable for firing depends on age, design, material from which the arm was fabricated, and condition. We will therefore limit this discussion to a manageable group, with well-known characteristics, suitable for practical hunting

Shooting the Old Winchesters and Marlins

and target practice. Reference here then is to Winchester rifles of Models 1873 through 1895, and certain models of Marlin repeating rifles introduced between 1881 and 1895.

Probably no other single classification of discontinued non-military firearm is collected in larger numbers or more frequently fired. Although the earliest are now nearly one hundred years old, a sizable percentage are still usable. Assuming the bore is in decent condition and the action is not overly loose from excessive use (or abuse), accuracy will generally be adequate for hunting at typical woods ranges of a hundred yards or less. Those calibers for which new factory ammunition is still available are deliberately loaded to levels that render them safe in arms in good condition, and with the exercise of reasonable precautions dictated by a consideration of design and material characteristics, handloaders can readily prepare safe and accurate custom loads.

Those two words—"safe" and "accurate"—are the keys to success in reloading for the older rifles. These rifles were originally designed (with certain exceptions) for black-powder cartridges; the reloader must, herefore, remain constantly aware of pressure limitations, particularly in the Winchester Models 1873 and 1876, with their link-supported breech bolts.

Smokeless powders generate vastly higher pressures, with potentially disastrous results, leaving no room for the sloppy or reckless reloader. A clear understanding of the most likely causes of increased pressure is imperative. Too much powder, especially the quick-burning types, is the primary source of trouble, as it is with modern cartridges. But because you will frequently be using powders

A superb example of an original Model 1873 Winchester in deluxe grade with pistol-grip stock. All too rarely found today in this condition, such a rifle would almost certainly prove to be a good shooting piece.

having a faster burning rate in the older calibers, you must be especially watchful. Above all, be alert for double charges! With our dense modern smokeless powders, they're quite possible in many of yesterday's big-capacity cases, and they're deadly to both gun and shooter.

A logical question then is, why use such powders? Why not stick with the bulkier, slower-burning powders we've become used to with our modern rifles? In *some* cases we can, and wherever practicable I'll note that as we take up the various cartridges. But in general, it is important to recognize certain facts concerning propellant combustion:

First and foremost is that pressure affects powder burning. The lower the pressure, the more difficult it becomes to induce proper burning. Likewise, slower powder is more reluctant to burn well within straight-walled cases. And, of course, the larger the case and bore, the more this condition is aggravated. With accuracy so vitally dependent upon uniformity of conditions from shot to shot, it becomes obvious that consistency in ignition *must* be achieved. With most of the relatively mild loads of fast-to-medium-burning powders suited to these old rifles, "standard" rifle primers are perfectly adequate in furnishing that sought-after consistency. In fact, old hands at this cast bullet game long ago learned that mild primers gave *superior* accuracy with small charges of fast-burning smokeless. Even in big cases, it is seldom necessary to go beyond the "hot" W-W No. 120–8½ standard Large Rifle primers, and I've utilized Magnum primers only in those instances where a really slow-burning powder has been used.

So in reloading the old cartridges with smokeless powder, one encounters a strange paradox: too *low* pressures have to be guarded against almost as diligently as too high, even though not for the same reason. All of which serves to point up what should be our twin objectives: reasonable pressures and the best possible accuracy. Velocity will remain definitely secondary, mostly because these rifles won't tolerate the sort of pressures necessary to generate high muzzle speeds, but also because they aren't needed with the big heavy bullets.

Other factors affecting pressures are bullet size, weight, and degree of hardness. Undersize bullets are a waste of time and powder, and invariably prove inaccurate. Smokeless powder doesn't "upset" bullets to fill the rifling as black powder did. Best start by "slugging and miking" your rifle's bore to determine its actual groove diameter. The writer's experience has always been that while jacketed bullets should be the same diameter as the barrel grooves, cast bullets will deliver their best accuracy when sized from .001 inch to not more than .003 inch *larger* than groove diameter. A tight-fitting bullet, although it increases pressures somewhat, improves combustion, reduces gas cutting, and provides for a firm non-slip grip of rifling on bullet.

In big-bore, low-velocity cartridges, small variations of bullet weight have less effect on pressure than would occur with modern high-velocity rounds, and this can be readily equalized by making small changes in the powder charge. The tolerance of these old cartridges, some of which accurately handle bullets differing as much as 100 to 150 grains in weight (depending upon caliber), is truly amazing. As a rule though, start by selecting a bullet weighing close to the original factory load, to make sure that it matches the rate of rifling twist, and thus insure bullet stability. This is especially true of the so-called "Express" calibers, which used lighter-than-standard bullets in slower-twist rifling for increased velocity. Such barrels may refuse to stabilize bullets that are materially heavier.

I might note here, however, that the safest way to increase velocities with the old-timers is by reducing bullet weight. This helps to compensate for increases in charge when it is desired to up bullet speed by a couple of hundred feet per second without boosting chamber pressures. But don't expect phenomenal increases. Quite often such reasonable increases can be accomplished with little if any loss of accuracy.

In speaking of bullet hardness, the reference, of course, is to cast bullets. Here, two rules-of-thumb apply: Smokeless powder burns hotter than the old black, calling for a harder bullet alloy; the faster bullets are to be driven, the harder they should be. Cast bullets that are too soft have a tendency to "slug" or "jug" in the barrel, raising pressures and damaging accuracy. For this reason, I prefer alloys ranging from 1 to 15 (or 16) to 1 to 20 tin and lead with smokeless powder in the old rifles. If muzzle velocities will be above 1,500 f.p.s, I frequently cast them still harder, say, 1 to 10. Beyond 1,700–1,800 f.p.s., apply gas check cups to protect their base from distortion.

The velocities commonly attained with most of the old calibers do not require jacketed bullets. Cast bullets are far less costly, easier on barrels and, in the larger calibers (.32 an over), fully as accurate *provided* they are properly cast, inspected, sized, and lubricated. Years of experience have taught us that a well-made cast bullet, correctly loaded, can perform wonderfully, but by the same token, poor ones give results that are horrible to behold.

For this reason, I usually recommend that a shooter taking up bullet casting, or when testing a newly acquired rifle for accuracy, first run trials with jacketed bullets where they are available in the proper diameter. This method gives a good idea of what that particular rifle is capable of in the way of grouping, and the shooter knows what he has to work towards. If, we'll say, he is getting 2-inch groups of 5 shots with jacketed bullets, and his first attempt with cast bullets results in 4–5-inch groups, he shouldn't give up on the rifle (or cast bullets), because he knows that they can be made to do better.

About this time I can hear shrieks of protest coming from our collector friends at the suggestion of using jacketed bullets in the old soft-steel barrels, so let me take a minute to air my thoughts on this subject. I'm well acquainted with all the old wives' tales concerning how ruinous jacketed bullets are to mild steel bores, but I'm not about to buy all of it. Sure, there are some rifles that have been shot so many thousands of times by generations of shooters that their rifling has been literally worn away. But an old rifle with pitted and eroded bore is actually the result of corrosive primers combined with improper care and cleaning. It *wasn't* the bullets, nor in most cases was it due to smokeless powder!

This doesn't mean that I'm advocating the unlimited use of jacketed bullets; far from it, because barrels *can* be worn out. But here I'm not talking about continual usage or frequent strings of rapid fire, which should of course be avoided with old rifles. All I'm saying is that the soft copper jackets of bullets such as the .44/40, fired at low velocities with relatively small charges of powder, are not the villains they've so often been made out to be. With the curse of corrosive primers a thing of the past, and without the strongly erosive effects of high heat such as our modern high-velocity rifle barrels have to contend with, there is no reason under the sun why a few shots with jacketed bullets can't be fired now and then

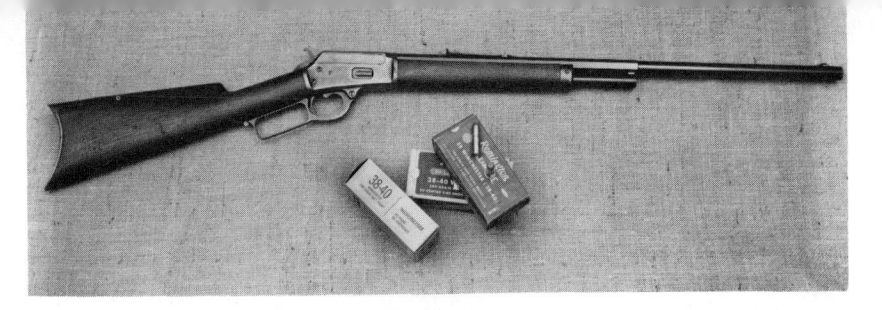

One of the seldom-seen Model 1889 Marlin rifles, this one in .38/40 Winchester caliber. The Model 1889 was the first Marlin to incorporate the now-familiar closed-top receiver with side ejection.

without in any way damaging a fine barrel. I've done it for over thirty years now and haven't lost a barrel yet.

Jacketed bullets can prove useful in still another way. Suppose your eighty-year-old rifle already has a bore roughened by pitting and erosion. I've known many instances where such a barrel will still show surprising accuracy with jacketed bullets while refusing to group cast slugs. In that case, the use of jacketed bullets gets a few more years out of the old barrel.

Before leaving the subject of bullets, I must repeat the often-aired warning that *only* flat-nosed bullets or those with extremely blunt round-noses should be used in tubular magazine repeating rifles because of the obvious danger of settting off the primer of a cartridge in the magazine if sharp-pointed bullets are loaded one ahead of the other. All of the rifles in the groups we have chosen to cover save two (the Winchester Single Shot and Model 1895 repeaters) have tubular magazines, so this warning is appropriate. Be sure to heed it!

The availability of specific components will be covered as we take up each cartridge, but I'm happy to report that, in general, the supply situation is still quite good. A fair number of the cartridges are offered as fresh new factory ammunition, either domestic or imports, and of those that have been discontinued, almost all can be formed from certain basic calibers of either primed or un-primed empty brass cases. Incidentally, this reforming of new brass is decidedly preferable to using old original ammunition of uncertain age and priming composition which may well be brittle enough to cause case head separations and/or bore erosion. Whatever else you may do, *don't* use cartridges or cases showing signs of corrosion; that's just asking for trouble.

Between them, RCBS and Lyman produce forming dies that will, with a single pass (or at most two), form the odd cases from standard sizes I'll be recommending further along. In this process, cases are given only a very light coating of case lubricant to avoid oil dents. Any necessary procedural instructions, including an indication as to whether trimming is needed, will be included with loading instructions for each cartridge.

Finally, there's the matter of equipment. The first requirement is a bench-type reloading press with sufficient leverage to reform and full-length resize cases. These are not the cheapest of tools, but over the long run you'll be glad you spent the extra dough for a stronger, easier working press with greater mechanical advantage, such as the RCBS "Rockchucker" or Pacific Multi-Power. If you'll be loading only low-pressure rounds where case expansion is minimal, you can get away with one of the original "tong-type" hand tools, which can still be picked up occasionally at some gun shops, but they aren't capable of full-length resizing.

A good powder measure is a real convenience, but an accurate scale is a *must*. You'll also want a case trimmer and one of the little inside-outside chamfering tools to prepare and maintain cases at proper lengths. If money is a problem, this work *can* be done with nothing more than a hacksaw and file, but the effort and time saved with the specialized equipment makes the additional expenditure well worthwhile. Some way of measuring case lengths will be necessary, whether it be a gauge or micrometer calipers.

If bullets are to be cast, tooling expenses increase considerably. A bullet mould will of course be required for each caliber, although one set of handles can be made to do for several moulds. Both Lyman and Ohaus make excellent moulds, far better, in fact, than any of the original moulds I've ever worked with. Today, they're properly vented and cast bullets that come closer to being perfectly round, thus requiring less sizing to true them up. In ordering a mould, be sure to specify the exact size you wish the cast bullets to be, allowing for the reduction brought about by sizing.

While its entirely possible to fire bullets "as-cast"—that is, without sizing—by standing them in a shallow pan of melted lubricant and using a "Kake-Kutter" to remove the excess, reloaders striving for the best possible accuracy will want to size their bullets. This can be done with considerable precision, simultaneously lubricating

Three examples of the old Ideal tong-type reloading tools. At top, a tool with double-adjustable chamber for the .32/40 cartridge. In the middle, another with single-adjustable chamber for the .405 Winchester. At the bottom, a tool with nonadjustable chamber, but incorporating a bullet mold, for the .38/55 cartridge. These tools still function perfectly but have the disadvantage of not being able to full-length-resize cases.

Waters' Model 1894 Winchester test rifle in .32-.40 caliber with full-round barrel and perfect bore. Fred Huntington's RCBS precision-made handloading dies deserve much of the credit for producing accurate handloads.

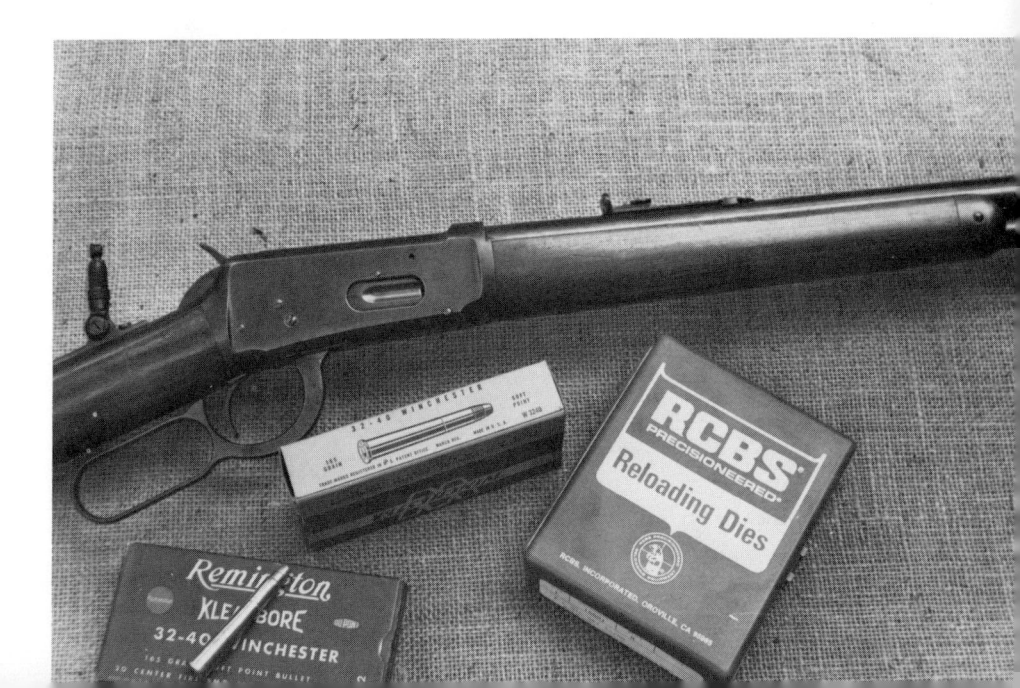

them without mess or additional time spent, by using one of the modern bullet-sizing and lubricating presses with sizing dies that swage bullets to the desired diameter rather than shaving them, as was formerly done. Lyman's No. 450 Lubricator and Sizer is probably tops in this field, together with the appropriate dies they produce in a myriad of sizes.

Our ancestors devoted a great deal of time and effort experimenting with various forms of bullet lubricants. Today, you'll do better to simply use one of the commercial lubricants, either the time-tested Lyman lubricant or one of the newer brands containing Alox.

For melting the lead alloy, you'll need a suitable lead pot, and here again if money is a prime consideration you can use a plain iron lead pot on top of the kitchen range, though the fumes and smoke that result may place your marriage in jeopardy. Better—and decidedly safer—is a separate pot with its own heating element, either electric or gas-fired. If it includes a thermostatic control holding the lead at an even, predetermined temperature, so much the better, though admittedly more costly.

And now we're ready to take up the specific application of all this advice as it pertains to preparing safe, accurate, and effective handloaded smokeless powder ammunition for the older models of Winchester and Marlin rifles. One final cautionary note, however: As a well-known ad urges, "Leave the driving to us," so I suggest that readers not undertake to do their own experimenting. Let me risk *my* rifles and *my* neck so you won't have to. Do *not* increase loads beyond charges listed here or in reliable reloading manuals. And please remember that neither the publisher nor myself can accept any responsibility for loads that *you* assemble!

.25/20 Winchester

Adapted to Winchester Model 1892 and Marlin Model 1894 rifles.
Original Ballistics:
  (1) Standard Load —86-gr. Lead bullets —M.V. 1,376 f.p.s. @ 20–22,000 p.s.i.
  (2) Old H.V. Load—86-gr. Soft-point —M.V. 1,712 f.p.s. @ 27–30,000 p.s.i.
  (3) 1929 H-S Load —60-gr. Hollow-point—M.V. 2,200 f.p.s.

Factory ammunition currently available with 86-gr. lead or soft-point bullets.

Present Ballistics: 86-gr. Lead or S.P.—M.V. 1,460 f.p.s. (No H.V. loads).
Components available: New empty cases and 86-gr lead or soft-point bullets; also, 60-gr. hollow-points.
Bullet Moulds: (a) Lyman 67-gr. (#257420) and 89-gr. (#257312)
 (b) Ohaus 70-gr. (#25070F) and 90-gr. (#25090F)
Bullet Diameters: Jacketed .257 inch; Cast .258 inch

(Reloading Data)

68-gr. Ohaus G.C. #25070F—9.0 #4227—1,650 f.p.s.
67-gr. Lyman G.C. #257420— 4.6 Unique—1,510 f.p.s. Small game.
89-gr. Lyman G.C. #257312— 4.7 Unique—1,467 f.p.s. Small game.
89-gr. Lyman G.C. #257312— 8.8 #2400 —1,708 f.p.s. Target load.
86-gr. Remington Soft-point —11.6 #4198 —1,489 f.p.s. Target load.
86-gr. Remington Soft-point — 9.5 #2400 —1,740 f.p.s. Varmint load.
60-gr. Winchester H.P.—10.0 #2400—1,935 f.p.s.

.25/35 Winchester

Adapted to Winchester Model 1885 Single Shot and Model 1894 repeating rifles
Original Ballistics:
 (1) Standard Load —117-gr. Soft-point   —M.V. 1,978 f.p.s. @ 32–34,000 psi
 (2) 1929 Express —117-gr. Hollow-point—M.V. 2,350 f.p.s.
 (3) 1929 Hi-Speed — 87-gr. Hollow-point—M.V. 2,700 f.p.s.
Factory ammunition currently available with 117-gr. Soft-points only.
Present Ballistics: 117-gr. Soft-point—M.V. 2300 f.p.s.
Components available: New empty cases and 117-gr. Soft-point.
Bullet Moulds:
(#257231)

(b) Ohaus 90-gr. (#25090F)

Bullet Diameters: Jacketed .257 inch; Cast .258 inch.

(Reloading Data)

89-gr. Lyman G.C. #257312—11.0 #4227—1,550 f.p.s.—Small game and plinking

106-gr. Lyman G.C. #257231—21.0 #4895—2,000 f.p.s.—Target load

117-gr. Winchester Soft Pt. —25.0 #4895—2,265 f.p.s.—Deer load.

.25/36 Marlin

Adapted to Marlin Model 1893 repeating rifles.

Original Ballistics:
  (1) Standard Load—117-gr. Soft-point—M.V. 1,855 f.p.s. @ 30–32,000 p.s.i.

Factory ammunition no longer available.

Components available: 117-gr. (.25/35) Soft-point.

Case Forming: (1) .25/35 Winchester cartridges may be fired in .25/36 Marlin chambers to fire-form (but NOT the reverse)—
  or—(2) Cases can be formed from .30/30 brass sized full-length in .25/36 or .25/35 die and fire-formed.

Bullet Moulds: Same as for .25/35 Winchester.

Bullet Diameters: Jacketed .257 inch; Cast .258 inch

(Reloading Data)

*Use same data as given for .25/35 Winchester.

.32/20 Winchester

Adapted to Winchester Model 1873 and 1892 repeating rifles, Model 1885 Single Shots, and Marlin Models 1888, 1889, and 1894.

Original Ballistics:
  (1) Standard Load —115-gr. Lead —M.V. 1,222 f.p.s. @ 17–19,000 p.s.i.
  (2) Old H.V. Load—115-gr. S.P. —M.V. 1,640 f.p.s. @ 25–28,000 p.s.i.
  (3) 1929 Standard —100-gr. S-P. —M.V. 1,330 f.p.s.
 *(4) 1929 Hi-Speed — 80-gr. H-P. —M.V. 2,000 f.p.s.
    *Note: H.V. and Hi-Speed load must NOT be used in Model 1873 rifles.

Factory ammunition currently available with 100-gr. lead or soft-point bullets may be used in all rifles in good condition chambered for this cartridge.
Present Ballistics: 100-gr. Lead or S.P.—M.V. 1,290 f.p.s. (No H. V. loads)
C.I.L. (Canadian) 115-gr. Soft point —M.V. 1,480 f.p.s.
Components available: New empty cases and 100-gr. lead or S.P. bullets.
Bullet Moulds: (a) Lyman 115-gr. (#3118) and 112-gr. G.C. (#311316).
(b) Ohaus 115-gr. G.C. (#31115F)
Bullet Diameters: Jacketed .310 inch; Cast .311-.312 inch
(Reloading Data)
115-gr. Lyman #3118 — 5.0 Unique —1,385 f.p.s.
—Small game and plinking
115-gr. Lyman #3118 —10.0 #4227 —1,381 f.p.s.
—Target !oad.
112-gr. Lyman G.C. (#311316)—13.0 #4227 —1,744 f.p.s.
—Do NOT use in Model 1873 rifles
100-gr. Remington S.P. — 9.5 #2400 —1,336 f.p.s.
—O.K. for Model 1873
100-gr. Remington S.P. —13.0 #4227 —1,720 f.p.s.
—Do NOT use in Model 1873 Winchester or Model 1888 Marlin rifles.

.32/40 Marlin and Winchester

Adapted to Marlin Models 1881 and 1893; also, Winchester Single Shot and Model 1894 repeating rifles.
Original Ballistics:
(1) Standard Load —165-gr. Lead—M.V. 1,427 f.p.s. @ 17–19,000 p.s.i.
(2) Old H.V. Load —165-gr. S.P. —M.V. 1,752 f.p.s. @ 30–32,000 p.s.i
(3) 1918 Rem. Hi Power—165-gr. S.P. —M.V. 2,065 f.p.s. @ 34–36,000 p.s.i.
(4) Final Factory —165-gr. S.P. —M.V. 1,440 f.p.s.
Only C.I.L. (Canadian) factory ammunition is currently available, with 170-gr. soft-point bullets at M.V. 1,540 f.p.s.
Components available: Winchester, Remington (.320 inch) and Hornady (.321 inch) 170-gr. Soft-point bullets.

Case Forming: Cases can be formed from .32 Winchester Special or .30/30 brass sized full-length in .32/40 die.
Bullet Moulds: (a) Lyman 181-gr. G.C. (#321297) and 151-gr. (#321298).
          (b) Ohaus 170-gr. G.C. (#32170F)
Bullet Diameters: Jacketed .320-21 inch; Cast .322-23 inch
          (Reloading Data)
181-gr. Lyman #321297 —13.0 #2400—1,365 f.p.s.—Target load
181-gr. Lyman #321297 —14.5 #4227—1,365 f.p.s.—Target load
170-gr. Remington S.P. —20.0 #4198—1,718 f.p.s.—Do NOT use in Ballards.
170-gr. Remington S.P. —29.0 #4895—1,887 f.p.s.—Deer load.
170-gr. Remington S.P. —28.0 #3031—1,925 f.p.s.—Max. - Do NOT use either of last two loads in 1881 Marlin or Ballard single-shot rifles.

.33 Winchester

Adapted to Winchester Single Shot and Model 1886 rifles, and Marlin Model 1895 rifles.
Original Ballistics:
  (1) Standard Load—200-gr. S.P.—M.V. 2,056 f.p.s. @ 33-35,000 p.s.i.
Note: This cartridge was originally designed (Introduced 1902) as a smokeless powder cartridge for use in the Model 1886 rifle.
1936 Ballistics: 200-gr. Soft-point—M.V. 2,180 f.p.s.
Factory ammunition no longer available.
Components available: *200-gr. (.338 Win.) Soft-point bullets.
  *Note: .338 bullets must have lead round points ground off to leave a large flat-nose for tubular magazine rifles. Also, only 200-gr. Herters bullets—so far as is known—have a crimping cannelure in the right location to give correct overall cartridge length for repeating rifles.
Cast Forming: Cases may be formed from new .45/70 brass in RCBS forming dies.
Bullet Moulds: (a) Lyman 201-gr. G.C. (#338320)
          (b) Ohaus 200-gr. G.C. #33200F
Bullet Diameters: Jacketed .338 inch; Cast .340 inch

(Reloading Data)
201-gr. Lyman #338320—24.0 #4198—1,650 f.p.s.—Target and plinging load.
201-gr. Lyman #338320—35.0 #4895—1,800 f.p.s. — Accurate light deer load.
200-gr. Herters J.S.P.   —40.0 #3031—2,175 f.p.s.
200-gr. Herters J.S.P.   —44.0 #4895—2,150 f.p.s.

.35 Winchester
Adapted to Winchester Single Shot and Model 1895 repeating rifles.
Original Ballistics:
  (1) Standard Load—250-gr. S.P.—M.V. 2,200 f.p.s. @ 39–41,000 p.s.i.
Note: This cartridge was originally designed (Introduced 1903) as a smokeless powder cartridge for use in the Model 1895 rifle.
Factory ammunition no longer available.
Components available: 200-, 220- and 250-gr. Soft-point bullets.
Case Forming: Cases may be formed from new .30/40 Krag brass, but will be 1/10 inch short. Full-length size, fire-form and reload with bullets of at least 200-grains weight seated out to 3.10 inch overall length.
Bullet Moulds: (a) Lyman 245-gr. G.C. (#358318)
                 (b) Ohaus 200-gr. G.C. (#35200F)
Bullet Diameters: Jacketed .358 inch; Cast .360 inch.
(Reloading Data)
245-gr. Lyman #358318—34.0 #3031—1,680 f.p.s.—Light load.
245-gr. Lyman #358318—39.0 #4895—1,900 f.p.s.—Deer load.
200-gr. Jacketed S.P.   —46.0 #3031—2,235 f.p.s.—Deer load.
250-gr. Jacketed S.P.   —49.0 #4895—2,150 f.p.s.—Big-game load.

.38/40 Winchester
Adapted to Winchester Single Shot and Models 1873 and 1892 repeating rifles; also, Marlin Models 1888, 1889 and 1894.
Original Ballistics:
  (1) Standard Load   —180-gr. Lead—M.V. 1,324 f.p.s. @ 15–17,000 p.s.i.

*(2) 1892 Special H.V.—180-gr. S-P. —M.V. 1,776 f.p.s. @ 21–23,000 p.s.i.
  *Note: 1892 Special H.V. load must NOT be used in Model 1873 rifles!
Factory ammunition currently available with 180-gr. Soft-points may be used in all rifles in good condition factory-chambered for this round.
Present Ballistics: 180-gr. Soft-points—M.V. 1,330 f.p.s. (No H.V. loads).
Components available: New empty cases and 180-gr. Soft-point bullets.
Bullet Moulds: (a) Lyman 170-gr. (#40188) and 172-gr. (#40143)
        (b) Ohaus 170-gr. (#40170F)
Bullet Diameters: Jacketed .400 inch; Cast .401 inch
        (Reloading Data)
172-gr. Lyman #40143—17.0 #2400—1,340 f.p.s.—Very accurate.
172-gr. Lyman #40143—19.5 #4227—1,390 f.p.s.
180-gr. Jacketed S-P.   —20.0 #4227—1,440 f.ps.
180-gr. Jacketed S-P.   —23.5 #4227—1,707 f.p.s.—Do NOT use in Model 1873 rifles.

.38/55 Marlin and Winchester

Adapted to Marlin Models 1881 and 1893; also, Winchester Model 1894 and Single Shot rifles.
Original Ballistics:
  (1) Standard Load   —255-gr. Lead—M.V. 1,321 f.p.s. @ 18–20,00 p.s.i.
  (2) Old Win. H.V.   —255-gr. S-P. —M.V. 1,593 f.p.s. @ 28–30,000 p.s.i.
  (3) Old Rem. Hi-Spd.—255-gr. S-P. —M.V. 1,700 f.p.s. @ 32–34,000 p.s.i.
  (4) Final Factory   —255-gr. S-P. —M.V. 1,320 f.p.s.
Only C.I.L. (Canadian) factory ammunition is currently available with 255-gr. soft-point bullets at M.V. 1,600 f.p.s.
Components available: None in U.S.
Case Forming: Cases may be formed from .32 Winchester Special brass fire-formed in .38/55 chamber. Formed cases will be slightly short. *(Do NOT fire-form in old Ballard rifles).

Bullet Moulds: (a) Lyman 249-gr. (#375248) and 265-gr. G.C. (#375296)
(b) Ohaus 250-gr. (#38250F)
Bullet Diameters: Jacketed .376 inch; Cast .378 inch

(Reloading Data)

249-gr. Lyman #375248—18.0 #4227—1,230 f.p.s.
249-gr. Lyman #375248—21.0 #4198—1,273 f.p.s.
249-gr. Lyman #375248—35.0 #4895—1,660 f.p.s.—Do NOT use in Ballards.
265-gr. Lyman #375296—35.0 #4895—1,640 f.p.s.—Do NOT use in Ballards, or 1881 Marlin rifles.

.38/56 Winchester

Adapted to Winchester Single Shot and Model 1886 repeating rifles; also, Marlin Model 1895 rifles.

Original Ballistics:
(1) Standard Load—255-gr. Lead bullets—M.V. 1,397 f.p.s.
(2) 1929 Std. Load—255-gr. S-P. bullets —M.V. 1,442 f.p.s.

Factory ammunition no longer available.
Components available: None in U.S.
Case Forming: Cases can be formed from .45/70 brass by sizing full-length in .38/56 die, or in two stages starting with .40/65 Winchester die.
Bullet Moulds: *Same as for .38/55 above.
Bullet Diameters: Same as for .38/55. (Jacketed .376 inch; Cast .378 inch).

(Reloading Data)

249-gr. Lyman #375248 — 30.0 #3031 — 1,530 f.p.s. — Target load.
265-gr. Lyman #375296—36.0 #3031—1,750 f.p.s.—Deer load.
265-gr. Lyman #375296 — 39.0 #4895 — 1,800 f.p.s. — Big-game load.

.38/70 Winchester

Adapted to Winchester Model 1886 repeating rifles.
Original Ballistics:
(1) Standard Load—255-gr. Lead bullet—M.V. 1,490 f.p.s.
(2) 1929 Standard —255-gr. Soft-point —M.V. 1,493 f.p.s.

Factory ammunition not available.

Components Available: None in U.S.
Case Forming: Cases can be formed from .45/70 brass by sizing full-length in .38/70 die, or in two stages starting with a .40/82 Winchester die, but will be approximately 0.34 inch short. Fire-form and reload with bullets seated out to 2.73 inch overall length.
Bullet Moulds: Same as for .38/55 above.
Bullet Diameters: Same as for .38/55 (Jacketed .376 inch; Cast .381 inch).

(Reloading Data)
249-gr. Lyman #375248—30.5 #3031—1,550 f.p.s.—Target load.
265-gr. Lyman #375296—39.0 #4895—1,800 f.p.s.—Big-game load.
Note: These loads based upon use of sized-down .45/70 cases.

.38/72 Winchester
Adapted to Winchester Model 1895 repeating rifles.
Original Ballistics:
   (1) Standard Load—275-gr. Lead bullet—M.V. 1,477 f.p.s.
   (2) 1929 Standard —275-gr. Soft-point —M.V. 1,483 f.p.s.
Factory ammunition not available.
Components available: None in U.S.
Case Forming: Cases may be formed from Speer-DWM 9.3 x 74-R brass by swaging (or turning) base to .460 inch diameter just forward of case rim, trimming cases to 2.57 inch, full-length sizing in .38/72 Winchester die, and fire-forming in .38/72 chamber.
Bullet Moulds: (a) Lyman 267-gr. (#375167) and 265-gr. G.C. (#375296)
                 (b) Ohaus 250-gr. (#38250F)
Bullet Diameters: Jacketed .376 inch; Cast .381 inch

(Reloading Data)
267-gr. Lyman #375167—32.0 #3031—M.V. ?—Target load
265-gr. Lyman #375296—39.0 #4895—M.V. ?—Big-game load

.40/60 Winchester
Adapted to Winchester Model 1876 repeating rifles.
Original Ballistics: 210-gr. Lead bullet—M.V. 1,533 f.p.s.
Factory ammunition not available.
Components available: None.

Case Forming: Cases can be formed from .45/70 brass by trimming to 1.87 inch and sizing full-length in .40/60 Winchester die.
Bullet Moulds: Lyman 200-gr. (#403168)
Bullet Diameter: Cast .406 inch
(Reloading Data)
200-gr. Lyman #403168—20.0 #2400—M.V. ?
Note: Like the 1873 Winchester, the Model 1876 is of comparatively weak link-action design. Do NOT exceed this load. Extreme care should also be exercised to avoid a double-charge!

.40/65 Winchester

Adapted to Winchester Single Shot and Model 1886 repeating rifles; also, Marlin Model 1895 rifles.
Original Ballistics:
  (1) Standard Load —260-gr. Lead-bullet —M.V. 1,367 f.p.s.
  (2) 1929 Standard —260-gr. Soft-point —M.V. 1,420 f.p.s.
  (3) 1929 High Power—253-gr. Hollow-point—M.V. 1,790 f.p.s.
Factory ammunition not available.
Components available: None
Case Forming: Cases can be formed from .45/70 brass in a single step by full-length sizing in .40/65 Winchester dies.
Bullet Moulds: Lyman 245-gr. (#403169) *Specify "Oversize" bullet.
Bullet Diameters: Jacketed .406 inch; Cast .408 inch
(Reloading Data)
245-gr. Lyman #403169—23.0 #2400—M.V. ?
245-gr. Lyman #403169—34.0 #3031—M.V. ?
245-gr. Lyman #403169—38.0 #4895—M.V. ?

.40/70 Winchester

Adapted to Winchester Model 1886 and Marlin Model 1895 rifles.
Original Ballistics:
  (1) Standard Load—330-gr. Lead bullet—M.V. 1,383 f.p.s.
  (2) 1929 Standard —330-gr. Soft-point —M.V. 1,457 f.p.s.
Factory ammunition not available.
Components available: None.

Case Forming: Cases can be formed from .45/70 brass in a single step by full-length sizing in .40/70 Winchester dies, but will be 0.3 inch short. Fire-form and reload with bullets seated out to 2.85 inch overall length.
Bullet Moulds: Lyman 290-gr.* (#403173) *Specify "Oversize" bullet.
Bullet Diameters: Jacketed .406 inch; Cast .408 inch
(Reloading Data)
290-gr. Lyman #403173—23.0 #2400—M.V. ?
290-gr. Lyman #403173—32.0 #3031—M.V. ?
Note: These loads based upon use of sized-down .45/70 cases.

.40/72 Winchester
Adapted to Winchester Model 1895 repeating rifles.
Original Ballistics:
  (1) Standard Load—330-gr. Lead bullet—M.V. 1,373 f.p.s.
  (2) Old Smokeless—330-gr. Soft-point —M.V. 1,423 f.p.s.
Factory ammunition not available.
Components available: None.
Case Forming: Cases may be formed from Speer-DWM 9.3 x 74-R brass by swaging (or turning) base to .460 inch diameter just forward of case rim, trimming cases to 2.58 inch, full-length sizing in .40/72 Winchester die, and fire-forming in .40/72.
Bullet Moulds: Lyman 330-gr. (#406150) and 288-gr. *(#412263) *Specify "Undersize" mould.
Bullet Diameters: Jacketed .406 inch; Cast .408 inch
(Reloading Data)
330-gr. Lyman #406150—36.0 #3031—M.V. ?
330-gr. Lyman #406150—42.0 #4895—M.V. ?

.40/82 Winchester
Adapted to Winchester Single Shot and Model 1886 repeating rifles; also, Marlin Model 1895 rifles.
Original Ballistics:
  (1) Standard Load—260-gr. Lead bullet—M.V. 1,492 f.p.s.
  (2) 1929 Standard —260-gr. Soft-point —M.V. 1,525 f.p.s.
Factory ammunition not available.
Components available: None.
Case Forming: Cases can be formed from .45/70 brass in a

Shooting the Old Winchesters and Marlins 245

single step by full-length szing in .40/82 dies, but will be 0.3 inch short. Fire-form and reload with bullets seated out to 2.77 inch overall length.
Bullet Moulds: Lyman 245-gr. (#403169) *Specify "Oversize" mold.
Bullet Diameters: Jacketed .406 inch; Cast .408 inch
(Reloading Data)
245-gr. Lyman #403169—23.0 #2400—M.V. 1,350 f.p.s.
245-gr. Lyman #403169—35.0 #3031—M.V. 1,300 f.p.s.
245-gr. Lyman #403169—40.0 #4895—M.V. ?
Note: These loads based upon use of sized-down .45/70 cases.

.405 Winchester

Adapted to Winchester Model 1895 repeating rifles.
Original Ballistics:
(1) Standard Load—300-gr. Soft-point—M.V. 2,204 f.p.s. @ 43–45,000 p.s.i.
Note: This cartridge was originally designed (Introduced 1904) as a smokeless powder cartridge for use in the Model 1895 rifle.
Factory ammunition no longer available.
Components available: None.
Case Forming: Cases may be formed from Speer-DWM 9.3 x 74-R brass by swaging (or turning) base to .461 inch diameter just forward of case rim, trimming cases to 2.58 inch, full-length sizing in .405 Winchester die, and fire-forming in .405 chamber.
Bullet Moulds: Lyman 288-gr. (#412263)
Bullet Diameters: Jacketed .412 inch; Cast .414 inch
(Reloading Data)
288-gr. Lyman #412263—25.0 #2400—M.V. 1,500 f.p.s.—Light load.
288-gr. Lyman #412263—43.0 #3031—M.V. 1,700 f.p.s.—Deer load.
288-gr. Lyman #412263—47.0 #4895—M.V. ?
288-gr. Lyman #412263—55.0 #4831—M.V. ?
Note: Use Magnum primers with #4831 powder.

.44/40 Winchester

Adapted to Winchester Models 1873 and 1892 repeating rifles,

Winchester Single Shot rifles, and Marlin Models 1888, 1889 and 1894.

Original Ballistics:
  (1) Standard Load—200-gr. Lead bullet—M.V. 1,300 f.p.s. @ 13–15,000 p.s.i.
  *(2) 1892 Spec. H.V.—200-gr. Soft-point —M.V. 1,569 f.p.s. @ 18–20,000 p.s.i.
    *Note: 1892 Special H.V. load must NOT be used in Model 1873 rifles!

Factory ammunition currently available with 200-gr. soft-points, may be used in all rifles in good condition factory-chambered for this cartridge.

Present Ballistics: 200-gr. Soft-points—M.V. 1,310 f.p.s. (No H.V. loads).

Components available: New empty cases and 200-gr. soft-point bullets.

Bullet Moulds: (a) Lyman 205-gr. (#42798) and 215-gr. G.C. (#429434)
              (b) Ohaus 200-gr. (#44200F).

Bullet Diameters: (a) For Winchester rifles: Jacketed .427 inch; Cast .428 inch
              (b) For Remington rifles: Jacketed .425 inch; Cast .427 inch

(Reloading Data)

205-gr. Lyman #42798 — 8.3 Unique—M.V. 1,200 f.p.s.—
  For Model 1873
205-gr. Lyman #42798 —19.0 #2400 —M.V. 1,460 f.p.s.—
  O.K. for 1873
215-gr. Lyman #429434—22.0 #4227 —M.V. 1,500 f.p.s.
  NOT for 1873
200-gr. Winchester S.P. —22.0 #2400 —M.V. 1,625 f.p.s.—
  (Use ONLY in 1892 Winchester, Winchester Single Shot, and 1894 Marlin)
200-gr. Winchester S.P. —24.0 #2400 —M.V. 1,770 f.p.s.—
  (Use ONLY in 1892 Winchester, Winchester Single Shot, and 1894 Marlin)

.45/60 Winchester

Adapted to Winchester Single Shot and Model 1876 repeating rifles.

Original Ballistics: 300-gr. Lead bullet—M.V. 1,315 f.p.s.
Factory ammunition not available.
Components available: 300-gr. jacketed hollow-point bullets.
Cast Forming: Cases can be formed from .45/70 brass by full-length sizing in a .45/70 die and trimming to 1.87 inch case length.
Bullet Moulds: Lyman 292-gr. (#457191)
Bullet Diameters: Cast .457 inch; jacketed .457 inch

(Reloading Data)

292-gr. Lyman #457191—22.0 #2400—M.V. ? (Do NOT exceed.)

.45/70 Government

Adapted to Winchester Single Shot and Model 1886 repeating rifles; also, Marlin Model 1895 rifles.

Original Ballistics:
- (1) Standard Load —405-gr. Lead bullet —M.V. 1,318 f.p.s.
- (2) Infantry Load —500-gr. Lead bullet —M.V. 1,201 f.p.s.
- (3) Express Load —350-gr. Soft-point —M.V. 1,344 f.p.s.
- (4) Express H.P. —330-gr. Hollow-point—M.V. 1,380 f.p.s.
- (5) Old Winchester H.V.—300-gr. Soft-point —M.V. 1,888 f.p.s. @ 23–25,000 p.s.i.

Factory ammunition currently available with 405-gr. soft-points, may be used in all rifles in good condition factory-chambered for this cartridge.
Present Ballistics: 405-gr. Soft-points—M.V. 1,320 f.p.s. (No H.V. loads)
Components available: New empty cases and 300-gr. H.P., 350-gr. and 405-gr. Soft-point bulle ts.
Bullet Moulds:. (a) Lyman 385-gr. (#457124) and 378-gr. G.C. (#457483)
     (b) Ohaus 385-gr. (#45385F) and 405-gr. (#45405F)
Bullet Diameters: Jacketed .457 inch; Cast .459 inch.
Note 1—Lyman bullets have blunt round-noses; Ohaus are flat-nose.

Note 2—500-grain bullets have purposely been omitted because they are not suited (in the writer's opinion) for lever-action repeating rifles which are designed around the 405-grain.

(Reloading Data)

378-gr. Lyman #457483—28.0 #4227—M.V. 1,400 f.p.s.
378-gr. Lyman #457483—44.0 #4895—M.V. 1,450 f.p.s.
405-gr. Ohaus #45405F—31.0 #4198—M.V. 1,360 f.p.s.
405-gr. Ohaus #45405F—45.0 #4895—M.V. 1,524 f.p.s.
405-gr. Ohaus #45405F—55.0 #4831—M.V. ?
350-gr. Jacketed S-P. —56.0 #4831—M.V. 1,287 f.p.s.
350-gr. Jacketed S-P. —46.0 #4895—M.V. 1,446 f.p.s.
405-gr. Jacketed S-P. —44.0 #4895—M.V. 1,400 f.p.s.
405-gr. Jacketed S-P. —55.0 #4831—M.V. 1,281 f.p.s.

Note: Use Magnum primers with #4831 powder.

.45/75 Winchester

Adapted to Winchester Single Shot and Model 1876 repeating rifles.

Original Ballistics:
  (1) Standard Load—350-gr. Lead bullet—M.V. 1,383 f.p.s.
  (2) 1929 Standard —350-gr. Lead bullet—M.V. 1,470 f.p.s.

Factory ammunition not available.

Components available: 350-gr. Soft-point bullets and 300-gr. H.P.

Case Forming: Cases may be formed from .348 Winchester brass by trimming to 1.87 inch case length, full-length sizing in .45/75 Winchester die, and fire-forming in .45/75 chamber.

Bullet Moulds: (a) Lyman 330-gr. H.P. (#457122) and 385-gr. (#457124)
                 (b) Ohaus 385-gr. (#45385F)

Bullet Diameters: Jacketed .457 inch; Cast .457 inch

Note: If cast of straight linotype metal, 385-grain Lyman bullets will weigh approximately 360-grains only.

(Reloading Data)

330-gr. Lyman #457122—22.0 #2400—M.V. ?
330-gr. Lyman #457122—28.0 #4198—M.V. ?

.45/90 Winchester

Adapted to Winchester Single Shot and Model 1886 repeating rifles; also, Marlin Model 1895 rifles.

Original Ballistics:
  (1) Standard Load —300-gr. Lead bullet—M.V. 1,532 f.p.s.
  (2) Old Win. H.V.—300-gr. Soft point —M.V. 1,992 f.p.s.
  (3) 1929 Standard —300-gr. Soft point —M.V. 1,660 f.p.s.
Factory ammunition not available. Standard .45/70 cartridges may be safely fired in .45/90 Winchester-caliber rifles.
Components available: 300-gr. hollow-point and 350-gr. soft-point bullets.
Case Forming: Standard .45/70 cases may be loaded for use in .45/90 rifles, but cases will be 0.3 inch short, therefore bullets should be seated farther out of the case neck.
Bullet Moulds: Lyman 292-gr. (#457191) and 330-gr. H.P. (#457122)
Bullet Diameters: Jacketed .457 inch; Cast .459 inch

(Reloading Data)

292-gr. Lyman #457191	—28.0 #4227—	M.V. 1,440 f.p.s.
330-gr. Lyman #457122	—40.0 #4198—	M.V. 1,700 f.p.s.
330-gr. Lyman #457122	—44.0 #4895—	M.V. 1,490 f.p.s.
300-gr. Hornady JHP	—46.0 #4895—	M.V. 1,530 f.p.s.
300-gr. Hornady JHP	—50.0 #4895—	M.V. 1,700 f.p.s.
350-gr. Hornady or Herters JSP	—56.0 #4831—	M.V. ?

Note 1—These loads based upon use of .45/70 cases rather than .45/90's.
Note 2—Use Magnum primers with #4831 powder.

Custom-made cases in several of the more common obsolete calibers can be had from case-forming specialists such as "W"-Everlasting Cases, Rte. 1, Box 1018, Carnation, Washington, 98014; Robert Pomeroy, Morrison Ave., East Corinth, Maine, 04427; and Russell L. Campbell, 219 Leisure Drive, San Antonio, Texas, 78201. Although these custom cases are considerably more costly than standard brass, they have the great advantage of being in the proper length, and of course a full-length .45/90 or .40/82 case is definitely preferable to a reformed .45/70 case 3/10-inch too short.

Reloading die sets for every one of the calibers I've listed here, plus the .50/110 Winchester, can be obtained from RCBS, Inc., P.O. Box 1919, Oroville, California, 95965. I should mention that the .50/110 was purposely left out of his write-up because of the very considerable difficulty in forming satisfactory cases for this caliber from currently available brass. I consider this a job for the commercial custom caseformers.

At one time during the early 1960's, an outfit calling themselves The Connecticut Cartridge Company produced a whole series of new cases—some drawn and some turned—from virgin brass, for the obsolete American calibers, and they were truly excellent. It is to be regretted that they discontinued production.

The Lyman Division of The Leisure Group, located at Middlefield, Connecticut, also produces well-made reloading dies for many of the old cartridges, and are known around the world for their most complete offering of bullet moulds. A relative newcomer to the bullet mould field is the Ohaus Scale Corporation, 29 Hanover Road, Florham Park, New Jersey. They have succeeded in producing a truly fine selection of moulds in calibers from .22 to .45, many of which are perfectly adapted for use with the old rifles.

From all this, it should be evident that the Winchester and Marlin rifles introduced during the final quarter of the last century are not just "wall-hangers." They still have the capability of serving their owners well, whether the target be paper or game.